TWIN SACRIFICE
Jennifer Lane

PSYCHED PUBLISHING

Published by Psyched Publishing

First published, February 2018

Chapter one of *With Good Behavior*, copyright © 2010
Used by permission of Omnific Publishing

ISBN: 978-0-9979970-2-6

10 9 8 7 6 5 4 3 2 1

Book Design by Coreen Montagna

Printed in the United States of America

To male survivors of abuse: You are not alone.

"If you want to keep a secret, you must also hide it from yourself."
~George Orwell, 1984

1. Match

The searing sting of his wrists woke him.

Matthew's stomach roiled as he scanned the room. He touched crisp bedding and smelled pungent antiseptic. In his scramble to sit up, he kicked down the sheet, freeing his arms from the covers. The IV was a solid clue to his whereabouts. But once he saw his bandaged wrists, he knew not only the where, but the why.

He'd gone too far.

Now fully aware of the jam he'd put himself in, he collapsed back on the mattress and dreaded the aftermath. It arrived seconds later in the form of a lithe, auburn-haired beauty stalking toward him from the corner of the room. She must have seen him stir.

He braced himself for the blaze of fury in her copper eyes.

"What the *hell* were you thinking?"

He forced a swallow down his dry throat. "Sorry."

"Sorry? You tried to off yourself, and that's all you got? *Sorry?*"

He scratched at the bandages wrapped around his wrists, wondering how well he'd pulled off the cuts concealed beneath the gauze.

"Stop that." She slapped his hand away. "Or I'll get them to restrain you."

He sighed as he let his hands fall to his sides. "That won't be necessary, Kate. I'm not suicidal. I don't want to die."

Her forehead creased, and she lowered to the bed next to him. "Then why'd you do that to yourself?" She drew his hand into hers and stroked his fingers. "Why, Matthew?" Her eyes searched his. "Was it something I did?"

"God, no! It's not your fault."

Her shoulders dropped an inch, but she kept her hawkish gaze trained on him.

"It's…complicated," he added. "I didn't mean for it to get this far."

She flung his hand down. "What's *wrong* with you? I never get to see you anymore—if you're not working crazy hours, you're at the gym, lifting weights nonstop. You're distant and moody all the time, and now this? You go and do this, right after Justin, right after he—" Her face contorted as a choking sound caught in her throat.

He reached for her and exhaled when she didn't fight him. Her body tucked into his, warm and close on a cold March day. As he patted her back, he savored the feel of her in his arms, her cocoa butter smell.

When she spoke, his hospital gown pressing against her mouth muffled her words. "I can't lose you, too. I can't."

"You won't. And we haven't lost Justin yet." His jaw clenched. "We *won't* lose him."

Kate pulled back. "How do you know? He seems really determined this time."

"I won't let it happen."

She shook her head. "You can't save him. You can't play psychologist to your family. You know that." She looked down. "And I shouldn't play lawyer to him. He's like a brother to me."

"Justin has the best attorney in Ohio: *you*." He squeezed her shoulder. "You have no choice. You have to try. It's been the three of us for as long as I can remember."

"Just the three of us against the world," she agreed.

Matthew's chest tightened as he looked down at his bandages. *A bald man grabbed a boy, shaking him awake…the boy's whimper…*He looked back up. "Sometimes it feels more like the world's against us, not the other way around."

She cupped his chin. "Listen to me, Durante. It's not right what's happened to Justin, but he'll come out of this—he'll be ready to stand trial soon. And then I'll do everything I can to get him acquitted. It's no good with just two of us. We need all three, just like when we were kids."

He wanted to believe her. But he'd never seen his twin brother so hopeless, so full of despair. So numb. Harangued by guilt and public hatred, Justin was determined to kill himself. And until recently, Matthew had felt helpless to stop him.

With the building pressure of plans left undone stirring in his chest, he moved to get out of bed.

Kate frowned as she pushed him back down. "Uh-uh, you're supposed to stay. The nurse told me not to let you leave."

"But I'm fine. Just let me get this IV out—"

"You're *not* fine, dumbass!" She clutched his shoulders.

Though he was taller and heavier, he allowed her to pin him to the bed. He knew she was right. He was far from fine.

She released one of his arms and smoothed her hand down his shoulder-length black hair, which must have worked its way loose from his ponytail during the ambulance melee.

"Matthew?" Her voice trembled. "Why'd you do this?"

He swallowed and looked away. She scooted back on the mattress to give him some space. Voices from the hallway and a faint beeping noise punctuated the silence between them.

"Do you believe me when I say I wasn't trying to kill myself?"

She had her attorney face on—that prying, shrewd gaze she wore when interviewing witnesses—and she seemed to consider his words. "Well, you did call me before you passed out. I guess that's evidence you have *some* sense of self-preservation. You're lucky I wasn't in court."

"Thank you." He looked at her. "And even though I asked you not to, thank you for calling nine-one-one."

"You're welcome. And you still haven't answered my question."

"I know. You deserve an explanation." His fingers drummed on his thigh. "You remember that time when we were sixteen, when we caught Justin…?"

She flinched. "When we caught him with the scissors."

He nodded. His world had blown apart that first time he'd discovered his brother cutting himself. The pain had been almost like Justin was cutting Matthew's skin. "I was…" His lower lip trapped beneath his teeth. "I was trying to understand why Justin hurt himself like that. Why he keeps trying to destroy himself."

The toss of her hair highlighted its red hues. "But that makes no sense. We already know why Justin's messed up in the head: he blames himself for your parents' deaths."

Matthew grew quiet, wishing he still believed that—wishing he hadn't discovered the true source of his brother's mental illness.

Bile climbed up his throat as he recalled his client's anguish during a recent psychotherapy session. As the college student had related his experience at the hands of his foster father, Jefferson King—the man who'd also been foster father to Matthew, Justin, and Kate—a sickening realization had taken hold.

Matthew now saw Justin in a new light. And he saw their childhood in a new darkness.

"You're right. We already know what changed Justin for the worse," he said. "Maybe I just had to experience it for myself, try to get closer to him some way. I miss him, you know? And when I started cutting, I don't know what happened, but I went deeper than I'd planned…"

Her expression darkened. "I think…" She tapped her index finger on her chin. "I think you're full of shit."

His eyes made a quick shift, feigning shock. "Kate—"

"Don't try to snow me. I know you. You've been acting weird for months now, and this little suicide trip is the icing on the cake—it's the *slice* of cake, you prick. What if I'd been in court? What if I couldn't answer my phone?"

"I would've called the squad myself."

"No, you wouldn't, liar. You men are all the same, never asking for help."

Matthew knew her hostility was a mask for fear. Still, he squirmed under her glare.

She continued, "If it wasn't for me, you'd be lying *dead* on your bathroom floor!"

The weight of her words pushed him back into the bed. He'd never seen her so angry. But she'd be even more upset after he carried out his plan.

"How could you do this to me?" she railed. "I could've lost you. You could be lying dead in your condo, with…with freaking Slim snacking on your face."

An inappropriate laugh bubbled in his throat, though he didn't let it escape.

She breathed hard, staring coldly at him.

"Hey, don't go hating on my full-figured cat," he ventured. "She can't help it if she's fat."

After a minute, her mouth twitched. "Slim's not fat; she's big-boned."

He exhaled. "So, if I died, how long you think she'd give it before she started 'snacking' on my corpse?"

"You're disturbed. Seriously disturbed. Maybe *you* belong in there, not your brother."

A blond nurse bustled in. "Ah, here we are. All awake. How're you feeling, Mr. Durante?" She had an Ohio State University Wexner Medical Center badge clipped to her scrubs.

"Why have I been admitted? They told me they'd release me from the ER."

His sharp tone didn't seem to faze her. "That was before the attending got a good look at your wrist — he's worried you injured a tendon. We gave you some pain meds, and we've got you scheduled for a consult with a hand specialist tomorrow."

"Tomorrow?" He heard desperation in his voice. "But I have to work in the morning."

"Work will have to wait." The nurse fiddled with the IV bag. "This should counter the fatigue from the blood loss. What do you do, by the way?"

Matthew gave Kate a sideways glance. She sat poker-faced.

He closed his eyes. "I'm a psychologist."

The nurse looked at his bandaged wrists. "How nice." She checked the IV site on his arm. "The social worker's on the floor. Are you ready to see her now?"

"No."

The nurse didn't miss a beat. "Great. I'll send her right in."

He sulked after she sashayed out of the room. "Nurses aren't fans of suicidal psychologists, I take it."

"I don't think she'll sign up for therapy with you anytime soon," Kate said.

"At least she didn't ask, 'Are you analyzing me now?' I *hate* that."

A few minutes later, a woman knocked on the door before peeking into the room. "Mr. Durante?"

He rolled his eyes at Kate. "That's me."

Tight, wiry curls stuck out in a cute mess atop the social worker's head, framing her girlish face. "Or should I call you Dr. Durante?"

He grimaced. Apparently, the nurse had ratted him out. "Matthew's fine."

She reached out to shake his hand. "Mimi Adams, Matthew. I'm a licensed social worker, and I'd like to chat with you a bit." She moved into position at the other side of the bed.

"I'm the girlfriend," Kate supplied. "Kathryn Summers."

They shook hands, and Mimi asked, "You're the girlfriend who called nine-one-one?"

"Yes. Unless there're *other* girlfriends I don't know about." She doubled down on her glower by smacking him upside the head.

"Ow!" He rubbed his crown. "You're the only girlfriend, okay?"

"I better be, Durante."

Mimi watched the interaction, seeming intrigued, then pulled a chair over. "Matthew, would you like Kathryn to be here while we talk? Or would you prefer if she waits outside?"

Kate crossed her arms. "Oh, I'm staying."

"This is really the patient's call." Mimi turned to him. "Matthew?"

He felt the heat of Kate's stare. "Kate's the reason I'm still alive, so yes, I want her here." *I just have to make my performance all the more convincing for the human lie detector over there.*

Mimi sat, her pen poised above her notepad. "Sounds like you've had a rough time lately?"

He shrugged. "Not really."

Kate's eyebrows pulled together. "Not really? What about Justin?"

"I don't want to talk about him."

Kate scowled. "You have to talk about him — if you don't want a repeat performance of this suicide attempt, that is."

"Oh, so *you're* the psychologist now?" Matthew asked. "Telling me how to live my life?"

Kate blanched.

"What's this all about?" Mimi interrupted. "Who's Justin?"

Matthew played with his bandages.

"Matthew's twin is Justin Durante," Kate said.

Mimi frowned. "I'm sorry, that name sounds vaguely familiar, but…"

"The King Combatics explosion?" Kate prompted. "The man accused of detonating the bomb that killed the scientist?"

Mimi paled. "The bomber?" Matthew caught her recoil from the corner of his eye. "That's your brother?"

Slowly, defiantly, he raised his head. His eyes locked on hers. "Yes. He's my brother."

"I'm sorry."

"Well, *I'm* not," he snapped. "He's the best brother I could ever wish for." He looked at his girlfriend. "Thanks, Kate. Thanks for bringing that up."

"She needs to know. She needs to know about Justin, locked up in a psych hospital until he restores competency…" Her lips trembled. "She needs to know he tried to kill himself a week ago, sawing through his wrists with a plastic knife."

He shook at the image. "Why? Why in the world does she need to know that?"

"Because that's why *you* attempted suicide! I know you and Justin better than anyone, and it doesn't take a psychologist to see your survivor's guilt. That guilt made you pull something this stupid."

Damn. She didn't even have all the facts, yet she was dangerously close to the truth. Her intelligence was the biggest threat to his plan.

"Is that true, Matthew?" Mimi asked. "Is survivor's guilt the reason you cut yourself?"

"Truth is, I don't know," he lied. "I do know I don't have any suicidal thoughts now. There's no way I'd try this again."

Mimi's eyes hooded with apparent suspicion. "And *I* know you're a psychologist—quite aware of what to say to get discharged."

Matthew slumped. Why hadn't he stopped once he'd drawn blood? He wished he'd been strong enough to use a plastic knife like his brother. But he'd had to switch to a metal blade, and then he'd gone too far. He hadn't planned on having to explain himself to a damn social worker.

"King Combatics," Mimi said when he didn't respond. "I'm remembering more now. They're investigating the company's ties to terrorists, right? Something about a flight that went down last October?"

"Yes." Kate's eyes narrowed. "The bomb that detonated on the plane—its triggers were manufactured by King Combatics, but Jefferson King claims they were stolen." She sighed. "They haven't been able to prove otherwise."

Matthew grimaced. The bomb had wiped out all exculpatory evidence when it leveled the King Combatics warehouse.

After thirty minutes of answering Mimi's questions, including denials of depression interspersed with claims that his life was wonderful, Matthew got the social worker to admit he wasn't in imminent danger of harming himself.

"But I want you starting outpatient therapy once you're discharged," Mimi said. "You need some help dealing with your brother's crime."

"Alleged crime," Kate amended.

Matthew said nothing, just stared at the wall.

"I'll put some referrals to local therapists on your discharge instructions." Mimi rose.

"Thank you," Kate said.

"You have no intention of seeing a therapist, right?" she added once they were alone again.

"I'm sorry for putting you through all this. I don't want to hurt you. Besides Justin, you're all I got."

Her features softened. "You…scared me today." When she swallowed, his gaze followed the curved hollow at the base of her throat and traveled up the elegant length of her neck to land on her glittering eyes. "Don't do it again."

You created those tears, idiot. "I won't. I promise." Seconds ticked between them. He slid over to one side of the bed and thumped the mattress. "Cuddle?"

Her eyes tapered. "You can't spoon with that damn cat for one night, and you want me as a substitute?"

"It's not my fault I like something soft and furry, with a bite. And the cat's pretty nice, too."

"Hey. I shaved my legs yesterday." She stared at him for a long minute before she kicked off her shoes and snuggled against him.

"Which reminds me," he added, "would you go over to my place and feed Slim tonight, since I'm stuck here?"

Her back curled into his chest. "I think she can go without food for one night."

"She'll claw up the closet door if you don't fill her bowl. And can you grab my calendar from my car and bring it to me? Looks like I need to cancel tomorrow morning's clients."

"Jeez, you're bossy."

"I love you, Kate." He leaned over her shoulder to kiss her collarbone.

"Well, I don't love you, asshole." She paused. "But even if I did, my love isn't blind. I'm on to you. I'm gonna figure out your little game."

His stomach knotted. This was no game.

2. Despair

Back home the next evening, Matthew could hear the cat's insistent meows even before he unlocked the door of his two-bedroom townhouse.

Once inside, a furry gray butterball rushed him, darting between his legs as he closed the front door. He tried to place the stack of mail and the hospital's discharge instructions on the kitchen counter, but he almost tripped with the cat underfoot.

"Stop it, Slim!"

The cat shirked away, her green eyes wounded, and Matthew sighed.

"C'mere." He squatted and hefted her twenty-pound girth with a groan. Scratching her ears, he cooed in a singsong voice, "How's Daddy's fatty catty?"

Sated purrs emanated from the furball held like a babe in his arms.

He rubbed her sizeable belly. "There, there. Daddy's home." He halted his petting when he noticed a splotch of red matted in her paw. "What's this? Did you get hurt?" But his inspection only earned him meows of protest, no injuries. Looking up, his gaze landed on the first-floor bathroom. His heart thudded.

As he approached the crime scene, he paused before entering the bathroom. Expecting to see stains of dried blood, he instead found the beige tile floor clean, wiped, and scrubbed. The knife he'd used had vanished.

"Kate."

So *that's* what had taken her so long last night during her errand to feed the cat and pick up his schedule book.

Guilt squeezed his stomach. He didn't deserve a woman as amazing as Kate Summers. She'd spent most of the night with him in the hospital before leaving in the early morning to prep for court. He was glad she hadn't had to wait with him all day for the consult with the hospital's hand surgeon. Dr. Weiss had chastised him for letting the cuts come within centimeters of a major tendon in his wrist, and then pronounced him a lucky (albeit troubled) man.

By the time Matthew had gotten out of the hospital, he'd had to cancel every one of his eight psychotherapy clients for the day. He'd now have to reschedule, squeezing them into an already-booked calendar over the next few weeks.

He didn't have much time left.

After dodging Slim's hisses and swipes as he wiped her paw clean, Matthew placed her on the floor and went into the kitchen. He ignored the discharge instructions and rifled through the stack of mail. When he landed on a letter from his bank, he felt a brush of fur near his ankles. Adamant meows interrupted his focus.

The meow's increased in volume and frequency as he reached for a bag of treats. He squatted to pour a few beef-flavored nuggets onto the floor, realizing too late that he'd positively reinforced Slim's pain-in-the-ass meowing. Behavior modification with the cat was a total fail. Instead, she'd trained *him* very well.

Now the only sound was her sharp teeth crunching the nibbles, leaving Matthew to return to his letter in peace.

Dr. Durante,

I'm pleased to inform you that we have been able to fulfill your request: your home mortgage has now been paid for twelve months, with the agreement that you will resume monthly payments next April. We appreciate your business.

His satisfaction faded into melancholy as he looked over the comfortable condominium, his home for the past two years. The rich eggplant-colored sofa and loveseat were coated with gray fur, and white stuffing bulged out of the armrest, the victim of Slim's claws. Then he took in the aging psychology volumes on his bookshelf—many recovered from his mother's office—followed by the abstract paintings on his wall, favored by his chemist father.

His phone still had some juice, so he listened to his voicemail. First was a message from a psychology journal, disappointed that he'd canceled his subscription and offering him a discount for resuming it. Matthew deleted that message, but he couldn't ignore the next one. That trembling voice—sounding younger than his twenty years of age—got Matthew every time.

"Hi, Dr. D. It's Cody Keystone. Sorry I'm calling your cell phone…I know I shouldn't unless it's a crisis, but I left some messages at your office number after you canceled today, and, um, you didn't call me back, and, uh, I really need to talk to you. I had a rough night…didn't sleep at all…I don't know how I'm gonna make it through classes if I don't talk to you soon. Crap. This was probably a mistake. I shouldn't bother you. I'll be all right, don't worry…"

Matthew groaned. He'd fretted nonstop over what to do with Cody, and the boy's desperation after missing just one session made it clear there'd be no easy way to terminate their therapy. It would get ugly when he had to deliver the bad news in their next session, which he needed to reschedule pronto. He wondered if it was too late to call him.

He glanced at his watch and frowned. Though it wasn't too late to call a college student, he realized that visiting hours for the day had long since passed. He'd have to wait until tomorrow to see Justin.

The next day, the dark clouds that had gathered since dawn unleashed a torrent of spring rain as Matthew eased his vehicle into a parking space. He'd just cleared a security checkpoint at the entrance to the hospital, and high fences crowned with coiled barbed wire closed in all around him. He switched off the frantic wipers a moment before he shut off the engine, but he could still see the looming hospital through the water streaming down the windshield. A shudder climbed up his spine.

He slid down the cuffs of his long-sleeve shirt to hide his wrist bandages, then grabbed his umbrella and made a mad dash to the concrete building. *Mad* dash? This place had already infiltrated his thoughts.

Cold water had seeped into his shoes by the time he arrived at the entrance, panting.

A guard's stiff-arm stopped him, and the man pointed to a slab of concrete by the door. "Umbrellas stay outside."

"What if somebody steals it?"

A stony stare. "The criminals are *inside*, not outside."

Matthew nodded as he thought about his twin. "Gotcha."

Inside, fluorescent lighting bathed the drab surroundings of the circa-1920s asylum in a humming, unnatural pall. He signed his name in the visitor log and handed over his driver's license to be scanned. He surrendered his jacket and emptied his pockets before walking through the metal detector. The last step was a thorough frisking. Matthew tried not to wince as the guard's rough hands passed over the hidden cuts on his wrists.

Another guard accompanied him to the visitation room, leading him to a cheap plastic chair that had been bolted to the floor.

"Stay put," the guard barked. "The accused will be brought in shortly."

Matthew gave him a grateful smile. "Thank you."

The wait felt interminable, probably because he was jumpier than normal, his mind awash with plans and worries. He observed the room — thick steel door, scuffed white walls, musty smell, and tinny Muzak piped in through some invisible speaker. Pervasive loneliness pressed his shoulders and nailed him to the chair. No wonder Justin had tried to kill himself multiple times in here.

To be fair, Justin had attempted suicide in jail, too. That behavior had gotten him remanded to this facility, to restore competency to stand trial. The judge had agreed with Kate's motion that Justin wasn't competent to mount his defense due to his self-destructive actions. But since arriving here four months ago, Justin's subsequent suicide attempts had only delayed the inevitable: a guilty verdict. Kate had said the evidence against him was overwhelming. She was a sharp defender, but even she wouldn't be able to acquit him. If he made it to trial.

Finally, the metal slab of a door pushed open. Other than the buzzed hair on the patient's head, Matthew stared at his mirror image shuffling into the room in chains. Justin was just shy of 6'4", with the same sky blue eyes, crooked nose, and full lips. His once-chiseled physique had withered over the months since his arrest, but he was still strong enough to warrant cautious handling by the guards.

The guard who guided Justin into the room hadn't seemed like a total bastard in Matthew's past interactions with him — at least there was that. Still, Justin barely seemed to notice when the man dumped him in the chair. His blank expression indicated they had him on some antipsychotic med again, which tightened Matthew's chest.

Smoothing his long, black hair, and pleased to find no wayward strands escaping from the ponytail, Matthew cleared his throat.

"Officer Shaw, would you please remove my brother's chains?"

The red-haired guard frowned. "That's against protocol, Dr. Durante, since the visitation room is off the secure unit."

"I'm aware of that, and I'm also aware that you'll be here the entire time, supervising the visit. The door's locked, right? What could possibly happen?"

Shaw's frown deepened. "I've already got Dr. Pierre coming down to meet with you after visitation, as you requested. What more do you want?"

"I'm grateful for that. C'mon, unlock the chains. Use your *ginjah ninja* skills if my brother tries anything."

Shaw rubbed his ginger-red hair and smiled just a little at that.

As Matthew eyed the wrist bandages visible under the cuffs of Justin's white jumpsuit, his throat constricted. "Truth is, I want…I just want to hug my brother, and have him hug me back, before…"

A hint of sadness flickered in Justin's eyes.

"…before he succeeds in killing himself," Matthew got out. "Before I lose him forever."

"Now look, Dr. Durante, we got him on a one-to-one — nothing's gonna happen—"

"He was under twenty-four-hour surveillance a week ago, wasn't he?"

Shaw sighed. "How could we know he'd confiscate a plastic knife and try to saw off his damn hands with it?"

"You couldn't know," Matthew said softly. "Face it, you can't keep him safe. I can't, either." He looked down. "I've come to accept that."

He swallowed, then looked up. "But I can't accept walking out of here without a proper goodbye. Please let me hug my brother. Please, Officer."

Blotches reddened the guard's freckly complexion as he seemed to consider the request. Matthew held his breath.

"Just for the length of the visit." Shaw whipped out a set of keys and knelt by the chair.

"Thank you, ninja sir." Matthew gulped a breath of relief.

As Shaw unlocked the cuffs, he glared at Justin. "You try anything, Durante, no visitation for a *month*."

Justin's face remained impassive, but once Shaw removed the chains and backed away to a nearby wall, Justin drew his hands together on his lap. At first he stroked the inside of his wrists, likely easing the lingering pain from the tight handcuffs. Then a faint smile crossed his face as his fingers dug deep into his bandaged cuts.

"Stop it!" Matthew reached out to pry Justin's hands free. He clutched his wrists to restrain him.

Justin flinched, then blinked across at him, appearing to notice him for the first time.

"Told you that wasn't a good idea." Shaw smirked.

Matthew's face got hot. "Thank you, Officer."

"Sorry," Justin whispered. "I, I don't want to hurt you, Matty."

Matthew felt his lip quiver. "I know you don't." *You just want to hurt yourself.* "Can I give you a hug, Justin? Would that be okay?"

Justin nodded. "Don't want to hurt you. Sorry I'm such a fuck-up."

"You're *not*." Matthew pulled him up and gathered him in his arms under Shaw's vigilant watch. "You'll be okay."

Though at first Justin remained limp, after a beat he snaked his arms around Matthew's back. Matthew guessed this hug was the only comforting touch Justin had received in some time. Rough hands holding him down were probably the only physical contact he knew. Justin seemed to melt into him.

"This'll be over soon," Matthew whispered in his ear as he clutched him tighter. "I need you to spit out your meds."

When they pulled out of the hug, Justin's eyes held a hint of confusion, mixed with their typical flatness. The brothers returned to their chairs.

"So, how ya doin' in here?" Matthew attempted a smile.

It seemed like Justin had trouble swallowing—probably due to the dry-mouth and swollen-tongue side effects of whatever drugs they'd forced down his throat.

He shrugged. "'Kay." He squinted like he was in a brain fog. "How's Kate?"

"She's good." Matthew felt the weight of his heavy heart with each beat. "Still as feisty as ever."

"That's our Kate."

The cuts on his wrists, less than two days old, burned with each heartbeat. Matthew tugged down his shirtsleeves. "You haven't tried anything in the past week, right?"

Justin looked away. "Sorry I keep screwing up. Don't want to bring you pain, bro, I just can't keep doing this. I can't…"

They'd rehashed this conversation countless times, with Matthew pleading for Justin to stop attempting suicide and Justin refusing. This time Matthew just stayed silent.

When he didn't voice his typical protests, Justin raised his head. "What, you're not going to tell me I deserve to live? That it wasn't my fault Mom and Dad died? That *I* didn't start that fire?"

"You had no idea those chemicals would explode. You didn't make Dad go back in there for her—*he* chose that. It's not your fault!" Matthew huffed a breath as he listened to the echo of his words. Then he slumped in his chair, mad at himself for being goaded into his usual role.

This pointless discussion helped no one. It only served to titillate Officer Shaw, who stood near the wall, nodding. The guard had likely pieced together Justin's childhood fire-starting with the crime that had landed him in The Columbus Hospital for the Insane: the lethal explosion at King Combatics' warehouse.

"It *is* my fault," Justin mumbled.

Matthew's stomach flipped. He now knew Justin's self-blame extended well beyond their parents' deaths, as if that burden alone wasn't enough. It saddened him that his brother kept punishing himself for events beyond his control…for sacrifices he'd made, benefiting Matthew and Kate both.

"How's the food in here?" Matthew faked a grin.

"You don't wanna know."

"Worse than Dad's cooking, even?"

A small smile lightened Justin's face, and in those few seconds, Matthew caught a glimpse of the twin he'd known the first twelve years of their lives. The Justin who was such a know-it-all, taking the lead in their relationship even though he was mere minutes older than Matthew. The Justin who was fearless, knocking them into all sorts of trouble with his thirst for adventure and intellectual stimulation. The Justin who had a booming laugh, filling up the room with his charisma and stupid jokes.

That brother had ceased to exist when the fire had engulfed their parents and they'd gone to live with their dad's boss, Jefferson King. Now that old Justin was gone, replaced by a shell of a man who wasn't much longer for this earth.

Matthew leaned in. "Remember that time Dad broke the microwave?"

"With the grapes?"

"Yeah, when he thought he'd found a new way of making wine. Mom was *pissed*."

"Dad and his chemistry experiments." Justin winced. "He always wanted to see what worked together."

Matthew thought about his father's tall form stooping over his workbench in the basement, absorbed for hours in chemicals and combinations. Dad had used to wave them over to show off his latest bubbling or crackling concoction. Justin had asked all kinds of questions, while Matthew had stifled yawns.

His jaw clenched as he looked at what his brother had become. "*We* work together, you and I. Ever since we shared a womb, we've been together. Without you, I don't exist. Don't you see? There's no reason for me to live if you're gone."

Justin looked down, his voice weaker than a whisper. "I don't justify your existence, Matthew. I only pull you down. I'm an anchor, man."

Matthew looked away, biting back tears.

"You'll see," Justin promised. "You'll be better off when I'm gone."

"*No.*" Matthew bared his teeth as he shot off his chair.

"Hey!" Shaw's shout startled Matthew. "Visit's over." He approached Justin, chains in hand.

"No," Matthew repeated.

Shaw's eyes flared. "You sit your ass down, or I'll restrain you, too."

Matthew took a step back as his pounding heart flooded his chest. He met Shaw's glare for a moment, then exhaled as he collapsed into his chair.

He watched the guard slide on the restraints. The patient appeared serene, and he knew his brother had accepted his death long ago — he only needed to find a surefire way to destroy himself. He knew Justin would figure it out someday. Someday soon.

He, on the other hand, was wild with despair. No way in hell he'd accept losing his brother. No, he would fight. He would do whatever he could.

Once Shaw led Justin out of the room, Matthew paced the cracked linoleum. He was probably the one needing a tranquilizer, not his brother.

There was a knock on the door, and in walked Justin's psychologist, Dr. Francine Pierre. She'd pulled her long blond hair into a sleek ponytail, showcasing her intelligent blue eyes and pouty lips. Matthew continued to be amazed that a woman so beautiful would work in such a frightening environment, though she did seem to thrive on challenge.

"I only have a few minutes, Dr. Durante." Her arms crossed over her chest. His fear must have shown because her voice lightened, her soft French accent growing more pronounced. "How'd your visit go?"

"How's my brother doing?"

She sighed. "You of all people should know about confidentiality limitations."

"He's still not letting you speak to me?"

She looked at the dingy wall.

"Can you at least tell me what you have him on? He looks like a freaking zombie."

"Medication questions should be directed to Dr. Majumdar —"

"Who won't talk to me at all," Matthew fumed.

The corners of her eyes creased. "I know you worry about him. I know how hard it must be seeing your brother accused of such a crime, locked up in here —"

"Are you a twin, Dr. Pierre?"

She blinked several times. "No."

"Then you know squat."

Her mouth tightened. "You may not believe this, but we're trying to help your brother, Dr. Durante. We are. Now, is there anything else I can help you with today?"

"Keep in mind what we both learned in grad school." His eyes hardened. "You can't treat a dead patient."

She held his gaze for a moment before she walked off, calling over her shoulder, "A guard will be here to escort you out."

Once she left, he closed his eyes. He wished he could quell the tremors shaking his heart.

3. Deceit

*M*atthew sat in the therapy office waiting room and tried not to stare at the couple across from him. The woman wouldn't look at the man, who read a month-old *Sports Illustrated* from the office's magazine rack. Both wore wedding rings.

"Huh," the man said. "They predicted the Reds would get last in their division, but they're tearing it up at spring training." At his wife's chilly Do-you-think-I-care? look, he glanced down and muttered, "Sorry." A few seconds later he added, "Guess that's *another* thing you can bitch about to the therapist."

The woman had likely caught her husband cheating, and the man had agreed to couples counseling to try to salvage their crumbling marriage. He'd seen it countless times. Given the wife's hostility and the husband's apparent ineptitude at remorse, Matthew gave the marriage a ten-percent chance. Many couples waited until it was too late to start counseling, leaving everyone feeling like they'd failed when the inevitable split occurred — especially the psychologist.

To distract himself from these dismal musings on marriage, Matthew took out his cell phone and stared at it before sending a text:

Well, I'm here. About to get my brain shrunk.

He slipped his phone back in his pocket, having learned long ago not to expect his girlfriend to respond during the busy workday of a criminal defense attorney. He jumped when his pocket vibrated.

Good. Your head's far too big anyway.

Chuckling, he typed:

Oh yeah it is, baby baby.

Kate's response:

Gross. You need help.

"Matthew Durante?"

A kindly gray-haired man peered down at him. The man's shaggy beard parted from its matching moustache when he grinned.

"That's me." Matthew stood and took the offered hand in a vigorous handshake.

The psychologist maintained his smile as he pointed down the hall toward his office, and his congenial demeanor made Matthew wonder if he was one of the people who *didn't* associate the name Durante with the man accused of bombing a warehouse. Matthew had caught curious stares from the couple across from him when the psychologist said his name.

As they strolled down the hallway, he studied George McCallister. The man's easy gait belied his professorial carriage. Reading glasses hung from a chain around his neck to rest on his protruding belly, and he wore a Glen plaid suit jacket. He could have been a full-fledged Freud lookalike except for the missing pipe and patches on the jacket's elbows.

"Did you find the place okay?" George asked as they entered his office.

"Yeah, no problem."

They sat in opposing easy chairs. "So, what brings you in today, Matt?"

"I go by Matthew." When the psychologist nodded, he sighed. "My girlfriend wants me to get some therapy."

"I see. And how do *you* feel about being here?"

Matthew weighed his question. He would've followed up with something similar if he'd been the therapist. "Not thrilled, to be honest. No offense."

"None taken. It's hard for us guys to pony up and talk about *feelings*." George emphasized the word with a disgusted, effeminate waving of his hands.

Matthew felt himself grin.

"You ever been in counseling before?"

"Nope." He waited a moment before asking, "So, how long have you been a psychologist?"

"Too many years to count. What is it now—thirty-four? I've probably been at this for longer than you've been alive."

"I'm twenty-nine," Matthew confirmed.

"Omph!" The big smile returned.

"Where'd you go to graduate school?"

George crossed his legs. "Okay, so you want to know about my credentials…that's fair. I went to the University of Maryland. I'm a licensed counseling psychologist."

"How about undergrad?"

George feigned umbrage. "Ohio State, of course!"

Matthew smiled again.

"So, what's your girlfriend worried about? Why does she want you to get therapy?"

"Um…" Matthew stalled. "Not sure. Do you get many guys in here whose girlfriends or wives make them go to therapy?"

"Sometimes." George sat back as he appeared to scrutinize him. "Seems tough for you to talk about yourself."

"Not at all. Ask me any question."

"The girlfriend you mentioned—how's your relationship going?"

Matthew shrugged. "Pretty good."

"You want to make her your wife someday?"

That question pierced his heart. God, how he wanted that. *So much.* But he knew he couldn't have a happy-ever-after with Kate… not when Justin needed him so desperately. "No. We wouldn't work together."

George's forehead creased. "How long have you been dating?"

"Fourteen years."

"You met her when you were *fifteen?*" George's lips parted.

"I met her when I was thirteen, when she came to live with the same foster family. We started dating a couple of years later."

"Wow. That sounds like a bond that'd be hard to break."

Matthew looked away, his throat tight. "Yes."

"But you 'don't work well together'?"

He felt his mouth curl into a faint smile. "She's bossy—a real pain in the ass when she doesn't get her way. She's overprotective, too…always in my business."

George squinted at him. "You know, when you say those things, you sound like you don't mind her being bossy and overprotective. Sounds almost like you enjoy it."

Crap. He'd shown his true feelings. He wished he could be more like his brother, who disguised his inner turmoil.

"You said you were in foster care. Did something happen to your parents?"

He swallowed. "They died when I was twelve."

"That must've been horribly painful for you."

"Yes."

After a beat, George asked, "How'd they die?"

Matthew tapped his fingertips on one thigh. He didn't want to get into this history. All he wanted was to test this psychologist, see how good he was. But something compelled him to answer. "There was a fire in our basement. We thought we got everyone out—even Marie and Alfie—"

"Marie and Alfie?"

"Marie Curie and Alfred Adler, our cats."

"Ah." George nodded.

"But then my dad realized my mom was still in there." It was quiet between them, and Matthew took a deep breath. "He went in for her, and…he didn't come back out."

George winced. "What a tragedy—you lost both of your parents at once." He smoothed down his beard, and Matthew stared at his feet. "How'd the fire start?"

He shook his head. "That's unimportant."

"Okay. So, then, what *is* important? Does your girlfriend want you to process your grief in here?"

Probably. But she really wants me to open up about my brother and why I slit my wrists, which will not *happen.*

Matthew sat up a bit. "I should quit wasting your time and tell you the real reason I'm here."

"Yes?"

He squared his shoulders. "Truth is, I'm dying of cancer."

"But you look so healthy!"

With a sad smile, Matthew said, "That's what the doctors say, too. But they also tell me my insides are a mess, and any day now I'll have to check into hospice."

"What kind of cancer is it?"

"Gallbladder — adenocarcinoma." He hoped he'd pronounced that right. His research had indicated it was a rare type of cancer, and lack of familiarity meant fewer questions from nosy clients — and nosy psychologists, for that matter.

The psychologist's slow nods gathered speed. "You're facing a death sentence. Is that why you tried to cut your wrists?"

Matthew recoiled as he darted his right hand to his left cuff. *Damn it!* The psychologist must have seen his bandages. "Not much gets by you, does it, Dr. McCallister?"

George said nothing.

He went with it. "Yeah, I tried to slit my wrists. I thought doing the deed myself would make things easier. I don't want my girlfriend to have to watch me endure a slow, painful death."

"I imagine you don't want your brother to have to watch that, either. You look just like him…You must be twins?"

The psychologist surprised him once again. So George *did* know about Justin Durante, psychotic bomber. Yet there was no judgment in those warm, brown eyes. Instead of the flash of anger he typically felt at the mention of his brother, Matthew found himself blinking back tears.

"It must be terribly difficult to live in the shadow of Justin's crime — alleged crime," George added.

He cleared his throat. "It's not too bad."

George leaned forward. "You don't have to pretend in here, Matthew. It seems your life's been one tragedy after another. You lose your parents when you're only twelve, your twin gets arrested for terrorism, and now you're dying of cancer? I'd say counseling is long overdue."

He clenched his jaw. All he did anymore was pretend, and pretense would be hard to get away with under George's dissecting gaze.

"But of all those tragedies, I'm guessing you're here to talk about one thing: your brother. You can't die in peace knowing he's rotting in there. It's impossible to say goodbye. He's all you've got left."

Matthew shifted, uneasy in the chair. *Time for misdirection.* "You're wrong—I've already made peace with my brother. He killed Dr. Frederick, and he needs to pay his debt to society." Matthew paused, wondering if George had read the more detailed *Dispatch* article about Justin's arrest or simply recognized him from television.

"Do you know what I do for a living?"

"No."

Television only, then. "The real reason I came in? I need to find a competent therapist to refer my clients to when I go to hospice. I'm a psychologist, you see."

George's eyebrows shot up. "You're a psychologist?"

"Yes. I apologize for not coming forward with that at first, but I wanted to be certain I could trust you. I have some very troubled clients, and I want to make sure they're taken care of when I'm gone."

George gaped at him.

"Are you accepting new clients, Dr. McCallister?"

"Uh…yes, I suppose."

"Good. I'll give you a call to brief you on my clients' backgrounds once I get signed releases from them." Matthew stood.

"Hold on! I need to ask a few more questions. Won't you stay?"

He glanced at his watch. "I have to get to my office soon. You got five minutes." He sat again.

George looked down at his notes, and Matthew bet he thought, *Five minutes? I need five* years!

"You tried to cut your wrists," the doctor said. "Are you still having suicidal thoughts?"

"No, that was stupid. My girlfriend made me see that."

"Are you sure? No suicidal urges?"

"None of that. I want to live, for as long as I can, anyway." *I need to carry out my plan.*

"You really don't want to be in therapy right now?" George asked. "You have a lot to deal with, son."

"I don't want to spend my last days getting analyzed. There're many people more deserving of your services."

"I think you're very deserving, Matthew. Uh, how do I say this? I'm worried about you. I'm concerned you're too impaired to see clients right now."

He grinned. "That's why I'm referring them to you, Doc." He stood again.

George got to his feet as well, but hesitated to shake his hand. "You're always welcome back if you change your mind. I'm sorry I won't have the pleasure of getting to know you."

"Me, too. But you're really helping me by taking on some of my clients. It'll give me huge peace of mind, believe me."

"I hope you find some peace during your last days, Matthew." George held onto his hand as he looked into his eyes.

The man's physical and emotional warmth consumed him. He nodded, and part of him wished he could stay in therapy. "Thank you, George."

Cody paused. "You're still listening, right?"

Matthew blinked a few times at his sandy-haired client. Where had he just been? "Yeah, go ahead."

"And then Steve called me a fucking loser right there in the locker room. Told me I didn't deserve to be on the team."

"Wow. That *was* a bad day. Steve's still pissed about the alcohol incident?"

Cody nodded.

"Steve's the one who got busted for buying you booze the night you went to the hospital, right?"

"Yeah. But that happened in December — freaking four months ago. He's never gonna let me forget it."

"You almost *died*, Cody. I don't want you to forget your overdose either. Thank God your coach took it seriously and mandated counseling for you both."

He scoffed. "Yeah, it's sooo great."

The pronounced eye-roll made Matthew smile. "As I recall, Steve's going to the student counseling center for his mandated counseling. You know, *you* could go there for free."

"Are you trying to get rid of me?"

Matthew laughed off the comment. "Speaking of alcohol, how's your social life now that the season's over?"

"We're back in the pool, you know. Just 'cause Big Tens and NCAAs are done doesn't mean we stop training. We're always in-season."

"Right, almost forgot how dedicated you swimmers are. And nice try avoiding the question. How *is* your social life? Have you been able to identify a sober social support network?"

"Everything's cool. You don't have to worry."

He sighed. "So you've been drinking again."

Cody looked down.

In a softer voice, Matthew asked, "You're using alcohol to help you fall asleep?"

He nodded.

"Flashbacks?"

The tall, muscular swimmer seemed to shrink, his voice small. "Yeah."

"Are you remembering to use your grounding strategies? Deep breaths? Reorienting yourself to the present?"

Cody looked up with a sheepish shrug. "Sorry, I forgot."

"That's okay. It's hard to remember when you're freaking out from a flashback. How about you put those grounding skills papers near your bed, to remind yourself how to get through flashbacks and nightmares?"

"'Kay."

"Good. And let's review the facts on how alcohol affects sleep."

A hint of anger crept into Cody's voice. "We already went over this."

"Yeah, we did, but you're still drinking to help you sleep, so we need to go over it again."

The boy pouted for several moments. "Alcohol helps you fall asleep faster, but it affects with the quality of your sleep — it interferes with your REM cycles."

"Excellent." Matthew gave him a stern look. "And could you remind me what happens if you get caught drinking again?"

Cody stiffened. After ten seconds of glaring, he mumbled, "I could lose my scholarship."

"I know how much you love swimming. That seems like a pretty big risk, don't you think?"

"Why're you such a jackoff today? You're treating me like I'm eight years old!"

Surprised by Cody's outburst, Matthew sat back. "I didn't mean to do that. Sorry." He drew in a breath, wondering why he'd pushed his client so hard. He felt more like a lecturing parent than a collaborative therapist. A grim sense of urgency gnawed at him.

"I've been distracted today — I apologize. It's because I've got some stuff on my mind. I need to tell you something."

The boy's anger seemed to shift into curiosity.

"I…I'm…" Matthew's mouth felt dry. "I need to stop seeing clients. I'm afraid I have to refer you to another therapist."

Cody's eyes got huge. "W-W-Why? You don't want to see me anymore, right? I'm too much trouble. Sorry, I didn't mean to burn you out—"

"Cody, no. This has nothing to do with you. I wish I could keep seeing you — I don't want to refer you."

"Then don't. Please, don't make me see another therapist. Nobody understands what I've been through like you do."

"There are lots of trauma counselors out there. It's true we had the same foster father, but that doesn't mean I'm the only one who can help you."

"Yes, you are! I can't tell anyone else what happened to me…I, I can't. You said it didn't happen to you, but you know him. You know what a bastard he is."

Matthew indeed knew the depravity of Jefferson King.

"I never would've looked you up like I did if I knew you'd do this to me. How can you just leave?"

Matthew grimaced as he recalled their first session almost four months ago. He'd asked why Cody had come off-campus for counseling.

"I read that article about your brother, you know, when he was arrested. What a coincidence that Justin blew up the King Combatics

plant, considering he'd been Dr. King's foster kid for six years." Cody's unflinching stare had immobilized him. *"And how ironic one twin brother was psycho while the other was a psychologist."*

Matthew had been furious, thinking his new client was only there to throw his family heartache in his face, until Cody had explained the reason for seeking him out: *"I was Dr. King's foster kid, too."*

When Cody confessed that Dr. King had sexually abused him, Matthew had been stunned. He'd had to report the abuse to Child Protective Services despite Cody's protests. Matthew had explained that he had no choice in making the report, especially knowing that King had two more foster children at the time. When he didn't hear anything about the CPS investigation, he'd sniffed around and discovered that the teenage boy living with King had run away shortly after Justin had been arrested. But the teenage girl had continued to live with King, so the investigation must have led to a dead-end.

Cody's wounded, glassy eyes drilled into Matthew once again, breaking him out of the memory. "I wish I never came here," Cody said. "You don't care about me. You never did."

"You're wrong. I do care about you, and I feel horrible that I have to leave. I'm so glad—so *honored* that you came to see me. But I can't continue as your therapist. I have my reasons."

"Yeah? Like what?"

Time to rip the Band-Aid off. He couldn't hate himself more. "I have cancer."

The boy's eyes filled with tears.

I'm a monster.

Cody swiped at his face. "You have cancer? But you'll be okay, right? Right?"

Matthew looked away.

He gasped. "You're, wait, you're not, um, you're…"

"My doctors want me to take some time off. Chemo's not an option, but they're trying every other treatment, even the experimental ones—"

"Oh, my God—you're *dying?*" Cody started sobbing. "How could this happen? You're a good guy. This isn't supposed to happen. This isn't fair!"

Matthew let him cry it out for several moments. "I imagine this is difficult to take in. I'm sorry I can't keep seeing you, but it wouldn't be right to keep going when I'm this sick. I can see you one more time after this, okay? We'll have one more session, and we can talk about terminating, get you set up with someone else. I met a great psychologist—George McCallister. I think you'll really like him."

Cody was crying so hard he could barely get the words out. "I don't…" He sniffed. "I don't want to see *George!*" He lunged for his backpack and rushed out of the room, leaving Matthew to stare at the slammed door.

"*That* went well." He cradled his face in his hands.

4. Betrayal

A week later, Matthew whisked an item out of a crinkly bag and yanked off its department store tags before he buried them in the trash. As he held the silky material in his hand, stomach acid surged up his throat.

After a thick swallow, he announced to the empty bedroom: "You can do this."

Slim lay sprawled on her side near the chest of drawers. Her tail swished as her green eyes tracked him.

Matthew crossed over to his bed. He shoved the item under the pillow, then dashed out of the room, flipping off the light switch behind him.

Later that night, Kate's eyes roamed up Matthew's light blue button-down shirt and black suit jacket, which fit sleekly over his muscular frame. His lack of tie allowed a peek at the smooth grooves lining the recently enhanced muscles of his chest.

She watched their waitress, Angel, flirt with him right in front of her. Matthew's apparent obliviousness to the ho-bag's charms vexed her. Usually he'd pick up on slutty moves like Angel's lean-in cleavage display as she pointed out a full-bodied wine on the list. Normally he'd notice the soft lick of her lips and the toss of her bleached-blond hair.

Kate waited for a playful wink from Matthew as he tried to dodge the tip of her pointed shoe kicking his shin under the table. But tonight none of that happened. The waitress frowned as he distractedly selected a bottle of pinot noir and then all but ignored her to stare at his phone.

Angel gave a terse "Right away, sir," and left in a huff.

"What's up with you tonight?" Kate asked.

Matthew's eyes widened before he pocketed the phone. "What do you mean?"

"You're quiet."

"Sorry." He chewed on his lower lip. "Rough day at work."

"Yeah?"

"I had to terminate with a client." He grimaced. "He's an abuse survivor, so I didn't want to initiate a hug, but he seemed like he needed it."

Given the privacy requirements of his profession, Kate didn't want to pry. But the question left her mouth before she could stop it. "What happened? His insurance benefits run out?"

"No." He gave a heavy sigh. "I had to fire him. He's an addict who needs more help than I can provide, so I kicked him out." He frowned. "Makes me sound like a coldhearted bastard."

"Not at all."

"I probably shouldn't say more."

"I have confidentiality restrictions too, Matthew. You know I'd never tell anybody what you say, right?"

"I know. It's just…I shouldn't talk about my clients."

She smiled at him. "I know you care about them. You want to do right by them."

When he ducked his head, she wondered why he seemed embarrassed.

She reached across the table to clasp his fingers and stroked the back of his hand. "Could you put work away, for now? Just enjoy our night together?"

"Of course." He nodded. "How could I pay attention to anything but your ravishing beauty?"

She shook her head, then glanced at her feet. "Should've worn boots tonight. The bullshit's getting thick."

His laugh as he caressed her hand loosened the tension in her shoulders. The light in his eyes—its shiny blue even more vivid next to the hue of his shirt—showed a glimpse of his usual self.

"I'm glad we're here together," he said. His smile faded. "I want to cherish this night."

Her shoulders tightened again. *Why does it sound like he's leaving me?*

Angel returned and uncorked their bottle of red. As she poured a taste for Matthew, Kate caught a whiff of its plum bouquet.

He swirled the wine in his glass and took a sip, then nodded. "Excellent recommendation, Angel."

She smiled brightly, and when she clasped her hands behind her back, her voluptuous breasts pushed forward. "Let me tell you about our specials tonight."

Though Matthew's eyes had landed on her unavoidable chest only for a second, it was long enough for Kate to notice. His muted *Oomph* as shoe hit shin caused Angel to pause before resuming her description of balsamic-braised pork tenderloin with shallots.

After they'd placed their orders, Kate watched Matthew reach down under the table, probably to rub his bruised shin.

"Glad you *didn't* wear boots tonight," he muttered.

She sipped the fragrant wine. "Nice place you've taken me to." Her vision narrowed. "Any special occasion?"

He straightened. "Just a night out for the two of us. Does there need to be a special occasion?"

"As in our fourteen-year anniversary?"

His face fell. "It's April seventh?" He looked at his phone. "Shit."

April seventh…their first kiss. Years ago, she'd peered over her shoulder at the lanky teenager, his eyes alight with intrigue as she led him behind the toolshed in Dr. King's backyard. She'd known the second her intentions became clear because his hand started shaking in her grasp. Her heart had pounded like a jackhammer as he lowered his mouth to hers, sweet and possessive. He'd tasted like nacho chips.

"*Kate.*"

Her eyes snapped open.

"Oh, God, Kate, I'm so sorry. I've just been so preoccupied lately, I—"

"It's okay." Her lips glued together. "You've been working a lot."

When he stretched for her hand, she almost stole it back.

"It's *not* okay," he said. "I'm an idiot. Work's never more important than you."

As Angel arrived with the breadbasket, they broke contact. The waitress seemed to sense the tension and lingered at their table for an awkward moment.

Once she left, Matthew's hand trembled as he reached for his wineglass and lifted it. "To fourteen years." His eyes seemed conflicted—at once devoted and desperate.

Kate hesitated. *Every romance is full of little disappointments,* she'd read in a magazine. *It's the big moments that make a relationship worth it.* She realized the past few months of her romance had included quite a few little disappointments—small letdowns that had accumulated into something larger, something more salient. For the first time, she wondered if their relationship was indeed worth it. Such blasphemous thoughts after fourteen years together astounded her.

Pasting on a smile, she lifted her glass and clinked his. Despite her disloyal thinking, his crystal blue eyes stole her breath every time. They were shards of fine glass, soulful and sultry.

Though he'd grown taller since they'd first met, now filling out his angular frame and needing to shave every day, those eyes hadn't changed at all. They were the same eyes that had gazed at her behind that shed, blinking in the sunlight before he'd leaned in and touched his lips to hers.

"Fourteen years is a long time," she finally said.

He grunted.

"A long time to be together…" Her voice faltered. "And not married."

Matthew winced as his hand grazed his chest. "Please, I don't want to talk about this."

"For someone who talks about emotional crap all day long, you're surprisingly tight-lipped when it comes to discussing our relationship."

His lips pressing together proved her point.

"Matthew, you used to be more talkative, more involved, more present. At this point I feel like I could get more out of *Justin*." He looked away, but she kept going, "And we both know how Justin's terrified of any conversation of substance. I thought you were different."

He splayed his hands out to the side. "What's the point of discussing this, Kate?" His voice rose. "We're clearly at an impasse. You want to get married now, and I want to get married later—when the time is right."

"But you thought the time was right seven months ago." She breathed out through her nose. "Don't you remember ring shopping?"

"And don't you remember what happened right after ring shopping?"

She squeezed her hands together as she thought of Justin's arrest.

He shot her an incredulous look. "How exactly are we supposed to plan a wedding while my brother's hauled off to a psych hospital? You want me just to forget him?"

"Of course not. Listen, it killed me, too, when he got arrested. I did everything I could to get him to trial." She swallowed. "I know I fell short."

"It's not your fault." He looked down. "Justin's guilty as hell."

A gasp climbed up her throat. "But you think he's innocent."

He looked up. "I changed my mind."

"Why?"

"I woke up to reality. You should stop living in fantasyland, too."

Who is this man? "How can you say that? Justin would never hurt that scientist—you and I both know he's the most harmless person around. He would never have murdered Elyse Frederick. He loved her."

"He *stalked* her."

Kate blew out a breath. *This again.* In addition to evidence tying Justin to the bomb, investigators had found a recording from King Combatics' security cameras that had survived the blast—an interaction between Justin and Dr. Elyse Frederick that Kate knew would damn him at trial.

The recording had showed Elyse flinching in her office chair. "Oh! You startled me," she'd said.

"Sorry." Justin stepped into the frame wearing a navy blue maintenance jumpsuit and clutching a broom.

"You shouldn't be here, shouldn't come so close." Elyse gestured to a device on the table. Her long brown hair had swayed as she shook her head.

He inched closer to her. "If it's that dangerous, you shouldn't be here, either."

"That's sweet, Justin." Her face lit up when she smiled.

He seemed under a spell as he gazed at her. "Sorry if I'm disturbing you, but it's after midnight. Don't you need to be in bed?"

She glanced down as her cheeks flushed.

"I mean, go home…"

"Dr. King needs these bomb triggers by tomorrow."

Justin seemed to pale as he stepped back. His jaw went slack.

Elyse frowned with apparent confusion. "He's a slave driver, you know?" She set down her tool and stood.

Justin jumped back a foot. "I'll let you get back to work, ma'am."

"*Ma'am?*" One corner of her mouth quirked. "I told you to call me Elyse."

"It's late." His voice shook, and he winced, standing taller as he gripped his broom. "I'll walk you to your car when you're done."

"I'll be fine."

He gave a resigned nod as he looked down. The audio barely caught his mutter. "Damaged goods. You deserve better."

She leaned forward, like she couldn't hear him, then reeled back with a gasp when a crack resounded.

Justin had gaped at the jagged broom in one hand and the split-off top piece of the handle in the other. His head had shot up, and when he noticed her fear, he'd taken off running.

Matthew's voice broke in to her memory. "Guilty or not, he'll be convicted of the crime."

"Most likely. For now he's doing the time." A long sigh deflated her. "And I feel like our relationship's been arrested right along with him." She gazed into his troubled eyes. "When will our imprisonment be over, Matthew? When will we be free?"

His rapid blinks made it seem like he struggled not to cry.

Her voice dropped. "When will you come back to me?"

"I want to come back." He swallowed. "But when Justin set off that bomb, things changed. He needs me more than you do."

"What does that even mean? Why can't we *both* have you?"

Angel appeared at their side, holding two steaming plates. She set down their entrees and slunk away from the table.

Kate forced a few bites down her throat.

After dinner, when Matthew turned his Honda Accord north on High Street, she shot him a confused look. "You're taking me to your place?"

"Yes. That's not okay with you?"

She stared at him for several seconds. "I think I'd rather go home."

Considering her request, he eased the car over to the shoulder and let the engine idle as the heater pumped warm air on his feet. The idea of calling it a night and taking her home was quite appealing, but also quite avoidant. *Coward.*

"I, um, I'd like you to come to my place, if you're willing?" He searched her eyes. "I know this has been the shittiest anniversary ever, but maybe we could turn it around?"

She seemed to deliberate.

He made a last-ditch effort. "Slim misses you."

Her eyes narrowed. "You and that damn cat."

Knowing he'd convinced her, he smirked as he merged the car back with traffic.

They arrived at his condo and came in through the garage just like they always did, but their well-practiced walk inside seemed awkward tonight. Matthew heard a *thump* from upstairs — Slim hopping off his bed — soon followed by the fuzzy gray cat's waddle down the stairs.

"Hey, Slimmy," Kate cooed, reaching down to scratch behind her ears. Slim halted on a step, trying to sniff Kate's hand before allowing her to touch her.

Matthew angled his head as he watched the interaction. Though he'd caught Kate petting his cat more than once when he'd been out of the room, she'd often ignored Slim when they were together, claiming the cat was mean and messy. She kept her own apartment pristine and often looked disparagingly at the rips in his sofa armrest.

He noticed her hand shaking as she held it out for a cat scan. How could she be nervous around *him?* He scowled as he realized his recent behavior had bothered her. It had bothered him, too.

Shrugging out of his suit jacket, he hung it on the post at the bottom of the stairwell. He grasped her hand and yanked her flush against his body. Kate inhaled as she blinked up at him. When he nudged in to kiss her, he felt the tension in her shoulder blades and the tightness of her mouth. He proceeded slowly, letting his breath warm her skin as he kissed along her jaw, ending at the curve under her ear.

"Sorry I'm a thoughtless jerk," he whispered. "I love you." He breathed in her cocoa butter scent. Eventually, her shoulders relaxed, and the closeness of her body warmed him.

He barely noticed Slim's insistent meows.

As he tasted the remnants of red wine on Kate's mouth, he trapped one corner of her lip between his teeth and gently tugged. Her hands snaked up to smooth his hair.

He slid her blouse down to expose the milky skin of her shoulder, and leaned in to scorch a trail of kisses from elegant clavicle to sexy shoulder. She responded by pulling off his ponytail holder and running her fingers through his hair. Her fingertips worked a deep massage at the roots, causing his eyes to close and his head to tilt back. He hoped the stubble of his five o'clock shadow didn't feel too rough against her lips, which now grazed his neck. She could still undo him with that sassy mouth of hers.

His eyes popped open when she unbuckled his belt. With a naughty glint in her coppery eyes, she grabbed his hand and led him toward the sofa. His heart thumped—that wasn't the location he'd planned. He shook his head and pulled her in the opposite direction, toward the stairs. But she looked over her shoulder at the sofa and back at him several times.

Why doesn't she want to go to the bedroom? He heard his voice shake. "You don't want to?"

She paused. "Of course I want to."

Yet when he pulled again at her hand, her feet stayed in place.

"Matthew, I…" She bit her lip, then blurted, "Why buy a cow when you get the milk for free?"

He stared at her for a few seconds. "You're worried about giving your milk away? But I *want* to buy the cow! I want to marry you. God, I want to be with you the rest of my life. Don't you know that?"

"*How* would I know that?"

He pulled her to him again as he drew up their hands and clasped their fists between their chests. "Because you know me. You *know* me, Kate. No matter what happens, don't ever forget who I really am, okay?"

Her eyes grew big. "That sounds ominous."

"It just means I love you. I want you to feel my love, deep inside of you. You're the only woman for me. You're the only woman I'll ever want."

"You've told me that before, but it's getting harder to believe." Her cheeks colored. "Make no mistake—we *will* marry soon."

He hid his flash of sadness with a smile. "Fine. But first, come to my bed, cow. I'm thirsty for some of your milk."

She shoved their entwined fists into his chest. "You're such a prick."

He glanced down at his protruding belt flap and lifted his eyes with a devilish grin. "Thank you, Elsie. To the bedroom, then?"

She growled, her face flushed with desire.

He guided her up the stairs and managed to avoid stepping on the protesting cat.

"Wow, you actually made your bed," she teased.

"Clean sheets too, madam." He gave a little bow before scooting over to the dresser and lighting a eucalyptus-scented candle, followed by turning off the overhead light. He was back in her arms before she'd finished unbuttoning her blouse.

"You need to let me do that," he said. He shooed her hands away from the bottom button and finished the job himself. Sliding the gossamer purple blouse off her shoulders, his mouth made a beeline for the alcove of warm skin between her breasts, nudging his nose into the dark and delicious nook.

She tucked strands of wayward hair behind his ears and leaned down to kiss the top of his head. Her fingertips dug into his skull when he kneaded her breasts through the silky fabric of her bra. *She likes that.*

He stood and reached behind her to fumble with the tiny clasps of her bra while her hands glided down to unbutton his shirt. She seemed to have trouble, and he looked down to see the buttons bulge over his pectoral muscles. She was still struggling with the third button when he felt the clasp of her bra release.

When she got the shirt off him, she shook her head. "Time to buy bigger shirts, bodybuilder boy."

His hands paused their scrabbling on her skirt zipper. "You like my new muscles?"

"They're nice, I guess. But I always loved your body the way it was." Frowning, she added, "You know, it's kind of weird…you're looking more like Justin every day."

His chest squeezed as he pulled back from her.

"What's wrong?"

He turned away from her and looked down at his clenching fists, which rippled the taut muscles of his forearms.

"Matthew?"

"Maybe you're right." He gulped. "Maybe I should take you home."

Her hands darted up to cross over her bare breasts. "You change your mind just like that? What's your deal tonight?"

He closed his eyes. *Don't do this. Don't hurt her this way. Just take her home.*

A strange coldness entered her voice. "Maybe I should get myself some boobs like that waitress. Maybe then you wouldn't change your mind."

"God, no!" He stepped closer. "You're perfect, Kate. I *love* these." He cradled the swell of her breasts in his palms. "Promise me you won't ever change these beauties."

"You're confusing the hell out of me! What's your problem?" She caught his wrists and forced his hands to rest between them, twisting them so his palms faced up. The bandages had come off, exposing the serrated scars from the cuts he'd made on his wrists, jagged and deep. "Are *these* related to your bizarre behavior tonight? Are you still not right?"

He tried to avoid her gaze.

"When Justin got arrested, I know it was awful, but at least we were together. You were still there for me. But these last few months, you've changed." She let go of his hands. "I feel so alone."

"Oh, Kate." He embraced her, then cringed as she stiffened in his arms. "Please, don't be mad." She shuddered. "I'm sorry for hurting you. I never meant to hurt you, of all people. I love you so much."

Her face buried in the crook of his neck, their bare chests smashed together. In a flash her lips were on his, greedily kissing and sucking as if she sought comfort in his familiar touch.

He couldn't help himself—his hardness returned. It seemed she could feel him pressing into her because she groped for his belt as she deepened her kisses. He found her zipper again and succeeded at removing her skirt just as she scooted his pants down his legs.

Matthew pulled her backward toward the bed, managing to shed his pants in the process. Without removing his lips from her skin, he lowered himself onto the duvet with her on top of him. The pressure of her lithe body was exquisite, and he clutched the curve of her bottom as she dropped wet kisses down the hard line of his chest.

He knew just what to do to get her going. One hand massaged her perky behind while the other swirled inside of her. Her increasing breaths gave him the feedback he needed. *Her* hands, meanwhile, were doing some magical things to him down below.

Panting, he fumbled for the end table, somehow sliding open the drawer and feeling for the box of condoms.

Kate yanked his arm and replaced his hand on her bottom. She shook her head with a breathless murmur, "We're covered."

His brain was low on blood supply, now funneled below, and feeling cloudy and weightless, he strained to understand her meaning. But in a heartbeat she'd guided him inside of her, and all remnants of thought ceased. There was only feeling—rocking, squeezing, pulsing…soaring…floating. He was indeed covered. And she was screwed.

He wanted to climb inside her. After rolling her beneath him, his skin smashed on hers, he took her more aggressively than ever before. Urgency possessed him, and her bucking hips and clawing fingernails down his back only encouraged him. Her vocalizations, at first soft and breathy, grew deeper, more feral. When a strange noise escaped her mouth, a high-pitched vibrato note that held incessantly long, increasing in intensity and volume, he halted his pillaging of her body.

The echo of the operatic cry reverberated in his ears before they both burst out in laughter. He gazed down into her burnished eyes, shining in the candlelight. "Are you first or second soprano?"

"First," she replied with a grin. "I'm always first, Matthew."

"You are." He kissed her cheek, relishing the feel of her body beneath his. He squeezed her like a departing soldier clutched his pregnant wife, and beads of sweat dotted his hairline from her body's heat. With a desire to hold onto this memory, he held her for a long moment. Then he unwrapped his sweaty body from hers and rolled onto his back.

She smiled as she stretched her limbs with a dancer's grace. When she sat up, she frowned at the crumpled duvet beneath them. "We should've taken this down first." She peeled down one corner of the duvet, and Matthew sat up as well to help her uncover the sheets.

"I have to wash it soon, anyway. There's cat hair everywhere."

As she tugged at the duvet, one of the pillows dislodged, revealing a flash of black on the sheets. She squinted at him before she picked up the black bra. The bulging D cups meant it wasn't hers.

Matthew felt his stomach drop, watching her discover the bra. Her cheeks flushed as she turned to face him. Her jaw unhinged and her mouth seemed unable to form words. She threw down the offending piece of lingerie and crawled to the edge of the bed.

When her betrayed eyes met his again, the storm of pain raging in them horrified him. "You're not saying anything," she rasped. "You're not denying it."

Unable to look at her, he turned away. "I'm so sorry." This hurt way more than he'd expected.

"It all makes sense now," she spat as she rose to her knees. "The extra hours at 'work,' heading to the gym all the time, the fucking aloof, distant *thing* you've got going on. I thought it was *me*, I thought…" A tormented sob swallowed her words.

The mattress dipped, and he braced to get hit, hoping the bruises wouldn't interfere with his plan.

But no angry fists came at him. He looked up to find Kate's clothes and shoes already gathered in her arms as the milky white skin of her backside zoomed for the door.

"Kate, wait!" He scrambled off the bed and fumbled with his pants. "I'll drive you home." He heard her thunder down the stairs, and after a moment she slammed his front door before he could find his other shoe. "Kate!"

He raced downstairs and out the front door, calling for her while hiking up his beltless pants.

"Kate!" He sprinted up and down the empty streets of his condominium complex as he searched.

He kept calling her name until he was hoarse and his neighbors emerged from their condos, drawn out into the night by the hollering shirtless man — the crazed psychologist whose brother was crazy and psycho.

But she was gone.

She was gone.

He doubled over and crouched down, scrunching his eyes shut and rocking in the middle of the street.

5. Shock

This time it wasn't raining.

Six days after he'd betrayed Kate, Matthew hustled to the entrance of the Columbus Hospital for the Insane. Despite the weight of his thoughts, the brightness of the spring day distracted him. Wisps of clouds streaked the brilliant blue sky, and the cozy warmth of the sun drew his eyes to the celestial canvas. Craving one last look at nature's beauty, he inhaled the smell of freedom.

In an instant, he careened forward and caught his fall with outstretched hands. His chest followed, landing with a thump on the concrete sidewalk.

Dazed, he glanced over his shoulder at the small metal box protruding from the ground next to him.

"You okay, sir?" a deep voice asked, and Matthew looked ahead to see a guard jogging toward him.

Before the guard arrived, he was back on his feet. He brushed his stinging palms against the seat of his pants. "I'm fine. Just tripped, I guess."

"Did you break any skin?"

"No." He gave a tight smile. "It was nothing."

The guard eyed him for a moment, then pinched the com-link near his collarbone. "Three to base. Get maintenance to check detector five."

The radio squawked back. "There a problem?"

Three smirked. "Visitor just tripped over it. Guess the motion detector did its job real good."

Matthew's heart raced.

"You need to stay on the sidewalk, sir. Whatcha in such a hurry for, anyway? Visiting hours are over."

"I know. Dr. Pierre told me to come right away." His hair was in disarray, obscuring his face, and he smoothed the strands behind his ears. "My brother tried to kill himself again."

Once the guard realized who he was, he stepped back.

Matthew wondered when such a repulsed reaction would stop hurting so much.

"I see," the guard said, all business now. "Let's get you inside, then."

He blanched when the guard clasped his arm and led him forward with long strides. He supposed he should get accustomed to the manhandling.

Once they entered the gloomy institution, the enormity of his mission pressed down on him. He strained for air as he handed over his wallet, keys, and cell phone. *This is really happening.*

Emerging from the metal detector, he retrieved his belt from the X-ray machine and threaded it through his pant loops as he attempted to hide the tremor in his hands. A different guard waited to escort him to the visitation room. "Uh…" Matthew glanced up at him. "I need to use the head first."

The guard looked him up and down. "This way."

Matthew followed the uniformed man until they stopped in front of a door. "You've got three minutes," the guard growled. "I'll be right outside."

"That's not necessary."

But the guard stayed put.

After Matthew scurried into the unisex bathroom, he wheeled around to reach for the lock but there wasn't one. Erupting into full-body shakes, he staggered to the sink and stared at himself in the cloudy version of a mirror.

With alarm, he noticed his hair was out of place, and he made a quick adjustment. "Pull it together," he whispered to his reflection.

He drew his trembling hands to the faucet and ran cool water over his palms. The running water soothed him, and he reminded himself to suck in some deep breaths. Cody's voice, woven with threads of pain and numbness, echoed in his mind.

"He told me he'd rape her if I didn't submit to him."

Matthew clenched his jaw. When he raised his eyes to the reflective surface, he noticed they'd darkened with fury. His trembling stopped on a dime.

"I'm ready," he said as he emerged from the bathroom.

The guard nodded and accompanied him through several locked stations, each time waiting to be buzzed through under the watchful eye of guards. At last they arrived at the familiar visitation room. Once the guard left, Matthew's only company was the chill of fear.

When he heard a clank of keys and groan of the thick steel door, he let out a breath as he saw it was Officer Shaw who accompanied Justin. Matthew did all he could to remain planted in his chair, trying not to spook the guard.

Justin looked straight ahead as he shuffled forward. The chains encircling his ankles, waist, and wrists clanked with each step. Shaw dumped Justin into the chair across from him.

Matthew waited until Shaw gave him a guilty glance. "Please, Officer Shaw? Remove the chains?"

Shaw scowled. "This can't become a regular thing, Dr. Durante. I'll lose my job."

"I agree," Matthew spat. "This can't become a regular thing. I'll lose my *brother.*" His glower matched the bitterness in his voice. "Oh, wait. This *has* become a regular thing. You guys want him dead, don't you?"

"Now listen, we stopped him before—"

"Please. I won't tell anyone if you take off the chains, and this room's not wired with cameras, right?"

Shaw grunted as he studied Justin.

To Matthew, his twin looked still as catatonia. In contrast, he felt restless as mania.

"Fine," Shaw muttered as he bent down to unlock the y-cuff. He removed the chains and stepped back.

"May I approach him?"

Shaw nodded.

Matthew popped off the chair and knelt as he grasped his brother's hand. "It's okay, Justin," he murmured, but got no response. When he reached to his brother's face, Justin flinched. Matthew nudged up Justin's chin to let the fluorescent lighting fall on his neck.

The ring of mottled bruises he found there made him suck in a breath.

Shaw cleared his throat. "He tried to use a twisted sheet—"

"To hang himself off *what*, exactly?" Matthew got to his feet while keeping hold of his brother's hand.

"He tried to jerry-rig the shower head. It never would've worked—"

"Bullshit! Did you see those bruises?" He let go of Justin's hand to point at his throat. "They're deep! Looks like he almost made it."

Quiet up to this point, Justin now mumbled, "Sorry."

Matthew ignored him and glared at the guard. "I want to see Dr. Pierre! *Now.*"

Shaw shook his head. "She's in session. She'll be here soon."

"You get her here now. Have you met Justin's attorney? Kathryn Summers? 'Cause she'll be all over you people once she discovers this repeated abuse."

"Abuse?" Shaw scoffed. "Your brother's doing this to himself."

"And *you're* supposed to stop him! You're neglecting your duty. Damn it, I better see Dr. Pierre in here right away, or I'll splash this prisoner abuse all over the media." Matthew aimed for the coldest glint he could muster as he pointed his finger at Shaw. "And I'll be sure to name *you* as the biggest abuser of all."

From the corner of his eye Matthew saw Justin gape at him.

"Get her here *now!*" Matthew bellowed.

When Shaw inched back, Matthew hoped the guard thought he was as psycho as his twin.

"Take a seat, Dr. Durante." Shaw scooted around the edge of the room toward the door.

Matthew kept his eyes narrowed as he watched the guard's retreat.

As Shaw neared the door, he pointed at Matthew. "The only way I get the doctor is you calm yourself down. Sit down, Dr. Durante."

He followed the order.

"Both of you stay seated. I'll get Dr. Pierre."

Once Matthew heard the comforting sound of the lock sliding into place, he grasped Justin's hands. Dr. Pierre's office was on the far side of the unit, but threatened lawsuits tended to speed up hospital response. "We don't have much time. I need you to listen carefully."

His brother's eyes were still unfocused and confused, but he did at least look at him.

Matthew swallowed the lump lodged in his throat. "I know. I know what you did."

Justin blinked as he stared back.

"I know Jefferson King raped you. Repeatedly."

His twin seemed to stop breathing.

Matthew tensed as he dropped Justin's hands and got to work. He slid off his loafers and unbuckled his pants. "I know you didn't tell anyone about the rapes to save me and Kate. I know you sacrificed yourself for us."

Justin paled.

"And I know why you tried to kill him with that bomb in his warehouse." Matthew stood, ripped off his jeans, and yanked off his socks. "I would've done the same thing. I would've bombed that sicko to hell."

Justin seemed to have trouble forming words. "I—"

"C'mon." Matthew ripped open the Velcro of his brother's prison jumpsuit.

Justin shrunk back, gulping for air. "What're you—"

"It's okay, Just." He gazed down into his brother's frightened eyes. "You trust me, right? I'm going to change your clothes now, okay?"

Justin's forehead creased, and he blinked up at Matthew like a bewildered little boy. "Why?"

Matthew realized he had to play dirty to get him to comply. "How many times did King rape you?"

Justin's lips parted.

"I know one time for sure," Matthew continued. "When we were fifteen, and I couldn't wake you up for school. He drugged you, didn't he?" His voice shook, and Justin's eyes glossed over with the sheen of dissociation. "That night he gave you too much."

Justin's entire body trembled, and his stare was vacant. His breaths came one short pant at a time. When Matthew drew him to his feet, he bobbed like a rag doll.

Watching his brother vanish before his eyes, Matthew couldn't help himself—he started crying.

"I'm so sorry, Just." He shimmied the jumpsuit down Justin's muscular shoulders then peeled it off his limp body, pushing him back down so he could remove his shoes and jumpsuit. White boxers and a T-shirt remained. "I'm so sorry you had to go through that alone."

Through a haze of tears he noticed his own boxers and T-shirt purchased from Wal-Mart were a good enough match to those his brother wore. His shoulders slumped.

His gaze shot to the looming steel door, praying it would stay shut for a few more minutes. Justin swayed a bit on the chair, apparently lost in hellish flashbacks. The Muzak played some happy tune, and Matthew found his frantic undressing moving to the beat of the song.

Matthew lifted his navy-blue turtleneck sweater over his head and threw it on his chair, then stepped into the jumpsuit and heaved it on. The tiny hooks of Velcro made a satisfying sticking sound. He slid on Justin's white slippers—a perfect fit—then went to dress his eerily immobile brother.

The only evidence Justin was still conscious was his stiff posture and the slow furling of his fingers into fists. Matthew crammed the turtleneck sweater over his brother's head and pushed his arms through the holes. Then he scooped each foot into the legs of the jeans, bunching up the denim and sticking Justin's feet into his socks and loafers, before drawing his brother to his feet to yank the jeans around his hips.

Matthew left his zoned-out brother standing there while he scrambled for the belt. After he wrapped it around his neck and joined both ends in his right hand behind his head, he lunged forward, feeling the belt bite into his windpipe. He coughed and wheezed, tears continuing to leak from his eyes. But he didn't let his panic stop him from lunging forward twice more, hoping the bruises would look authentic enough.

Despite the choking sounds caused by Matthew's theatrics, Justin's expression remained neutral. He hadn't moved at all. Once Matthew stopped gasping and could see straight again, he took the instrument of self-torture and began to thread it back through Justin's jeans. His heart pounded a furious cadence as he swiped tears from his cheeks.

With only a few moves left before the transformation was complete, Matthew paused his coughing to step forward and wrap his arms around his brother. He knew he had to bring Justin back or all his efforts up to this point would be futile.

As he cradled one hand on the back of his head, he whispered, "Justin, it's me. It's Matty. It's your twin brother. You're safe, buddy." He squeezed Justin's torso a little tighter. "I want you to take some deep breaths…that's it, good." He coughed as he rubbed Justin's buzzed hair. "Can you feel my hand on the back of your head? Can you hear my voice in your ear?"

Matthew loosened his hold and pulled back to fix his eyes on Justin, whose glassy stare was still present, though there was a hint of recognition in his gaze. "We're twenty-nine years old now." Matthew patted him on the back. "We're both adults. We're safe. That's right, be aware of your breath. Keep taking deep breaths."

He snuck a look at the steel door and refocused his attention on his brother.

Taking a step back, he reached for Justin's hand, hoping his next idea would work. A photo of their childhood cats would be a more vivid reminder, but the fire had destroyed all of their possessions. Turning Justin's wrist so that his hand faced up, Matthew stroked his palm. "Remember how soft Marie and Alfie were? Remember what it was like to pet them?" His touch was feather-light on Justin's palm. "To feel the vibration of Marie purring when you would pet her throat?"

Justin frowned as he curled his fingers to squeeze Matthew's hand. He rasped, "We had to take them to the pound when we went to foster care."

Matthew nodded and smiled. "That's right, Justin. Dr. King was allergic to cats."

Justin's eyes clouded. "It wasn't fair."

"No, it wasn't."

Justin squinted at him. "Why're you wearing my jumpsuit?"

"Here, have a seat, and I'll tell you." Matthew guided him to his original chair and switched places with him.

When Justin glanced down and noticed the turtleneck and jeans, his head snapped up. "What's going on?"

Matthew sniffed as he braced himself. "You sacrificed yourself for us. I love you for it. I want to pay you back. And I'm *not* going to lose you."

Justin tilted his head to one side as he stared.

There was no easy way to explain the plan, and time was ticking. Not taking his eyes off his brother, Matthew sat back in his chair and lifted his hands to his head. He peeled off the longhaired wig, revealing a buzzed cut that mirrored those of the patients at the Columbus Hospital for the Insane.

Justin's eyes expanded.

When Matthew brought the wig toward Justin's head, his brother came alive. "No! What the fuck are you doing?"

"We're changing places," Matthew said.

Justin gasped. "Like hell we are!"

Matthew matched his volume. "You're *not* killing yourself! I won't allow it. I'm getting you out of here the only way I know how."

"You can't do that! You'll never get away with…" His gaze trailed down to Matthew's neck and likely saw fresh bruises there. Then he touched his own neck, wincing when he made contact. With a sharp intake of air, he lunged for Matthew's wrists and twisted them, revealing angry scars on the underside, just like his own.

"This, this is insane! Stop this goddamn game. Give me my clothes back." Justin groped for his belt, but Matthew sprang forward and gripped his wrists. Justin shrunk back, seeming shocked by his strength.

"Too late," Matthew barked. "They're coming any second." He threw a glance at the steel door. "Listen to me. This is happening, and you can't stop it."

"Yes, I *can*." Justin strained against Matthew's hold.

"If you don't follow along, they'll arrest me, too. Then nobody will be there to watch over Kate."

Justin stopped struggling. "Kate." His eyes widened. "You're going to *leave* her? You're just walking away? You love her!"

Matthew swallowed. "I had to leave her." He looked down. "She thinks I cheated on her. So you can't let her see you, okay? Make sure you stay hidden when you check up on her."

Justin's jaw hung slack.

"We have to hurry. The condo's paid up for a year, so you have a place to live. There's some money on the kitchen table. But Justin, you have to find a job. Come back and visit me, and I'll help you, okay?"

"You're fucking nuts. *I'm* supposed to be the insane one, Matthew. You can't stop me from killing myself on the outside, you know."

"You won't kill yourself, dumbshit. Not when there's me and Kate to protect."

"No," Justin moaned as tears filled his eyes. Matthew hadn't seen him cry in years. "You're not sacrificing yourself for me. I'm not worth it."

There were voices outside the door, and the jangle of keys.

"They're here," Matthew hissed. He raised the wig. "Please. Don't put us both in prison. Don't leave Kate all alone. If you love me, you'll do this."

Justin sobbed, but he didn't stop Matthew from placing the wig on his head. Matthew adjusted the long hair, realizing how ridiculous it looked, as he heard the lock slide out of its bolt. He slumped back in his chair a second before Shaw strode into the room with the blond psychologist trailing him.

Shaw took a look at Matthew's blank stare and knelt down to start securing him in chains.

"You removed his chains?" Dr. Pierre asked with a shake of her head. "And left him alone with his brother?"

Shaw glanced up at her. "His brother begged me to take off the y-cuff. Then I forgot about it when he started freaking out, yelling at me to go get you." He clutched the chains and shot her a pleading look. "Don't tell Majumdar?"

Dr. Pierre stared at Justin, and it must have been the tracks of tears on his face that softened her tone. "You're obviously quite upset to see your brother like this. I'm so sorry, Dr. Durante. But we *did* stop Justin in time."

Something seemed to change in Justin when the psychologist spoke to him. He sat up taller. Had her warm, respectful address surprised him?

In contrast, the guard's glare at Matthew seemed to press down on his shoulders, and he found it hard to hold his head up. The clank of chains in Shaw's hands echoed in the room. He closed his eyes as Shaw locked the handcuffs into place and circled the chain around his waist. He could smell the guard's body odor. Once Shaw had manacled his ankles, he yanked him to his feet. The tight chain hunched his shoulders. How the hell was he supposed to walk, trussed up like a pig about to be roasted?

"You're not telling Dr. Majumdar about the chains, right?" Shaw asked the psychologist again. "His brother went ballistic. What was I supposed to do?"

Matthew didn't listen to Dr. Pierre's response. He stared at Justin and mouthed, "*Kate*."

Justin gulped and swiped tears from his cheeks as he stood.

Matthew recomposed his mask as Dr. Pierre told Justin, "You must understand, Dr. Durante, that acting like a madman doesn't help us keep your brother safe."

Justin blew out a breath. "Right. It's all *my* fault." Despite the forced sarcasm, it sounded like he believed it.

"I'm not saying that. I…" She ran her hand over her mouth. "It's time for your brother to attend group therapy. Would you like to meet in my office and we can discuss this further?"

Matthew tensed. Group therapy would be a barrel of laughs—manic, maniacal laughs.

"No, thank you," Justin said. "I just want to go home. I'm tired. Tired of watching my brother try to kill himself. I won't let it happen again."

Does that mean he won't off himself? Matthew held his breath as he held eye contact. All he wanted was for his brother to live.

When Shaw led him away, Justin blurted, "Can I hug him?"

Shaw halted and frowned.

"One last time?" Justin added.

Dr. Pierre nodded. "Go ahead."

Justin approached him, seeming uncertain at first, but then stepped forward and encircled him in a strong embrace. His mouth right next to Matthew's ear, he whispered, "Don't think you're getting away with this, asswipe."

As Shaw dragged him away, Matthew almost tripped, distracted by his brother's last comment. It sounded just like something Justin would've said when they were eleven—full of spunk and domination, back before their lives were ruined. But what could Justin do? Matthew had set the plan in place, and there was no stopping it now.

Shaw led him past a guard station, and once they passed into the violent offender unit, Matthew felt the hairs bristle on the back of his freshly shorn neck. Several sets of eyes honed in on him as Shaw shuffled him to a group room down the hall, and he flinched when he heard an unsettling laugh somewhere behind him.

He had arrived at his new home.

6. Reflection

Jefferson King glared at his attorney as he chucked the front section of *The Columbus Dispatch* across the table. "When will this be over?"

Barry ran his hand through mouse-colored hair. "Soon. You lucked out with that explosion. All possible evidence went up in flames."

"Bringing my company to a complete standstill is *hardly* a stroke of luck, counselor. And the feds wouldn't find anything anyway. We both know allegations connecting me to terrorists are totally specious."

Barry's eyebrows lifted. "Nice vocab. They don't hand out mechanical engineering PhDs to just anyone, eh?"

"My doctorate's in chemical engineering."

"Ah—I stand corrected. Not sure your smarts fool the FBI, though. They don't seem to buy your theory about Sharik al-Islam stealing from you."

He almost growled at the shorter man. "Of course those triggers were stolen. I wish the feds would clue in to reality. *Me* in bed with terrorists? What a fucking joke. I'm the biggest patriot there is."

Barry stared at him.

"I'm paying you a lot of money to just sit there, Mr. Reynolds. I'll ask you again: when will this unwanted attention end?"

"And I'll give you the same answer, Dr. King. *Soon.* We crushed the Children's Protective Services investigation, and we'll win this one, too."

"Please tell me you've hunted down the person who made that report to CPS."

"Still working on it."

Jefferson clenched his teeth. *It has to be Gideon. When I find that boy…*

"Back to the terrorism investigation," Barry said. "It's been over six months since they found the devices on the plane, and this'll blow over soon. The only reason it's still hot in the media is Durante's upcoming trial. The press went apeshit over him being your foster son. As soon as he's competent, they'll nail him."

Jefferson aimed for an icy glare. "It's taking too long to die down. Maybe terrorists will strike another US target—that'd certainly divert attention away from me."

Barry studied him for a moment, a strange look on his face. "Oh yes, if more Americans were killed in a terrorist attack, you'd be all but forgotten by the media."

We're working on it. "Goodbye, Mr. Reynolds."

The attorney snatched up his briefcase and left.

Jefferson grabbed the newspaper and headed to the trash, but the photo on the front page made him pause. Right next to the photo of his own craggy bald head was a handsome young man's mug shot.

Justin.

"Either kill yourself or keep your mouth shut, kid." His heart thumped as he stroked the pad of his thumb across the boy's chiseled jaw. He folded the paper in half and whipped it with a thump into the wastebasket.

$$Ⅱ$$

Justin strained for air as he stepped out of his brother's Honda into the one-car garage. He wondered how he'd been able to drive at all after somehow walking out of the hospital as a free man less than twenty minutes ago. When he'd passed a police cruiser on the highway, he'd broken into a hot sweat. He was grateful he'd gotten away with spitting out his meds the past few days or he never would've had the wherewithal to navigate here.

Still stunned by Matthew's actions, Justin alternated between gagging nausea and unrelenting relief. When he reached for the doorknob at his brother's condo, he could already hear insistent meows.

"Hey, cat." As he stepped into the small foyer, Slim rushed toward him, but at the last second she halted. She circled as she sniffed his feet, and her green eyes flickered.

"Remember me?" He squatted and extended his hand. "Damn, I think you've gotten even fatter since I went away." He smiled faintly. "You're not a cat, you're a *cow*." He scratched her gray fur. "Or a manatee, maybe. Sea cow."

Matthew likely would've chastised him for hurting her body image, but this time silence swallowed his comment.

"Sorry." Justin scooped her up and hoisted her onto his shoulder.

He stroked down her back. He closed his eyes, lost in the comforting sensation of her soft fur and rumbling purr. He remembered Marie Curie's softness as he'd petted her on the porch after his mother had shooed him outside. That was probably one of the times Mom had yelled at him for spilling chemicals all over the basement floor.

What he wouldn't give for his mother to yell at him again.

He wasn't sure how long he'd petted Slim—it could've been a minute or an hour—when he opened his eyes. It was so quiet here. No damn therapist asking him questions, no nurse shoving meds down his throat, no spine-shuddering screams splitting his ear drums…

Setting the cat down, he crept into the family room.

His head itched, and when he went to scratch, he touched synthetic hair. He yanked off the stupid wig and flung it on the dining room table. At once he felt cooler and more like himself. Slim galloped over and leaped onto one of the chairs, peering over the edge of the table with a glint in her eye.

"Uh-uh." He snatched the wig and decided to hide it in the hall closet. "I don't want it ending up like those trashed sofas, you beast."

Meandering into the kitchen, he paused at the counter when he saw an envelope with his name on it. His brother's assured scrawl tightened his throat and made it difficult to swallow. His hands shook as he withdrew the handwritten letter from the envelope.

Justin,

I know you're mad at me.

I know you don't understand why I did what I did. But please believe me. I had no choice. You were hell-bent on killing yourself, and I refuse to lose you.

"Bullshit," Justin huffed. "That's no reason —"

Stop yelling Bullshit and listen to me. You would've done the same thing. You did do the same thing. You sacrificed yourself so King wouldn't hurt Kate or me. I'm deeply troubled that your sacrifice ended up destroying you, leaving you so full of shame that you hate yourself, leaving you no reason to keep living.

Justin's heart raced. How had his brother known Dr. King had threatened to do the same thing to Matthew and Kate? Matthew had always been tuned in to his thoughts, a combination of keen psychological intuition and twin insight, but this particular telepathy was uncanny. He thought he'd hidden things better. He kept reading.

I've decided I'll be your reason to stay alive, Justin. I need you. Kate needs you. You gave me twenty-nine years, and it's only fair that I give you twenty-nine more (or however long I survive in prison). I love you. After all you've done for me, I feel so relieved to do something for you. Will you allow me the gift of taking care of you, for once? I know you must be furious, but I'm hoping you might also feel grateful to be out? Maybe you feel a smidgen of relief to be free?

His face got hot. He did feel relief. Matthew now rotted away for a crime he hadn't committed, and *he* felt relief.

Justin shook his head. "Selfish bastard."

Matthew the shrink had always gone on and on about his emotions, constantly asking him how he was feeling, though he never could answer. Matthew's obsession with his feelings must have led him to pull off this insane switch in the first place.

Justin's hand curled into a fist as he spoke to his twin's ghost. "You sound like a goddamn girl."

He scanned the next few words, encouraged by their business-like appearance.

On to some logistical stuff—you should know what's going on in case you run into anyone involved with my former life. I had to come up with a reason for shutting down my practice. I told my clients I had end-stage cancer, specifically gall-bladder cancer (adenocarcinoma), and that I had to terminate with them before I went to hospice.

"Shit."

I referred some of my clients to my office mate, Nancy Wallace, PsyD, and the rest to George McCallister, Ph.D. Their numbers are on the last page of this letter, along with all the other information you'll need to assume my life.

You obviously know why I couldn't use the cancer cover story with Kate. I had to come up with something worse, something that would keep her away, so she'd never return to me.

The writing seemed to fade at this spot, and when Justin resumed reading, the ink was darker, as if Matthew had stopped and restarted later, after changing pens. Justin could only imagine the pain. Once *he'd* gone nuts, Kate was the only person keeping Matthew going. To lose her must have devastated him.

I had to come up with a way to make Kate stay away. This isn't easy to say, but I might as well come out with it. I pretended I cheated on her, and unfortunately, I gave a convincing performance.

You can say it—I'm a complete ass for what I've done to Kate. I'm so sorry. I'm sorry I've taken her away from you, too, but I didn't know how to keep her in our lives, considering what I was about to do. You know I'd never hurt her intentionally, but I didn't know another way. Once I get settled at the hospital, I'll ask for another attorney. And don't you dare go running to tell her what I've done. You know that would hurt her even worse. She'd never be able to say goodbye. She'd never be able to move on with her life.

I can only pray Kate will find another man, a healthier man, to keep her happy. Fate brought her to us, and I think she deserves better, don't you? She's suffered a lot, too, and she deserves more than two broken brothers weighing her down. We always knew she was the bright star among us. Somehow, the foster system made her strong. Somehow, she emerged with an attitude that takes no prisoners.

We had a different experience, though. Jefferson King did take prisoners. Namely, <u>you</u>. I always thought your mental health struggles stemmed from the fire, from losing Mom and Dad. I always wished they were still around to help you get back to being the boy I knew growing up. I hated myself for failing to ease your guilt about losing them. But I didn't have all the facts.

Justin grasped the counter to brace himself.

No wonder you have all the symptoms of PTSD. No wonder you take out all that rage on your body. No wonder you seem to think you're the lowest piece of shit on Earth. Would it help for me to tell you it wasn't your fault? That you're not a bad, dirty person just because a very bad man tried to ruin you? Probably not. I'm sure a therapist or two has told you the exact same thing, but obviously you don't believe it. Obviously you blame yourself, thinking you don't deserve to be happy after what you endured, thinking you don't deserve to live.

Justin clenched his teeth as he screwed his eyes shut and fought the flashing images in his head, the goddamn feelings assaulting his body—the scratch of the expensive sofa cushion on his belly, the hands roaming down his back, forcing him down, forcing him to be still. The rough hands invading him, owning him, infesting him, groping him. He wanted to scream *Get the fuck off me!* but the words trapped in his throat, frozen like a lump of sodium persulfate from his father's basement lab. Still, the hands kept coming.

Slim meowed as she rubbed against his ankles.

Gasping for air, he blinked in the small kitchen. Through eyes blurred by tears, he glanced down at the letter, the thick stationery puckered by his grip.

After he exhaled, Justin knelt on shaky legs to scratch the cat behind her ears. His panting breaths settled and fell into a rhythm with each stroke of cat fur. After a beat, he resumed reading as he continued to pet the cat.

When I finally realized what had happened to you—the true source of your pain—I was blind with fury. I considered buying a handgun and breaking through his layers of security to blow his balls off. I didn't care if I'd end up in prison for killing that bastard. No wonder you tried to blow him to bits. To end his pathetic weapon-making existence by exploding him into tiny little pieces would have been beautiful irony. Too bad he wasn't in the warehouse when the bomb went off.

But if we were both locked away, I wouldn't get to see you. I already miss you—how could I go for the rest of my life without seeing you? I miss my better half. I miss my twin. And that's when it dawned on me. We're twins. We're mirrors of each other, two halves of a whole. Without you, it's like looking in the mirror and seeing nothingness—an empty space. Don't you know I've been helpless without you in my life? It dawned on me that I could turn the pain of losing you, the man who knows me like no other, into something good. I could pay my debt to you.

"Oh, Matthew."

I have to admit I caused some damage along the way to doing right by you. I've hurt Kate irrevocably. I did the same with a few clients, though I'd like to think they're in a better place now, with a therapist who can actually help them, who isn't so destroyed himself.

"Matty," Justin gasped as hot tears leaked down his cheeks.

Will you make the sacrifice worth it, Justin? Will you seize what's rightly yours—a rich, full life? Will you stop being prisoner to a sick criminal's depraved choices?

Or will you simply survive, stumbling forward in the world, numb to all life has to offer? Will you keep trying to kill yourself, despite my pleas?

The choice is yours. My life is in your hands, as it always has been. If you choose to end your life, it will only be a matter of time before I end mine. And I'll figure out a way to succeed in killing myself in here, unlike you, because we both know I'm the smarter one.

Despite his tears, he snorted.

I need you to find a job, Justin. You have to be the strong one now, okay? I know you can do it. And deep down, you know, too. You're the one who got us through Mom and Dad's deaths. I'll always remember Azrael.

I tried to write this letter without lecturing, but I have to say a few things here. You need to take care of your body, because it's the only one you get. Your body made the ultimate sacrifice to protect Kate and me, and now it deserves to be treated better. Eat some food, Justin. I've got some in the cupboards, and you can use the money in the envelope to go to the grocery store and pay the bills until you get a job of your own.

"He's treating me like a damn nincompoop."

Try to be inconspicuous. Try to smile more so you don't scare people. I've got three months left on my gym membership — try to get some exercise. I know that lifting weights was the one thing that used to calm your mind.

There are a thousand things I'm probably forgetting to tell you, but it's all I can remember for now. If you can begin to forgive me, maybe you'll visit me inside? Even if you don't forgive me, will you visit me in the hospital, during the trial, and in prison? Please? Unlike you, I'll fight the charges, but it doesn't look good.

You know, I listen to my clients pour their hearts out every day, and I try to be honest with them, too. But outside the therapy office, I dodge and deflect my true feelings, pretending everything's okay, pretending nobody can touch me. We spend so much of our lives avoiding the things we want to say, the things we really mean.

Now that I'm finally doing what's right, I want to stop messing around. I want to be real with you. You mean so much to me, Justin. I hope you know how much I love you. I'm truly blessed you're my brother. You would do anything for me, and I'm trying to learn how to return the favor. I'm trying to learn how to be as strong as you, as impossible as that is.

After all my babbling, it comes down to one question: Will my love sustain you, despite the cruelty you've endured in this life?

Only you know the answer to that question.

With fondness and admiration,

Your brother, Matthew

Justin's legs trembled as he got to his feet. He took in shaky breaths, and his brother's words looped in his mind.

"Matthew," he whispered as he drew the letter flush against his chest. "What have you done?"

7. Restoration

Kate squinted at her office laptop. "*Can't* be right. That was a damn good deal!"

She looked up with a flash of relief that nobody had passed by to discover her talking to herself. For the past two weeks, she'd felt out of it, distant and foggy, and she didn't want any partners questioning her commitment.

But this was ludicrous! The assistant district attorney had refused the plea bargain, meaning her client had to go to trial? And Jim hadn't even bothered to call her. All she'd received was a curt email:

No deal. Your client's going down.

"Screw *you*, Jim," she muttered as she typed a swift reply.

I look forward to it, Mr. Kennedy.
Thank you for your attitude of cooperation and compromise.

As she clicked send, her indignant smile faded. So they'd found Emilio Sanchez's blood at the crime scene. When she'd interviewed her client yesterday, Sanchez had played with a bandage on his finger and admitted that he'd cut his hand during the robbery.

Who really cared, anyway? It was useless to fight the system.

She exhaled as she slumped back in her chair. This defeatist attitude was unlike her. But she'd been fatalistic about multiple areas of her life lately, ever since Matthew...

Her jaw clenched. Flames of betrayal flicked up her neck and flushed her cheeks with a crimson glow. How *could* he? The past two weeks she'd been numb, sleepwalking through her days. Before Matthew had deceived her, she'd thought it impossible to feel any worse about their faltering relationship. But when she'd found that huge-ass bra hiding under his pillow, she realized she'd been wrong.

Everything had gotten much worse.

Actually, her entire life had been crap since the day after Justin's arrest, when she'd seen the security video of him and that scientist Elyse. Her knees had almost buckled, knowing they'd later hear that word Kate dreaded—the word indicating her abject failure. The word that would lead Justin to a life sentence. The word that had haunted her for twenty years...

"Guilty," the judge had pronounced as he frowned at the auburn-haired woman standing in front of Kate. Her mother had been beautiful once, but now her thin hair hung in strings down her skinny back.

Thirty feet away, Kate quivered. Only nine years old, she looked up at the more robust woman at her side, the social worker.

The woman's eyes seemed to slant at the corners. She reached to scoop Kate's small hand into hers.

"Guilty? What's that mean?" Kate asked.

"It means your mother's going to prison, honey."

"Katie!" her mother wailed.

Kate watched in horror as two burly bailiffs hauled away her only remaining parent.

"I'm so sorry!" she cried over her shoulder. "I'll get clean, baby! I promise. I'll come back for you!"

Kate dropped her head to stare at the floor. Someone had left a shriveled piece of gum near the half-wall separating the spectator section from the front of the courtroom. The fuzzy, chewed remnants were neon green.

"C'mon, Kathryn," the social worker said as she nudged her toward the exit. "I'll take you home."

Though her legs had somehow followed, her chest had seized, leaving her gasping for air. Home? She didn't *have* a home anymore.

"So when're we going to double date again?"

She flinched, then looked up to find a man in her doorway—Pete Dixon, the firm's investigator.

"Whoops," he said. "Didn't mean to startle you." Pete's mouth curled into a smirk. "Daydreaming on the job again, Summers?"

She blinked a few times. "There's not much else I can do to save this client. Might as well dream about an acquittal—that's the closest he'll get."

"That bad, huh?" He stepped into the office and eased himself into a chair by her desk.

It seemed his hairline had receded farther since only yesterday, but his snarky grin and sparkling hazel eyes made up for the expansive forehead.

"Anything I can do to help?"

"Don't think so. This one might make the list of dumbest criminals. Not only does he nick his finger with the knife he's holding on the cashier, but then he leaves his blood at the scene, probably smeared on the half of the money he didn't take."

Pete chuckled. "An *honest* thief! Why didn't he take all the loot?"

Kate rolled her eyes. "He said he only needed four hundred for the engagement ring."

Pete laughed harder, but she felt her shoulders sag. Sanchez's girlfriend wouldn't be getting that engagement ring anytime soon. Kate knew the feeling.

To redirect the conversation, she asked, "Any word on King?"

"No, dammit." Pete remained stone-faced. "According to my contact at the FBI, there's no evidence to refute King's claim that terrorists stole those triggers. Not much survived the blast except a few recordings that make Durante look guilty as hell."

A tendril of guilt licked her spine. She hadn't visited Justin since Matthew had dumped her. She needed to check in on him soon.

"You still haven't answered my question."

She chewed on her lip. "Which was…?"

"When're we going to double date? It's been months, and Eve's been after me to ask you." When she remained silent, Pete rubbed the back of his neck. "Frankly, I think she's pushing for it just 'cause she wants to see Matthew. Eve might have a crush on your boyfriend."

Kate looked down, wrestling with tears.

"Hey, you know that was just a joke, right?" Pete cleared his throat. "Are you okay?"

She sighed as she met his gaze. "Matthew and I…well, we're history."

"What?" His lips parted. "That can't be."

She tossed her hair over one shoulder. "It can be. It is. It's over."

"But…" He appeared to search for words. "But how did that happen? You two seemed made for each other."

Her mouth pressed into a firm line. "Obviously not."

"You finally put the hammer down, then." When she didn't respond, he blanched. "He wasn't stupid enough to break up with *you?*"

Her heart thudded. "He cheated on me." When the words left her mouth, she felt her nose burn and tears pooled in her eyes.

She turned away from Pete, but not before he'd seen the evidence of her weakness.

"Oh, Kate. That bastard." He fidgeted while she scrambled for a tissue in her purse. "Want me to punch him?"

With a bitter smile, she shook her head. "He'd probably retaliate with a swift uppercut, given his newfound muscles." She dug around in her purse, located a package of tissues, and wiped her nose. "I should've listened to the advice columns. They say you should worry when your partner starts working out more. Prepare to get dumped."

Pete winced. "He's an idiot. What can I do, Kate?"

She looked up at him and sighed. "Can I have some time alone, I guess?"

"Sure, you got it." He stood. "You need someone to talk to, I'm your man."

"Thanks."

Her shoulders slumped when he closed the door behind him, and more tears followed. Clutching the tissue, she swiped at her cheeks and rocked in her chair. She frowned when she noticed the time.

"Stop, stop, stop," she hissed. "Stop your stupid crying." She had to get to the courthouse to visit a drug dealer who'd retained her. With a trembling hand, she reached into her purse for her compact.

Her wan smile did nothing to hide the blotchy skin and sunken eyes she saw in the small mirror. She was just slightly younger than her mother had been when she'd gone to prison. Her mother had never come out.

Maybe Deidre Summers had figured it all out. If life hurt this bad after losing her man, maybe the soothing salve of drugs was the way to go. Maybe her new client could hook her up with some contacts. At least *she* wouldn't leave a child behind to fend for herself in the foster system.

But she couldn't lose herself to drugs, not when Justin still counted on her. She had a meeting with him later this week — if he was still alive by then. Stealing one last look at her listless reflection, Kate snapped the compact shut. She grabbed her handbag and briefcase, then hustled out the door.

Matthew tugged at his collar. What was this jumpsuit made out of, sandpaper? It scratched and chafed his neck worse than the first two had. He'd learned they received a clean jumpsuit every three days.

The ancient, gray-haired psych tech assigned to watch him kept his eyes on Matthew between bites of his own sandwich. Matthew didn't know Geezer's name yet, but he did know this suicidal one-on-one watch was getting old fast. He couldn't sneeze without staff checking him for injuries.

"Can I have your pudding?"

Matthew stifled a smile as the boy next to him tapped his paper plate — Daniel was nothing if not predictable. When the eighteen-year-old had latched onto him during their first group therapy session, Matthew had realized his brother had acted as some sort of protector. Typical Justin.

Seconds after Matthew spooned the brown, plastic goo onto the boy's plate, Daniel vacuumed it up with a spork. He patted his belly with a contented sigh.

Matthew pointed to a pile of beige noodles. "Eat your beef stroganoff."

"Fuck *that*." Daniel shivered, then gaped at him. "Eww, you're eating that shit?"

He forced a swallow of gristly grey meat coated in chalky sauce. When the lump made it down his throat, he swigged some water. "Gotta get protein, my man." He patted Daniel's back. "Gotta stay strong."

His heart thudded when Daniel's eyes darted left—he knew the cause of the boy's vigilance. Matthew's peripheral vision caught a flash of gnarled teeth and gleaming black eyes. Even the dim lighting couldn't hide Shaddox's leer.

"At least drink your milk." He pointed to the carton near Daniel's plate and felt the boy's shoulders slump next to him.

"Gross," Daniel said.

Matthew shook his head as he downed the last sip of sour milk. "Read the label." He held it out for Daniel. "How many grams of protein does it have?"

Daniel leaned away from him as his eyes filled with hurt.

"What?" Matthew's forehead scrunched. "What'd I say?"

Daniel stood and grabbed his plate off the table. "Asshole," he muttered.

What just happened? A low chuckle drew Matthew's attention to the left. When Shaddox gave him a snaggletoothed smile, gray meat pressed up his throat.

Geezer nodded at him. "Time for your individual, Durante."

He shot to his feet. Meeting with Francine was far preferable to spending time in the company of killers. He threw his plate into the trash and walked toward the hallway.

"Think you can fool me?" asked Geezer from behind him.

Matthew wheeled around as his heart rate kicked up.

Geezer squinted and tossed his thumb over his shoulder, pointing in the opposite direction. "Dr. Pierre's office is this way, psycho. Don't try to screw with me." His bony fingers grasped Matthew's shoulder and pushed him on his way.

Shit. He should've remembered the directions to Francine's office from his first individual session. But he hadn't had the opportunity to get rid of his morning meds, and they were screwing with his focus. "The meds make me foggy," he mumbled as they passed a CO.

"Save it for someone who gives a shit."

Though Geezer was new, he sounded like he'd worked here for years.

After Francine opened her office door, the psych tech led Matthew to a chair. Francine sat across from him and looked up at Geezer, whose hand continued to press down on Matthew's shoulder.

"Thank you, Harold," Francine said.

But Harold didn't move.

Francine maintained a pleasant smile. "Harold, we got this."

The man's grip tightened. "This one's up to something, Dr. Pierre. I can feel it. I'll stay right here."

"That's so sweet of you to protect me." When she uncrossed her legs and stood, Matthew pushed against Harold's hold to try to get to his feet as well.

"Stay seated, Justin," she said, her stern gaze nailing him to the chair. She turned her attention to the psych tech. "I've been meeting with the accused for months now, and he hasn't threatened me once." A flicker of sadness crossed her face. "The only threat he seems to pose is to himself."

Matthew swallowed. He hadn't thought about how his brother's suicide attempts had affected anyone beyond him and Kate, but Francine seemed to share the same guilt and helplessness he knew so well. He prayed Justin hadn't offed himself on the outside. They would inform him if his brother had died, wouldn't they?

Harold still didn't budge, so Francine crossed over to her desk. "Really, we'll be fine." She picked up an envelope. "Would you take this to Dr. Majumdar, then wait outside until the session is over?"

The psych tech accepted the envelope with a frown. "I'll be right outside. Don't forget to use your panic button if you need it."

"Of course. Thank you." She waited for him to leave, then took her seat.

Matthew tensed as she studied him.

"How're your bruises?"

He touched his throat. The raw abrasions from the belt had almost healed, leaving a lingering trace of tenderness.

"You seem to be feeling better." She smiled. "What's your rating today?"

My rating? What was she talking about? He squirmed under her watch.

"It's okay, Justin. You're safe here."

His tongue felt thick and furry as he swallowed.

Her eyes tightened. "So you're not talking today?"

"Sorry, Dr. Pierre. I…can't…"

The creases above her eyelids disappeared. "I told you to call me Francine when we're alone."

Interesting. It seemed unwise to relax professional boundaries around criminals like his brother. Matthew would've insisted on being called Doctor in a place like this. But now that he looked closer, he did notice warmth in her eyes that went beyond the unconditional positive regard they'd been trained to provide for clients. Almost a look of…lust? He inhaled—did Francine have the hots for Justin? Her look reminded him of Kate's smolder.

Kate. His heart squeezed. How was she holding up? Did she still hate him? Did she miss him at all? He doubted she felt drowned by sorrow like he did every night in his plastic twin bed. Waves of regret would wash over him, filling his lungs, making it hard to get air—like he was breathing through a straw. The night watch guy had thought he was having panic attacks, and maybe he was—panicked that he'd taken his brother's place.

"Looks like you've got a lot going on in that mind of yours," Francine said.

He scoffed. "My stupid mind's like a sieve."

"I doubt that." She gestured to the computer on her desk. "Stupid minds can't fix computers. It's running great, by the way."

He frowned at her. She'd let Justin repair her computer?

"It seemed like you were sad, just then. Did you have a sad memory?"

His lips pressed together. Obviously, he couldn't tell her about Kate.

"So I'm guessing that makes your rating higher today? Where are you, on a scale of zero to ten?"

Ah. She was asking him to rate himself on some sort of feeling scale. He'd used that measure with clients. But he had no idea what feeling he was supposed to rate.

"Sorry." He tried to swallow. "These meds…can't remember… what're the anchors for the scale?"

Her head tilted. "Zero is no suicidal urges, ten is an urge so intense that you're searching my office for a way to kill yourself this second."

Jesus. How could he answer without arousing her suspicion? On the outside, he would've said zero, no problem, but he had to admit that suicidal thoughts had crept into his head the first night of captivity. If he gave her a number like two or three, though, she might think he was bullshitting her. "What was I last time?"

She referred to her notes. "Nine." Her eyes turned down as she looked up at him. "That was before you tried to hang yourself."

He touched the raised ridges of skin on his neck.

"You haven't attempted since then. Good job." She reached for a little red box on her desk and handed it to him. "Go ahead and pick out a sticker."

His eyes zoomed up—she had to be kidding. She was giving him a *sticker* for not killing himself? His shock must have shown because she chuckled.

"I know you're not a child, Justin. But I'm trying to reinforce positive behavior." Her smile faded. "Staying alive doesn't feel like a reward for you, I realize. Not with a trial awaiting you once you're declared competent."

More than that, Matthew knew Justin just wanted the horrifying flashbacks to end. Francine hadn't mentioned sexual abuse in their first session, and wasn't alluding to it now. Was it possible Justin hadn't told her about it? How would he ever heal from the abuse if he didn't process it in therapy?

He opened the box and thumbed through a collection of smiley faces and kittens. "You know I'll get killed if I wear one of these stickers on the floor."

Her eyebrows lifted. "You'll reach your goal, then: dying in here."

He hid a smile and peeled a ridiculous cartoon kitten from its backing. He pressed it below the collar of his jumpsuit.

"I'm at seven today," he said after he returned the box. He would've gotten up to put it on her desk, but he had the sense that standing might make her feel threatened.

"Seven." She nodded. "Why not eight?"

It was a good follow-up question. He tried to get into Justin's head to consider how he would answer, but realized he could answer from his own heart. "I'm lower than eight because I don't want to let my brother down. He doesn't deserve this."

"Matthew told me I'd never understand your relationship because I don't have a twin."

He cringed at her wounded expression.

"But I do know you love him," she said.

Matthew's chest ached with longing. Was that true? All he wanted was to be worthy of Justin's love. "*How* do you know?" he couldn't stop himself from asking.

She leaned back in her chair. "Well, you talk about Matthew constantly. You seem to respect him for all the schooling he went through, for trying to help people. You've told me you admire him for being there for Kate, for visiting you in here, and for loving you, despite your belief that you don't deserve his love."

As she blinked, the ache seeped deeper into his chest. He sniffed, but he wouldn't let himself cry. Justin rarely cried.

"And you told me about that stuffed animal you bought for Matthew when you were teenagers," she added. "When he was missing your cats after the fire."

"Azrael," Matthew said with a soft smile. Justin had scraped money together to buy him the stuffed animal, the mischievous cat from *The Smurfs*. Dr. King was allergic to cats, so Justin had bought Matthew the next best thing. Azrael had been an inside joke because they'd secretly referred to their foster father as Gargamel, the evil wizard from the show.

Francine's eyebrows pulled together. "Do you know what that name, Azrael, means?"

He'd heard the meaning somewhere but couldn't access the memory. He stared at her, wishing his brain didn't feel so foggy.

"The angel of death," she said. "Were you suicidal when you bought the stuffed animal for your brother?"

His thoughts meandered—why couldn't he remember? "No, that's not it." He blew out a breath. "Azrael means...God's help. That's what he told..." *Crap. Get your story straight.* "That's what I told Matty when I got him the cat. He needed help."

A tuft of burnt orange fur tickled his chin as he clutched the plush animal...

"He held on to that damn cat every night."

"Matthew really struggled after your parents died?"

He pursed his lips. Justin's strong arms holding him from behind, after he'd bolted up from the mattress, screaming. *"Shh, Matty, don't wake him up. Calm down. Calm down."* Justin had seemed terrified about waking up Dr. King. Matthew trembled as he remembered. "Matty cried all the time. Had nightmares. What a wimp."

"You were twelve. Your world shattered when your parents died—of course Matty cried. Didn't you?"

He didn't remember Justin crying.

"Didn't you have nightmares?" Francine asked.

"No." *Those likely came later for Justin.*

"But you do now—a symptom of post-traumatic stress disorder. Are the nightmares about the fire?"

How should he answer that? Her rapid-fire questions were confusing him. If Justin hadn't told her about the sexual abuse, what *did* she know? "I don't have nightmares."

Her eyes darkened. "Try that again."

Oh. The night watch had probably ratted Justin out. He had to be more careful around this psychologist.

He massaged his temples. "Sorry, I forgot about them."

"You're having memory problems?"

"It's these damn meds."

She shook her head. "Dr. Majumdar is an excellent psychiatrist. Your medications are what you need, no more, no less."

"Wrong. They're giving me too many meds—they're messing with my head."

"So you're an expert in psych meds now?" Her chin dipped.

More than you know. "How can I be an expert when I don't even know what I'm taking?"

"We've reviewed your list of meds countless times."

"I already told you, they mess with my memory! I don't remember them."

She sighed, then looked down at her notes. "You're taking Xanax, clomipramine, looks like atorvastatin—"

"Why am I taking a statin?"

Her eyes rolled up to meet his. "For high cholesterol, I presume."

"My cholesterol is low."

"Hmm." She shrugged. "You'll have to ask your psychiatrist, then. I'm sure he has a good reason. You're also taking haloperidol, propranolol, and Ambien."

Whoa. Those were some heavy hitters — no wonder he couldn't think straight. It also seemed like a redundant combination of meds. Pure overkill, really. How could he find out more without revealing too much? "Haloperidol — I think Matthew told me they don't use it anymore? Too many dangerous side effects."

"They still use it." She nodded. "Especially when newer medications don't work."

"But they never even tried the atypical antipsychotics on me."

Her eyes widened.

Crap. Justin shouldn't have known any of that. "I mean, uh, that's what Matthew thought."

As she crossed her legs, her mouth quirked. "Aren't we lucky your brother's a psychologist. So what does *he* think you should take?"

"Definitely not as many meds, especially not haloperidol. I'm not psychotic. I have PTSD."

"Thank goodness you're finally accepting your diagnosis. But you're claiming you don't have nightmares?"

Her challenging stare made him hesitate. It would be difficult to assume his twin's identity in the best of circumstances, but with the cocktail of mindfuck chemicals they had him on, it was near impossible. Still, his muddled brain clung to a kernel of something, a nagging thought about the medications she'd just listed. Why a beta-blocker *and* a tricyclic *and* a benzodiazepine, all on top of an antipsychotic? In addition to a cholesterol drug? And he knew the sleep medication could cause bizarre side effects.

"Justin?" Her voice drew his attention. "Were you dissociating just then?"

His vision narrowed. "Have you noticed a common thread weaving through the medications they have me on?"

She blinked.

"They all have the same side effect." He paused. "Memory loss."

She frowned. "That can't be true."

When he continued staring at her, she stood and circled around her desk. Her fingers flew over the keyboard as she likely tried to gather evidence to dispute what he'd alleged. After a few minutes, she peered around her monitor.

"How'd you know that?"

He ran his tongue across his front teeth. "Truth is, I like chemistry."

She considered his response. "I'll have to talk to Dr. Majumdar about your medication. We're trying to help you uncover memories, not suppress them. There's a reason for your PTSD, and I believe it goes beyond your parents dying in a fire." She returned to her seat. "And you figuring that out about memory loss is even more evidence that you have a fine mind. But you never attended college?"

Short of attending his classes for him, Matthew had done everything he could to get Justin into college. But Justin hadn't believed he was worthy enough to invest in his future that way. He'd stumbled from one minimum-wage job to another until he'd accepted a maintenance position at Dr. King's weapons plant. At first, Matthew couldn't understand what had motivated his brother to be anywhere near their foster father. Then it had become clear why Justin had wanted to be in close proximity to his abuser's bombs.

"I didn't get scholarships like Matty and Kate did."

"Your foster father's loaded, though. Wouldn't he pay?"

Matthew shook his head, remembering all the Ds and Fs on Justin's report cards. Back then he'd thought Justin was just lazy, but now he realized traumatic memories had probably killed his concentration. "Even if he would pay, I didn't have the grades to get in."

Francine frowned. "What prevented you from performing better in school? I know you're as smart as your brother—it's in your genes."

"Neither of us is as smart as Kate, though."

"Speaking of Kate, she wrote me a letter."

Matthew's eyes lifted.

"She begged me to tell her why you fired her as your attorney."

The ache returned to his chest.

"Why'd you do that, Justin? I thought you were close to her."

He closed his eyes. His fingers twitched with the desire to touch her, hold her, feel her skin. When his eyes opened, Francine was watching him.

"It's the same reason you won't let me talk to Matthew, isn't it?" she said. "You don't want to let in the people who love you, thinking you'll hurt them less by keeping them at arm's length. Don't you know that hiding from them only ends up hurting them more?"

The hole in his chest was a deep cavern. Justin hiding his sacrifice had almost killed him when he'd found out. He knew that hurt all too well.

Francine sighed. "We're getting nowhere today."

His brother would typically apologize at this point, he guessed. "Sorry."

"You're supposed to work on apologizing less, remember?"

"Sorr—" He shrugged.

"Have you been practicing any skills when suicidal thoughts arise?"

He chewed on his lip. Which skills had she taught him?

"The ACCEPTS skill?" she prompted.

"I've tried to contribute more—that's one of the Cs, right?"

She smiled. "How have you contributed?"

"I, uh, encouraged Daniel to get more protein in his diet. But he got pissy with me."

"Daniel looks up to you. Maybe he was just having a bad day."

Maybe. It seemed easy to have a bad day in this hellhole.

"We're almost out of time," said Francine. "Back to the rating scale. Why isn't your suicide rating lower, like five or six?"

Matthew pressed his cotton tongue against the inside of his cheek. He wished Justin would visit him. "Life's too hard without my brother."

Her eyes softened. "You know that killing yourself won't bring him closer to you, right?"

"It'd stop the pain, though."

"Justin, pain is temporary. Feelings are fleeting."

He'd told his clients the same thing, and he used to believe it. But he had to admit, Justin's emotional pain would never leave. Not when he'd been abused for years, and not when he'd killed an innocent woman in an effort to exact revenge against the abuser. A man as sensitive as Justin would never recover from that.

But at least the pain of confinement had ended for him. Matthew had helped him the only way he could.

8. Recall

One hand fisted the sheet and the other clutched his dick. Justin's breaths came quick and loud—from arousal or fear, he wasn't sure. A wall of pressure pushed down on him, and he let go of the sheet to swat behind him. When he brushed against cool fur, he froze—what the fuck was that?

A noise in his ears increased in volume, grating on his brain. Then he realized it was repeated meows. He looked up to see Azrael looming above. The stuffed cat had come to life, blown up to supersize, and wore a black scarf draped over his ears.

Azrael meowed at him as he masturbated?

As he tried to make sense of the scene, a sharp sting pierced his nose.

"Ow!" His eyes flew open to find Slim's green eyes an inch from his. He reached up to cradle his nose. "Did you just bite me?"

More meows as her tail swished.

His heart still thumping, Justin wiped the drool from the corner of his mouth and pushed himself off the pillow to sit on the mattress. Near his hip was the worn orange stuffed animal he'd held as he'd fallen asleep. He drew Azrael onto his lap and shook his head.

"No wonder I had a freaky dream about you. But give a guy some privacy, huh?"

Slim crawled over his knee and fought for lap space with Azrael. Her deepening meows led Justin to scratch her ears.

"And no wonder I heard meows in my dream. You're not liking your diet, are you?" His long strokes down her back elicited motor-boat purrs. "I know you're hungry, Slimmy. But you don't have to feast on my nose."

He rubbed his eyes and looked over at the alarm clock. It was a little before four a.m. Three hours of sleep was an improvement from the night before, at least. Sleep had been elusive since he'd gotten out, making it difficult to come up with a plan to save his brother. Maybe it was too quiet in Matthew's condo. He blew out a breath, knowing he was fooling himself. The nightmares were the only reason his sleep was shit. They'd ratcheted way up since he'd left The Columbus Hospital for the Insane. And they kept getting weirder. A mega cartoon version of a stuffed animal, wearing a scarf and leering at him?

After he chugged some soymilk and threw a hoodie over his clothes, he headed for the door. Slim's meow made him turn around. She lingered by her food bowl with a pitiful drooping of her whiskers.

"You'll get breakfast when I return, sweetheart."

He heard a hiss as he closed the door leading to the garage.

The roads were empty, shortening his drive to a few minutes. But the parking lot held a surprising number of vehicles—insomniacs just like him. Once he walked inside and heard the pounding metal music, his shoulders relaxed. The gym was his safe haven.

"You cut your hair," came a voice from the front desk.

Justin's stomach dropped as he looked at the woman. *Crap. Forgot the wig.* "Yeah. Sweating too much doing cardio."

Her smile revealed crooked teeth. "It looks good, Dr. Durante."

"Just Matthew is fine." He swiped his brother's gym card through the reader.

When she started to yawn, she covered her mouth as she shook her head, spilling brown, wavy hair across her shoulders. Her subsequent sheepish look reminded him of something, but he couldn't place it. "Not supposed to yawn in front of the customers," she said. "Sorry. Night shift's kicking my butt."

He felt drawn to her for some reason. "You usually work days," he guessed, since she knew his brother. "How long you been working night shift?"

"Couple weeks. My mom started a new job and can't look after my little girl now. I gotta take care of her during the day."

He noticed dark smudges under her eyes. "When do you sleep, then?"

"Hah," she barked. "Good question. Sometimes I sneak some zzzs when Ellie naps." She sighed. "It probably won't last long. Mom gets fired from every job she starts, so cross my fingers I'll be back on days soon. At least I'm getting in good with my manager—he needs help on nights because one guy quit."

His gaze floated to the sign on the wall behind her: *Hiring Front Desk Staff.*

She yawned. "Sorry again."

She smiled as she shrugged, and he realized who she reminded him of: Elyse Frederick. Same hair color, same apology for yawning when she'd work late into the night.

"Here I go unloading my personal problems on you. You must get that all the time as a psychologist, right?"

He paused. "You have no idea."

"I'll let you get going. Have a good workout, Matthew."

"Actually…"

She looked up at him.

"I'm looking for work." One reason Justin hadn't visited Matthew yet, in almost two weeks, was that he didn't have a job. He couldn't face his brother's disappointment. He pointed to the sign. "How do I apply?"

Her eyebrows drew together. "But you already have a job. A busy one. You said you were swamped with patients."

He tried to think of something Matthew would say and remembered his brother's bitching about negotiating with health insurance companies. "Damn insurance—they keep reducing their reimbursement rates. Might need some extra income."

"Really?" She grinned. "It'd be fun to work together." She scrounged around in a drawer beneath the counter and handed him a flyer with a URL. "So you go to this website to complete the application, and make sure you use real references—they call them. And then if they hire you, they'll do a background check and fingerprinting."

"Fingerprinting." His airway squeezed.

She shook her head. "It's dumb, I know." She leaned in to whisper, "I heard there was a trainer who set up hidden cameras in the women's locker room a few years ago." She shuddered. "Total creep. Now they make sure everyone's legit."

Justin folded the paper and stuffed it in his pocket, knowing he'd never visit the website. "Thanks. Better get a move on—got lots of patients to see."

Another gym member had walked up to swipe his card, so Justin made a beeline for the locker room. He didn't know why it was so hard to breathe. It wasn't like he wanted the fucking job, anyway. He threw his hoodie into a locker and stalked toward the free weights—he was so jacked already, he didn't need a warm-up. After he pumped out several sets of power cleans, a dude with bulging biceps approached.

"Your lady do you wrong, man?"

Justin panted. "What?"

Biceps shook his head. "Never seen you go at it so hard. Sumpin must've pissed you off."

"Some days you're just mad at the world, you know?"

His grin matched the size of his arms. "You're in the right place, then. I couldn't sleep last night, either. Spot me, man?"

"Sure." Justin followed him over to the bench press. His eyes bugged as Biceps slung a hundred-pound plate onto one end. Justin lugged a matching plate from the stack of weights and heaved it onto the other end. But Biceps wasn't done yet—he added a twenty-pound plate on each side. "Two-eighty-five, huh?"

Biceps winced. "Cut me some slack. It's my warm-up set."

Damn. He hadn't lifted that much in months. He hovered behind the bench, standing idly as Biceps grunted the weight overhead for eight reps. After Justin helped him settle the bar back on the clips, Biceps popped up and nodded at him.

"All you."

Justin stepped back an inch. "Uh…nah, I'm working legs today."

Biceps squinted. "You did three-oh-five not too long ago."

His scrawny brother had benched over three hundred pounds? How was that possible? He must've trained nonstop. The weight of what Matthew had done for him punched him in the gut. It seemed like the air thinned around him as sweat slid down his spine, and the once welcoming metal music now crashed like cymbals in his ears.

"C'mon, man. You finally chopped off your girl hair; now it's time to man up."

Justin looked up as he sucked in a breath.

"I got you," Biceps said. "Don't pussy out on me."

His tongue swept across his lower lip. If Matthew could lift this weight, then he should have no problem with it. When he circled around the bar and laid back on the bench, Biceps smirked above him.

With a deep breath, his fingers curled around the bar and hoisted it off the clips. There was only a tiny tremble in his arms as he held the bar aloft then lowered it to his chest. He blew out a breath as he pushed up the bar, elbows straight.

"Guns, baby," Biceps growled.

By the third rep, the shaking of his arms intensified. A tremble tsunami took over on the fourth rep. He groaned.

"You got this!" Biceps hissed.

Justin bared his teeth as he struggled to lift the bar the fifth time. The bar moved barely one centimeter, then another, and a feral snarl unleashed from deep inside toward the top of its ascent.

"Fuck, yeah!" Biceps helped guide the bar back to its home.

Justin peeled his sweaty body off the bench. As he waited for his heartbeat to settle down, he shrugged. "Well, it wasn't three-oh-five."

The bodybuilder shook his head. "Sometimes you beat life; sometimes life beats you. But no matter what…" He looked Justin in the eye. "The harder you work, the harder it is to surrender."

Justin stilled. The words stirred a memory—a lecture from his father when he'd brought home a bad test grade. When his dad had told him he could do better, Justin had claimed he'd been unlucky because he'd studied the wrong material. His dad had said, *"You're in control of your luck. The harder you work, the luckier you'll be."* So later, when the social worker had told him and Matthew that their parents' deaths had been bad luck, Justin had known she was wrong. *He'd* caused their deaths, and he'd been responsible for everything that had happened since. And now Matthew was paying the price for his fuckups.

"Earth to Matt."

He looked up.

"You gonna spot me again, or what?"

He nodded. *Leave the past behind*, he told himself as he circled behind the bench, knowing his memories would keep flooding him no matter what he did. If only the past would stay in the freaking past.

Two hours later, his quivering legs took him out of the locker room toward the exit. Soreness had already settled into his muscles, and he wondered if he'd be able to walk tomorrow.

"Hope you apply soon!" said the woman from the front desk on his way out.

He turned to notice she'd piled her pretty hair on top of her head, making her look even more like Elyse. He gave her a weak smile and bolted to his car. Matthew's car. Once he tumbled into the driver's seat, he gripped the steering wheel. Pain shot up his chest as he remembered tousled brown hair, the floral scent of her perfume…

"Okay, Dad, I'm going home now—" Dr. Elyse Frederick had stopped short in the doorway of the maintenance office once she'd seen him shove a book under some papers.

He'd swallowed and tried to reflect her teasing tone. "About time, young lady." He'd caught her yawning when he'd emptied her trash earlier in the evening. "You need your sleep."

Her smirk vanished, replaced by a crease between her eyebrows. As she approached his chair, a field of flowers floated over him. She reached for the book, and he held his breath.

"You're reading this?" Her brown eyes searched his. The unspoken question hung between them: *Why're you reading a book about bomb triggers?*

"I, uh…" He licked his lip. "I wanted to understand what you do. What you work on every night. I wanted to talk to you about it." He stared at his feet. "It was stupid."

She flipped the book over. "Do you understand this material, Justin?"

He rose from his chair and backed up to lean against the filing cabinet. Her scent made it hard to think. "Some of it. The circuitry's kind of confusing. All the different bases and substrates — can't keep 'em straight."

She gazed at him as her mouth ticked up at one corner. "Your father worked here, right?"

He rocked back. How had she known that?

"I asked Darryl about you." The softest blush colored her cheeks.

So she'd asked around about him? He inched closer.

"Have you gone to college?" she asked.

This again. He shook his head. "Not smart enough."

"This is a graduate-level text." She returned the book to the desk. "Over most college students' heads."

When he said nothing, she leaned forward and clasped his wrist.

His heart hammered.

"Maybe you should think about trying school," she said. "Get a technician job here. We need help staying ahead of terrorists."

His thoughts scrambled, in disarray from her touch. He was also aware of the security cameras everywhere. Dr. King had told him not to bother the staff.

"I'll walk you to your car," he finally said.

They chatted about a sci-fi TV show they both watched as they headed to her Acura SUV. She looked up at him once they reached the car. "Thank you for protecting me."

He knew he should leave, but he didn't want to. She opened the car door and tossed her briefcase onto the front passenger seat. When she closed the door but still stood on the pavement, he froze. Could his heart beat any faster?

She grinned as she rested her arms against his chest and lifted up to press a kiss against his mouth.

Yes. His heart *could* beat faster.

He'd woven his fingers through her hair and returned the kiss, reveling in the softness of her lips.

A honk across the gym parking lot jerked him back to the present. Instead of silky tresses, his fingers clutched the cool leather of the steering wheel. The rising sun filled his car with ethereal shadows.

First his father, and now Elyse. Why wouldn't the ghosts leave him alone?

That night, Kate's finger trailed a drop of condensation down the side of her glass at a bar not far from her office. She'd just started her second double vodka, and she welcomed the slow slide into numbness. She couldn't believe she still felt such emotional pain a full three weeks after Matthew had dumped her. Her hand trembled with the urge to whip the glass against the wall.

The local news played on one of the TVs over the bar. With a little luck, they wouldn't mention the case she'd just lost. Her client, Sanchez, was going away for quite a stretch, only because he'd needed money to buy his girl an engagement ring. The girl had cried at the trial, and Sanchez had looked like he'd wanted to cry as well. *Idiots.*

A man slipped onto the barstool next to her. His thin brown hair was greasy, and his Army green jacket smelled like mildew. She hoped he didn't plan to hit on her.

"I'll have what she's having," he told the bartender before he grinned at her.

Fan-fucking-tastic. She scooted her glass away from him.

He scanned the mostly empty bar. It was just after five, so the legal professionals hadn't streamed in yet. "You're lookin' lonely here, all by yourself."

Apparently, he didn't read nonverbals so well. She sighed. "Don't feel like talking. I've had a long day."

"Really? What do you do?"

He didn't read verbals, either. She looked straight at him. "I'm a serial killer." *Killer of serial relationships.*

"Cool. How's the pay?"

She had to smile a little at that. "You looking for a new line of work?"

"Maybe." He shrugged. "Nah, I like what I do." He leaned closer, wafting his unwashed odor toward her. He patted his jacket pocket. "I help people feel awesome."

So he was a drug dealer. "Well, thanks, but I already feel awesome." She lifted her glass to show him — right before his drink arrived.

"To Team Awesome," he said, clinking her glass with his.

She moved her gaze to the TV and prayed he would leave her alone. When he started typing on his phone, she exhaled, then sipped her drink.

"*The Columbus Foundation hosted their annual awards presentation today,*" said the news reporter, "*celebrating philanthropists who make a difference in our community.*" Kate lowered her glass when a familiar face filled the screen.

"*After being nominated two years in a row, Dr. Jefferson King accepted the Harrison M. Sayre Award on behalf of his company, King Combatics.*"

She watched as he crossed the stage amid applause, his bald head shining in the lights, and shook the presenter's hand. She wondered if the reporter would mention the investigation into his company.

"*King Combatics has contributed thousands to Franklin County Children's Services,*" the reporter continued. "*They inspire us all to combat child abuse and neglect.*"

The reporter was all smiles. It appeared that King's generous donation overshadowed his alleged connection to a terrorist bomb.

The news story showed King's remarks at the podium. "*My wife, Natalia, and I have been heartbroken at the wretched conditions faced by poor children in our community. We have tried to help by donating to The Columbus Foundation, and we urge you to do the same. Financial donations are important. But what has truly made a difference in our lives is bringing foster children into our home.*" His ice blue eyes glistened. "*The loneliness and fear of losing your parents is a devastation few can understand. In* Oliver Twist, *Charles Dickens wrote, 'Let him feel that he is one of us.' Providing a new love — a sense of belonging — to lost children has been my mission. I hope and pray to spare their wounds.*"

The audience applauded, and the newscaster provided contact information for donations. As the reporter moved on to another story, Kate moved into a hazy memory.

Matthew's hand had shook in hers as they stood behind the toolshed. A soft drizzle had floated over her hair, and a drop of rain slid down his temple, mixing with the teardrops leaking from his eyes.

"Should we tell on him?" he'd asked.

Kate felt the hard metal of scissor blades in her rear jean pocket. She'd confiscated them from Justin when they'd caught him cutting the skin near his hip. He'd seemed so out of it when she yanked the scissors from his grasp. She pushed the image from her mind.

"I don't know." She skated her thumb across Matthew's cheek to wipe away his tears.

"He's not right." Matthew looked in the direction of the house. "It's been four years since the fire, and he's still not right." His hold tightened on her hand.

Watching him cry was killing her.

"I have to do something," he said.

He'd already told Justin the fire wasn't his fault a thousand times. She tried to think of a way to help Matthew feel useful. "I'm scared. Kiss me?"

The wetness of his cheek pressed against hers as he nudged in for a kiss. He hadn't hit his growth spurt yet, and was only a smidge taller than her.

"What's going on?"

They broke apart at the sound of their foster father's voice. Kate's heartbeat accelerated when she noticed his scowl. He wore a business suit, and a splash of mud had dirtied his expensive shoes.

"You're not allowed back here," he growled.

"Why not?" Kate challenged.

Matthew backed up a step. "Sorry. We didn't know."

"You do now. Get back to the house."

Kate wanted to argue, but Matthew spoke up.

"Um, Dr. King?"

"What is it?"

His harsh tone straightened Kate's spine.

Matthew paused. "Um, Justin…I'm worried about him. We found him…" He looked at Kate, who shook her head. "Well, he cut himself."

Dr. King's eyes narrowed. "I told you to be careful with the kitchen knives. That's a chef-grade set."

"Um…" Matthew seemed to search for words.

"No." Kate couldn't believe the man was so obtuse. She reached for the scissors and withdrew them from her back pocket. "Justin cut himself with these. It was on purpose."

Dr. King stiffened. "Why the fuck would he do that?"

Kate was shocked to hear him swear, and Matthew appeared equally startled. When they didn't answer, Dr. King shook his head.

"Give me those." He wrenched the scissors from Kate's grasp. "I'll lock these up. Keep Justin away from the knives." He shooed them toward the house.

"But—" Matthew didn't move.

"What?"

"Shouldn't Justin see someone? A…a counselor?"

Dr. King squinted at him like he was a cockroach about to be squashed by his Ferragamo shoe. "Of course not. He doesn't need a counselor—*I'll* talk to him. And don't tell anyone about this, especially Natalia. She can't handle the stress."

Kate rolled her eyes. Their foster father had told them not to bother his wife countless times, and Kate was still trying to figure out how a life of shopping and drinking alone in one's bedroom constituted stress.

Dr. King looked at his watch, then back at them. "Get out of here. Go do your homework."

Matthew took her hand and rushed her back to the house. They arrived at her bedroom, breathless.

"What's his *deal?*" she scoffed as they fell back onto her mattress.

"Gargamel's extra agitated today." He kissed the back of her hand. "I'm gonna see if Justin is awake yet—figure out why he did that. Make sure he doesn't do it again." His eyes tightened. "Then I'll come back and we'll do our French together, okay?"

Her voice rose with hope. "French kisses?"

He grinned at her. *"Oui, madamoiselle."* His warm breath tickled her hand as he kissed it again. Then he rolled off the mattress and out her door.

They went way beyond kissing when he returned. That evening was the first time she'd shown him her breasts. She'd done it at first to distract him from his worries about his brother, but the way his eyes lit up made her rip off her bra every French kissing session after that.

Her mind flashed to the last time they'd been together, in his condo.

"You're perfect, Kate." Grown-up Matthew had cradled her breasts. "I love these."

Her heart sagged as she clutched her glass of vodka. How long had he been lying to her?

Greasy Hair knocked into her shoulder while he pointed at the TV. "That guy who got the award. Didn't his foster kid blow up his weapons plant?"

She turned to give him a sharp look. Did he know who she was? Had Dr. King sent him to spy on her? No, that sounded crazy.

"What?" he asked as she kept staring. The piece of peanut shell stuck in his teeth made him seem more pathetic than threatening.

She pressed her lips together. "That's what he's accused of, yes."

"The guy sounds guilty as hell." He popped another peanut into his mouth.

Her throat clenched as she remembered the notice the state forensic psychologist had faxed a week ago: *Mr. Justin Durante has chosen new counsel. You're no longer on the approved visitor list at The Columbus Hospital for the Insane.* She'd locked down her emotions once she read it — it was just too much on top of Matthew throwing her away like a piece of trash. But confusion and betrayal climbed their way up her throat now, threatening to strangle her.

"What do *you* know about it?" she spat.

Greasy Hair leaned away from her, then shrugged. "Jack shit. Just like to run my mouth, act like I know what I'm talking about."

She exhaled. Her eyes found his jacket pocket. "What do you got in there?"

A lazy smile stretched his mouth as he took a look at the bartender on the other side of the bar before returning his eyes to her. "What do you want?"

She swallowed. "Any painkillers?"

"Lots. Percs for only ten each."

Ten dollars a pill? Maybe he was ripping her off, but at this point, she didn't care. "I'll take five." She reached behind to slide her purse strap off her barstool when a hand grabbed her wrist. She jumped and looked over her shoulder to find the firm's investigator staring down at her with a frown.

"Pete." She stole her hand back and rested it on her chest, feeling the wild thump of her heart. "What're you doing here?"

Greasy Hair had turned away from her, pretending to be absorbed in his phone.

Pete leaned in so only she could hear him. "Didn't your mother die in prison from a drug overdose?"

"How did you—?" She recoiled. "You're supposed to investigate the *clients*, not the lawyers."

"Sorry. Can't help myself."

Her eyes tapered. "How long have you been watching me?"

"Long enough." He slid onto the barstool on the opposite side of her. "I tried to find you in the office." He looked down. "Thought you'd need an ear after the Sanchez verdict."

Her anger toward him dissipated in an instant, and she realized how deeply she craved his attention. Now that the Durante twins had abandoned her, Pete was all she had.

"Where's Eve?" she asked.

He looked up at her with a smirk. "We broke up."

9. Pretense

Jefferson King glowered at the letters on his Words With Friends app. In addition to two blank tiles, he had O, U, R, V, and E. He should've had no problem using all seven letters considering he had two freebies, but he couldn't fit a new word into the existing spaces. There was room for a word starting with A, but how could his tiles form a word starting with that letter? He switched over to the browser on his phone and searched for *8 letter words starting with av*.

"Ah." He nodded as he returned to the game and slid his tiles to form *avoucher*.

His fist shot in the air as the app chimed.

"Suck it," he told the app. A ping on his phone alerted him that user MinivanMom had just played a word on another game he had in progress. His heart fluttered. *Safia*. He looked at his office door, but it remained closed.

He tapped on the game he'd been playing with her and read the message she'd just sent.

On for 6.5

She'd set the meet for May sixth, only one week away. The back of his neck tingled. But what was the location? He maneuvered his letters for a few moments and grinned when he was able to play the word *where*.

They'd had to move their meetings away from their normal location since the cataclysm a year ago. He still couldn't believe his bomb triggers had survived the plane explosion—a mistake that wouldn't happen again.

He looked up for a moment. The silence on the other side of the door pissed him off. No ringing phone, no bustling office. The government contracts had vanished once the feds retrieved King Combatics triggers from the crash site—a crash that had been designed to occur over the Arabian Sea, but had plummeted into the Yemeni desert instead. The American officials who had once paid him to fight terrorism now suspected him of aiding those same terrorists. He needed to be acquitted of wrongdoing and get his business back in the black. His plan with Safia could accomplish both in one blast.

Explosions had always fascinated him. He remembered standing next to his father at the entrance of a mine—one of many his father had owned in West Virginia. He'd only been nine or so as his father had rested his large hand on his shoulder.

"When you gonna blast it, Dad?"

His father's cool blue eyes had looked down on him. "Tomorrow morning. You're to be nowhere near here then, got it?"

"Yes, sir." Jefferson had swallowed as he watched a cardinal land on the branch of a nearby tree. He hoped the bird would fly far away before the blast occurred. "Whatcha gonna use?"

His father's eyebrow climbed toward the cloudy sky.

Whoops. His father had harped on him to use proper English. "What explosive will you use, sir?" Jefferson tried again.

"ANFO."

When Jefferson chewed his lip, his father smiled and said, "Ammonium nitrate and fuel oil, remember?"

"Oh, yeah." He cursed his stupidity. "*You're* gonna steer clear of the mine when it gets blasted, too, right?"

His father tousled his hair. "Of course. You have to treat explosives with respect. As Red Adair said, 'With bombs and fires, you only get one mistake.'"

The ping of his phone alerted him to a new word Safia had played. She'd built on an E from *where*, and had played the word *patience* for sixty-three points.

"You little cunt," he said with a grin. It was rare when they could play two words in a row to communicate instead of using the messaging function. He was studying his new tiles when his phone rang.

He blew out a breath and accepted the call. "Dr. King."

"Why do you answer the phone like that?" his wife asked. "So cold and businesslike. You know it's me."

"What do you want."

Her disgusted sigh irritated him to no end. He imagined her dark eyes narrowing.

"I'm calling about Julie. She's very disrespectful to me."

He rubbed his bald head as he pictured the slight blonde they'd taken in two years ago. "What do you expect, Natalia? She's sixteen."

"But she doesn't treat *you* that way," she huffed.

"That's because she knows I'm boss—I'd kick her ass to the curb if she even raised her voice to me. You let these kids walk all over you." He shook his head. "You're the one who wanted a girl in the first place."

He should've never allowed his wife to take Kate Summers into their home, along with rambunctious twin boys. But after the fertility treatments had failed too many times, Natalia had begged him for a girl. His guilt had made him cave, bringing that pain-in-the-ass foster girl into his home. With the big mouth on her, no wonder Kate had become an attorney. Julie was now the third girl they'd fostered.

Natalia said, "Julie was never like this before Gideon left."

At the mere mention of the boy's name, he got hard. Damn, he missed that sixteen year old. Gideon was his first foster child to run away. Check that—his first to run away and not be found. Cody had gotten away once, but when the police located him, Jefferson had made sure the boy never tried that shit again. That's where the second foster daughter had come in.

He touched himself through his trousers. "Any word on Gideon?"

"You're the one who's supposed to find him."

He shot to his feet. "I've tried! We've looked everywhere." His face flushed as he paced the thick carpet. Justin Durante had done this. He'd filled Gideon's mind with ideas, encouraged Gideon to defy him. Jefferson's jaw clamped. How dare Justin think he could interfere in his life after all he'd done for the boy and his brother?

$$\textcircled{\text{II}}$$

The next morning, Justin couldn't stop shaking. He sat in Matthew's car outside the King mansion, hoping he didn't vomit all over the front seat. How he'd gotten himself here, he didn't know. He only knew he had to be here after the dream he'd just experienced. He had to make sure the boy from his dream was safe.

Terrified green eyes…

The lanky boy had been running from him in the dream, and when Justin had caught up to him, he'd clasped the boy's shoulder and yanked him back, looking into those fearful eyes. He felt an urge to tell the boy something—what was it?

"You're not alone," he said to the dashboard. Then he flinched.

Wait—the dream had happened. He remembered saying those words to the boy months ago. Outside the boy's school. His breaths came quick and shallow, and he tried to rein in his thundering heartbeat. He grasped the parking brake with a steel fist. Part of him fought the memory, but part of him craved it. His eyes closed as his head thudded back on the headrest.

He'd first seen the boy in a photo from an online news story last August. He'd been using Matthew's computer, since he couldn't afford his own, as Matthew and Kate watched a TV show in Matthew's condo on a Sunday afternoon.

"He's got more foster kids?"

He must've said that out loud, because Matthew had paused the DVR and asked him, "What?"

Justin had licked his lips. "King." His voice shook, so he clenched his jaw. "He's got another foster son."

"And a daughter, I hear," Kate sneered. "One happy family."

Justin's stomach dropped. *Collateral.*

Matthew came up behind him to peer at the photo of the black-haired teenage boy standing between King and a blond girl. The boy's eyes looked dead. *Philanthropist Dr. Jefferson King nominated again for the Sayre Award*, the photo's caption read.

"Of course he's fostered more kids," Matthew said. "The man thinks he's a saint."

"Why didn't you tell me?" Justin roared. He stood so fast that his chair toppled backwards. He looked from Matthew's wide eyes to Kate tiptoeing toward him, and knew he'd freaked them out.

"I thought you knew," Matthew said as he bent over to right the chair.

Kate came up next to Matthew and studied Justin. "You never want to talk about him."

Justin couldn't breathe. "I…gotta go."

"Wait, Just." Matthew reached for his arm, but Justin ripped it away.

"Get the fuck off me."

Matthew stepped back, and the hurt in his eyes made Justin feel even sicker. He flew out of the condo and jumped into his beater car. He'd driven and driven and finally parked on a street in Bexley, just a few houses down from King's compound. It was his first time back in the wealthy neighborhood since age eighteen.

Justin stayed there all night, missing his shift at the fast-food restaurant, but it wasn't until the next morning that there was any activity at the mansion.

As the sun rose, King backed his Range Rover out of the driveway, and Justin could see two heads in the backseat. He tailed them to Columbus Academy, a private school nearby. The boy and girl rocketed out of the car, and King sped off.

Justin watched the girl bop over to another girl and enter the school, but the boy lingered outside by himself. He looked like a pariah, different and misunderstood, and Justin's heart squeezed. He barely remembered to put the car in park before he found himself walking toward the boy.

"You can't leave your car there," said a middle-aged woman.

He looked at her, then back at his car, which clearly didn't belong among the other luxury vehicles in the drop-off lane. "Fuck off," he said.

Her mouth dropped open.

"You're not alone," he blurted as he reached his destination.

The boy blinked at him.

He reached out his hand. "Justin Durante." When the boy made no move to shake his hand, he added, "I was King's foster kid, too."

The boy's face reddened as he shrank back.

"It's okay," Justin said. "I won't tell anyone. What's your name?"

The boy shook his head. A few cars honked behind him, but Justin ignored them.

"Can you tell me if there are any more boys in King's home?"

"Just me," the boy said, his voice unsteady.

"And the blond girl," Justin added.

The boy nibbled on his lip as the honks increased in volume.

Justin didn't have much time. "King threatens to hurt her unless you do what he wants."

Green eyes grew to saucer-size.

"Empty threats," Justin growled.

"H-h-how do you know?" The boy seemed to have trouble breathing. "He promised he'd hurt Julie, and I believe him. He's a bastard."

"He is." Justin heard the click of heels behind him. "That's why you gotta resist. Stand up to the bully."

"Sir," a woman snapped, and Justin looked over his shoulder. "You must move your car right now. Police are on the way." She pointed at the boy. "And you need to get to class before the bell rings, Gideon."

Justin had looked at Gideon, who'd reached for his hand.

"I'm Gideon Hall." His eyes had come to life. "Please help me."

Justin wrenched his eyes open, looking up at King's compound once again. Those pleading eyes had been a knife to the gut. He'd failed Gideon, despite his best efforts. The smartest thing he could've done was to go to the authorities and tell them King had abused him and Gideon. But he was too chickenshit to do it. No one could find out what had happened. So instead he'd gone to King that day and begged him for a job, thinking he could keep better tabs on the pedophile by working for him.

King had smirked at him. "I always knew you'd come crawling back. You're such a fuckup, Durante. You can't survive on your own."

He'd started working at the King Combatics warehouse, but being around King had stirred up quite a few unpleasant memories. He'd started drinking more, eating and sleeping less. Once the Yemen plane crash investigation had identified King's bomb triggers, King had scurried his wife and foster kids out of town. When the explosion had detonated at the warehouse, they'd found Justin drunk and incoherent in his car a block away.

Waves of helplessness washed over him as he remembered his failed attempts at untangling Gideon from King's web. He couldn't believe he was back here sitting and spying in front of King's house again.

Just then a flash of red in King's driveway caught his attention. The Range Rover's brake lights illuminated the fog of early morning, and its honk drew a blond girl, Julie, out the front door. Justin tensed as she hopped up into the backseat. He didn't know if he could stomach seeing Gideon, his failure. But King backed the vehicle down the driveway without waiting for the boy and zoomed off in the direction of the school.

Where's Gideon? Justin's lungs compressed. *Air, I can't get air.* Holy hell, what if the boy was dead? Maybe King had killed Gideon after he'd resisted his advances. *And the only reason Gideon would've fought him was me prodding him to do so.*

He should've known he couldn't fight such a powerful man. Elyse Frederick hadn't been his only casualty. He might have killed Gideon, too.

Justin's heart raced as he searched the car for a weapon. *Damn!* The glove compartment revealed no gun. He rummaged through paper and junk to emerge victorious with a Swiss Army knife. He sat back in the bucket seat as he clutched the cool, red, metallic object. How ironic that he would use a survival tool to end his life. He extended the blade from its casing and stared it down…much more effective than that plastic knife he'd confiscated from the hospital kitchen.

Sweat dribbled down his temple, and his shirt stuck to his back. His heavy breaths had started to fog the car windows. He ripped off the stupid wig and flung it onto the passenger seat. When the back of his hand brushed his cheek, he felt wetness. He hadn't remembered starting to cry.

"Sorry, Gideon," he whispered.

You're such a fuckup. He looked at the knife. *You don't deserve to live.*

A throbbing ache pressed down on his heart as he ran his fingertip over the top of the small blade. "Sorry, Elyse. You didn't deserve to die."

Vertical scars still marked the inside of his wrists, providing a neat landing strip for the knife.

"My life is in your hands, as it always has been."

"No, Matty." He tried to ban his brother's voice from his mind. Then he saw the flash of fear in Kate's eyes as she'd stolen the scissors from his grasp.

"Give me those, dumbass," she'd said.

They'll be better off without you, King's voice said, drowning out Matthew's and Kate's. Justin nodded. Shame filled his lungs with lead.

But his brother wouldn't shut up. *"If you choose to end your life, it will only be a matter of time before I end mine."*

"Don't put that on me," Justin panted. "I can't, I can't…"

"Will my love sustain you, despite the cruelty you've endured in this life?"

"It's too much," he sobbed. The knife shook in his hand as the scar inside his left wrist called to him. He'd go deep this time, down to the bone and beyond. No chance of seeing Matthew's devastated eyes staring back at him after he failed.

A light melody filled the car. It took a few seconds for Justin to realize the sound came from Matthew's cell phone. He placed the knife on the passenger seat, and his hand hovered over the phone before he scooped it up. The incoming number wasn't in Matthew's contacts. He swiped at his cheeks and tried to take a breath before he answered the call.

"Are you okay?" the male voice asked. The voice sounded younger than him.

His panting breaths must have been audible over the phone. He blew out some air. "Who's this?"

"Cody."

Justin squinted.

"Cody Keystone," the voice supplied when Justin didn't say anything. "Are you…lucid? I, uh, I heard about cancer brain…maybe I shouldn't be calling…"

This must be one of Matthew's patients. Justin fought to clear his mind before he spoke.

"Yeah, they're trying a new drug—it's kicking my ass."

The boy breathed out a long sigh. "Thank God you're still fighting."

Had Matthew told the boy he was dying? He tried to remember his brother's letter. That's right—Matthew had told his patients he was headed to hospice. What a cruel lie.

"Sorry, Dr. D, I know you told me not to call you anymore."

Cody's voice dripped with desperation, and Justin shook his head. How could his brother have abandoned people that way? He glanced at King's house through the side window. *Get off your high horse.* He was the one who'd let everyone down, who'd ruined everything. Matthew had been forced to lie because of Justin's screw-ups. His gaze floated back to the knife.

"But I couldn't sleep at all last night," Cody continued.

You and me both, kid.

"It made me sick."

Justin licked his lip. "What made you sick?"

"You saw it, right?"

"What?" Justin asked.

"Last night. That son of a bitch King got a humanitarian award."

Why was this kid mentioning King? Justin's heart pounded in his ears.

"Please, I need to talk to you. I know you said you can't, but I'm having more memories. You said that's good, right? I'm processing the trauma. But I can't think, can't stop throwing up…I have to talk to you. Sorry, I don't know who else…"

He wasn't sure how long he sat there, frozen, before Cody spoke again.

"Dr. D?"

Justin glanced at his keychain. "Meet me in my office in thirty minutes."

"Thank you," Cody breathed.

Twenty minutes later, the third key Justin tried unlocked Matthew's office suite. He'd been there once to take Matthew to retrieve his car after the shop had repaired a flat tire. Then, the Worthington office building had been busy. Now, at just past seven in the morning, the place was quiet. Matthew's office was off of a waiting room that connected to another office with a placard by the door: *Nancy Wallace, PsyD.*

The same key opened Matthew's interior office. A sofa, chair, and desk remained, but his brother had cleared out all personal items. A houseplant was the only sign of warmth left. As Justin closed the door and walked on trembling legs toward the plant, he noticed someone had watered it recently. His heart thundered, and he wheeled around, but the office was still empty.

What the hell am I doing? He couldn't pull off pretending to be a psychologist. He didn't know a damn thing about mental health—he only knew mental illness. He touched the Swiss Army knife in his pocket. But this Cody guy…he had to find out his connection to King. He had a suspicion he needed to verify. Maybe Matthew had notes or something he could read before Cody arrived. He knelt by the desk drawer and tried the smallest key on the keychain. When the file drawer slid open, Justin frowned. *Empty.*

A knock on the door sprang him to his feet. His eyes closed as he smoothed his hands over his wig. *Let's do this.*

He opened the door and looked up at a sandy-haired boy wearing an Ohio State letter jacket. His height and muscular frame made him look like a man, but the tears pooling in his troubled eyes were all boy.

"Cody?"

Justin gasped when the boy rushed into his arms.

"Thank God you haven't died," Cody said as he clutched him.

Justin's initial stiff posture gave way to hugging the boy back. A lump lodged in his throat as loss washed over him. Cody was another one of King's victims—he knew it. He only had to look into the boy's haunted eyes to know, and that confirmed his suspicion. Cody had led Matthew to discover what King had done to Justin.

"Sorry I've been such an a-hole," Cody said as he let Justin go. "Yelling at you for dying and all that." He sniffed.

Justin let out a breath. "You're just doing the best you can."

Cody rolled his eyes. "You always say that."

Justin started. Matthew had used the same words? Their psychologist mother had often said something similar: "*All you can do is your best.*"

"So the new drug's working?" Cody asked after lowering to the sofa. He snatched a tissue from the box Matthew must have left on the side table.

Justin figured he should close the door. Once he sat in a lounge chair catty-corner to the sofa, he shrugged. "Maybe. I've got more scans next week." The intensity of Cody's stare unnerved him. "I agreed to see you today, but I can't make promises about the future. You understand that, right?"

"You seem different."

Justin leaned back in the chair, feigning nonchalance despite the flip of his stomach. "The drugs make me feel weird. Hope I don't barf during our session."

"Eh, been there, done that." Cody shuddered. "It was your fault, too, making me tell you my traumatic memories."

Matthew had forced Cody to talk about the abuse? And it had made him so sick that he'd thrown up? This was exactly the reason Justin hadn't opened up to any therapist.

When Justin didn't speak, Cody raised his hands to the side. "I know, I know. Telling the memories over and over is a way to heal. I have to admit, the nightmares have decreased, like you promised."

Interesting.

"But last night—my nightmare was a doozy duce."

Justin braced himself. "You said King getting the award made you sick?"

"I read about it online. What demented fucks would give that monster a humanitarian award?"

"He's snowed lots of people."

Cody blew out a breath. "Including CPS."

Child Protective Services? How had they gotten involved? Justin's throat squeezed. King had threatened to kill him if he told the authorities about the abuse. He felt Cody's eyes on him, so he looked away to be able to think. Maybe King had killed Gideon because of CPS sticking their noses in, not because of Justin trying to intervene.

"I forgive you," Cody said.

Justin turned to him.

"I know I was mad when you called CPS, but you were right," said Cody. "The last thing I need is guilt hanging over my head from letting King destroy more lives."

Justin massaged his temples—he understood such guilt. He had to find Matthew's notes to learn more about his past with this patient. If CPS had investigated, why wasn't King locked up? He wondered what his brother would say to Cody now. What would Francine say? Something touchy-feely about the relationship, probably.

"I appreciate you forgiving me," he said. "I know we've come a long way."

Cody's smirk egged him on.

"You, uh, you want to tell me about the nightmare?"

Cody's face fell, but after a beat, he nodded. "It scared the crap out of me."

Justin battled the urge to run from the room.

"It was this woman…She was holding me down, forcing rum down my throat, like waterboarding or something." He looked up. "I swear, I haven't been drinking."

"Good," Justin found himself saying, when he really wanted some booze for himself.

"I was choking on it, and King was laughing at me because I couldn't fight her off. But I was, like, frozen."

Justin knew the frozen feeling well. "Fucking frustrating."

"I know, right? I couldn't freaking move." His hands shook in his lap.

Justin licked his lips. He didn't want to make the boy feel worse, but he couldn't stop himself from asking, "You said you've had more memories?"

Cody blinked. "The woman in my dream…I…I feel like I've seen her before. She seems important somehow."

A chill went up Justin's spine.

"Maybe not." Cody shook his head. "Maybe I'm making it all up."

"What did she look like?" The question tumbled out of Justin's mouth.

A line tightened Cody's forehead. "Dark. Um, black hair. Tan skin. Her hair was, like, in my face. Black. I couldn't see."

An uneasy feeling started in Justin's gut and snaked upward like a vise gripping his lungs. He heard a faint voice, but he was conscious only of a black-haired woman floating before him in a sea of memories.

"Dr. D?"

He looked at Cody, then became aware of the bare wall above the sofa. Matthew's office. He let out a breath.

"Do you think it happened?"

Justin realized Cody had repeated the same question.

"The woman," Cody said. "Is she real?"

"Uh, I don't know."

Cody scoffed, "I hate this shit. The nightmares, the memories." His hands twisted on his lap. "I just want it to go away."

It was like Cody had crawled inside Justin's head.

They continued talking about Cody's swimming and final exams in school, but then Cody's eyebrows furrowed.

"Aren't you taking notes today?"

Justin's heartbeat kicked up as he looked down at his empty lap. "I don't have a notepad."

"But you'll have one next week, right?"

"Next week?"

"C'mon, Dr. D. You did great today—no barf in sight. You can keep seeing me, right?" He stared at his feet. "Please?"

Shit, shit, shit. Matthew would kill him if he found out he'd met with one of his patients. But the boy needed him. And, to be honest, he needed Cody. He sensed that the woman in Cody's dreams *was* important. If they could figure out who she was, maybe they'd both stop having nightmares.

Justin didn't even know if Matthew's office would still be available next week. "How about next week? Monday at nine?"

Cody exhaled, then nodded. He rummaged in his backpack before handing some money to Justin. "Thanks for seeing me. A hundred's still the self-pay rate, right?"

One hundred dollars? Simply for talking to the kid? Should he take it even though he wasn't a psychologist?

"Dude." Cody shook the money. "I practically forced you to meet with me. I'll feel bad if you don't take it."

Justin didn't trust himself to speak, so he just accepted the money.

After they both got to their feet, Justin reached for Cody's hand and looked into his eyes. "You're not alone."

Cody's hand tensed in his. He looked like he wanted to say something, but instead he darted out the door.

Justin stood in the open doorway and saw a short, gray-haired woman emerge from the office across from his.

"Matthew!" Nancy Wallace's eyes widened, and she dashed toward him, almost bowling him over with her apple-shaped body.

This was the second person in an hour to hug him. Justin had never incited such excitement in others before.

"You look like shit," Nancy said, after she let him go.

He *felt* like shit. He wanted to sleep for days.

"But you're back?" Her eyes searched his. "The treatment's working?"

His lips pressed together, but he managed a slight nod.

Nancy turned to walk into her office, then spoke over her shoulder. "You were in such a rush when you left." She opened a desk drawer and withdrew a stack of files. "I did as you asked and called your clients to give them the bad news." She approached him. "You owe me—almost all of them started crying when I told them you couldn't see them anymore."

Justin accepted the stack of files with a wince. "Sorry."

"They'll be thrilled to hear you're back in business," she added.

Back in business?

"Lucky for you, I haven't rented out your office yet. Are you taking back the clients you referred to George McCallister, too?"

"Uh…" He cleared his throat as he thought about the five twenties in his pocket, sitting next to the Army knife. "Better start small first."

10. Resistance

"**B**ut I'm *not* mad," Daniel Vanderkay protested.

"Really?" Francine's chin dropped.

Matthew shook his head at his fellow patient's lack of emotional awareness—the boy radiated rage. The first day of May was a Tuesday, which meant group therapy. Group tension, more like it. Ezekiel Shaddox had maneuvered to sit across the circle from Matthew and leered at him nonstop.

"You look angry," Francine told Daniel. "You're clenching your fists, your shoulders are tense, and your face is red."

Sitting next to Matthew, Daniel looked down and unfurled his fists in his lap.

"What do you notice in your body, Daniel?" asked Francine, who sat on the other side of Matthew.

Daniel was quiet for a moment, then muttered, "Weed."

"Excuse me?"

He looked up at the blond psychologist. "Want weed."

"You're craving marijuana?" she asked.

He nodded.

"What do you notice in your body?" she repeated. She looked around the circle. "Each of you, pay attention to what's happening inside of you. Your body gives you clues about your emotions. And awareness of your emotions gives you power over your behavior."

Shaddox's hand drifted to his crotch as his half-lidded eyes bounced from Matthew to Daniel. A jagged scar shone on the hairless side of his skull.

There was no mistaking the emotion tied to the twist of Matthew's stomach: disgust.

When Daniel didn't answer her, Francine asked, "Is your heart racing?"

"Yeah," he admitted.

"Hard to breathe?"

From the corner of his eye, Matthew caught a nod from Daniel.

Francine tilted her head. "How would weed help you right now?"

"It'd chill me out."

"It would block the feelings?"

"Yeah."

Francine leaned in. "Where would the feelings go?"

"Away," Daniel mumbled.

"No, they wouldn't." Francine sat back in her chair. "Drugs don't take away the feelings. They mask them for a moment. But the feelings are still there, waiting to be dealt with. What's making you angry right now?"

The boy's fists tightened, turning his knuckles white.

Over the past seventeen days, Matthew had learned that Daniel had strangled his mother when he'd been tripping on drugs. It was unclear if he'd experienced drug-induced psychosis at the time. Hence his stay in psychiatric lockdown while the mental health system tried to sort out his culpability.

"She burned me when I was bad," Daniel rasped.

Francine glanced at Matthew before she returned her attention to the boy next to him. "Your mother?"

Daniel's eyes tapered. "With her curling iron."

Matthew closed his eyes. That explained the oval-shaped scars he'd seen on Daniel's back when he'd emerged from the shower. When he opened his eyes, he noticed Shaddox fondling his penis through his jumpsuit.

"Do you need to be restrained, Ezekiel?" Francine asked.

Shaddox grinned at her but slid his hands toward his knees.

Officer Shaw pushed off the wall he'd been leaning against and stepped closer to the ring of chairs.

Francine studied Daniel. "You're angry at your mother for hurting you."

Daniel's hands trembled as he flexed them. Matthew wondered how he'd found the strength to kill his mother with those small hands.

"And you chose to deal with your anger by being aggressive," Francine said.

Shaddox's laugh was deep and slow. "He killed the bitch."

Matthew felt Daniel tense next to him and surmised that the boy was glaring at Shaddox, given the man's widening smile. Francine looked at Shaw, and the red-haired officer shifted closer to Daniel's chair as he kept his eyes on Shaddox.

"Anger is a healthy emotion," Francine said. "We all experience it, whether or not we're aware of it. Aggression is a behavior that isn't healthy or effective. Aggression increases anger. Who else feels angry right now?"

Another man raised his hand, and Francine spoke to him. But Matthew didn't hear their exchange because he was riveted to the surging energy between Daniel and Shaddox. Daniel shifted in his chair, and Shaddox scooted forward in his.

"How about you, Justin?"

Matthew flinched as all eyes stared at him. He tried to clear the fog in his brain. *Damn meds.* Harold had caught him spitting them out a few days ago and now two psych techs supervised him at medication time to be sure he swallowed the putrid pills. Francine hadn't been successful at getting Dr. Majumdar to change his medication.

She gave him a gentle smile. "We're talking about effective ways to deal with anger. You like to do pushups, right?"

Matthew nodded. As his wrists had healed, he'd pumped out as many as he could in his cell every morning before they escorted him to breakfast.

"And your aggression toward yourself and others has decreased the past two weeks. Good job."

He was grateful she hadn't named suicide attempts as his aggressive behavior—the less the criminals knew about him, the better.

He was also relieved she'd lifted the one-to-one staffing on him once he'd made it two weeks without trying to kill himself.

"Good job," Shaddox mocked in a singsong voice.

Francine frowned at him. "Ezekiel, how do you manage your anger?"

As the man's stubby fingers glided along the jagged scar on one side of his scalp, Matthew wondered again where the scar had come from. He guessed one of Shaddox's purported sexual assault victims had fought back.

"I fantasize," Shaddox said as he ogled Daniel. His tongue snaked out to lick his upper lip. He looked at Francine. "Do you want to know what I fantasize about?"

Nope, thought Matthew.

"Only if it's appropriate to share with the group," said Francine.

Shaddox leaned to the left as he twisted to rest his right elbow on the back of the chair. His eyes roamed down Daniel's body. "Love," he said. "Soft skin. Bodies colliding."

"That's enough, Ezekiel," Francine said.

Daniel's white slippers tattooed a beat on the floor, and his hands gripped the chair. Matthew wasn't sure if his movements indicated fear or anger.

"Stop looking at me," Daniel sputtered at Shaddox.

Anger, then.

"Fantasies of kissing," Shaddox continued, his dark eyes glinting. "Licking. Sucking. Swirling."

Francine looked at Shaw. "Officer, please escort—"

Daniel interrupted Francine by popping off his chair and lunging for Shaddox. But Shaw was on top of the boy before he reached the predator.

Shaddox cackled as Shaw straddled Daniel, who was splayed out on the floor on his belly. Shaw cuffed Daniel and dragged him to his feet.

"Sorry!" Daniel moaned, but Shaw hauled him toward solitary. "No. Not the hole! Not the hole!"

Daniel's cries reverberated in the room after he left.

Shaddox smiled at Matthew and said, "Yes, the hole."

Queasiness overtook his stomach.

Francine stood. "Group's over for today. Stay put until the officers return."

As Matthew got to his feet and watched her leave, he hoped the state paid her a handsome salary. He couldn't imagine working in this environment. What hope did she have of affecting change in men who were already so destroyed?

Someone shoved him from behind, and he stumbled forward. "Hey!"

He righted himself and spun around only to find Shaddox charging into him, pushing him toward a door to the side of the group room.

"Get off me!" he yelled, but Shaddox overpowered him and launched him into the small space, a maintenance closet. Matthew tumbled to the floor.

He looked up to catch Shaddox snatching a white substance off of the lock on the side of the door—he must've jimmied it with gum or something. Matthew scrambled to his feet as Shaddox shoved the door closed, then flipped on the light.

"Time to make good on our deal," Shaddox said.

Matthew charged around him to grab the doorknob, but it was locked. His heart pounded as he jerked at the stalwart knob.

"Fighting me isn't part of the deal," he cooed as he came up behind and tugged at Matthew's collar.

Shrugging away, Matthew turned and swallowed. "What deal?"

"You know." His gnarled teeth shined in the light, and he reached for the Velcro of Matthew's jumpsuit.

Matthew panted as he fought him off. What deal had Justin made with this monster?

"You keep resisting," Shaddox hissed, "and I'll do the boy after I do you."

Matthew froze.

"That's right." Stubby fingers ripped the jumpsuit off Matthew's shoulders. "You don't want any harm to come to Danny Boy."

Oh, Justin. His stomach sank. His brother had continued to sacrifice himself for others. This time, it was a different tormentor, but same scenario. Cody's voice sounded in his mind. *"He told me he'd rape her if I didn't submit."*

When Shaddox leaned in to swipe his tongue across Matthew's nipple, Matthew pressed his back against the door, shirking away. He was taller, but the weight of Shaddox pushing into him communicated the man's strength.

"You made me wait too long. You're gonna pay for that." Shaddox looked up at him as he pushed Matthew's jumpsuit to his knees and reached into his boxers to seize his penis.

Matthew's breath caught in his throat, and a jolt of pain flared up his spine. The echo of Daniel's cries stopped him from wrenching the monster's hand off his junk.

"They stopped us the first time. Then you went and got yourself a shadow," Shaddox continued.

So he hadn't gotten the chance to rape Justin before the switch?

Shaddox shucked Matthew's boxers down his legs and took a step back to admire him. "Beautiful." His black eyes gleamed as they floated up to meet his victim's. The rasp of unclasping Velcro on Shaddox's jumpsuit competed with the rush of Matthew's pounding heartbeat in his ears. "But no more techs watching you every second. Now *I'm* your shadow."

Shaddox dispatched his jumpsuit in seconds, revealing light-brown skin with a smattering of chest hair, scars, and tattoos. His erection tented his boxers.

"I'll take you against the door." He swirled his finger. "Turn around."

But Matthew didn't move. Even the beta-blocker they had him on couldn't stop the heart attack he was about to experience.

"Move it, or I'll fuck the boy, too. And I'll be much rougher with him." He cupped his ear. "Can you hear Danny Boy's whimpers now?"

He couldn't do this, couldn't sacrifice himself for Daniel. He wasn't as strong as his brother. In an instant, his fist connected with Shaddox's jaw. The man careened into the steel shelving.

"You slut!" Shaddox bounced off the shelf and came for him. Matthew tried to evade his backhand but the jumpsuit shackled his ankles, tripped him up. His cheek exploded with pain.

When Shaddox shoved him, his forehead cracked on a bucket perched near the far wall on his way down. Warmth gushed down his face as he writhed on the floor. Then his breath huffed out of his lungs as Shaddox jumped on his back.

"No!" Matthew felt the man's sweaty skin cover him like a blanket and a hot rod pulse against his naked bottom. He squirmed to push off the floor, but his hand slid on wetness, and he gasped when he saw a smear of blood on the tile. "Get off me!"

Shaddox chuckled. "So you don't care about Danny Boy. That's okay, I'll take you both." He struck Matthew's head, then pushed down on him.

Matthew's ear rang from the blow, and he couldn't get air. *No. No. No.* He scrabbled for a hold to push up, but the wall of weight pressing down suffocated him. Acid splashed in his stomach as he felt Shaddox's rough hands on his butt cheeks. *Justin.* Justin had felt this same terror. This same violation.

"No!"

There was a crash, and then the weight lifted. He heard shouts and grunts, and he rolled to his side to see a psych tech manhandle Shaddox out the open door of the closet.

"Guards!" the tech yelled.

Harold? How had the older man subdued Shaddox?

Matthew panted as he watched Officer Shaw and another guard thrust Shaddox to the ground before cuffing and dragging him off, naked. The other patients gawked at the scene.

"Christ." Harold entered the closet, then pulled the door partly shut behind him. He knelt by Matthew and scanned the length of his body. "You okay?"

"He…" Matthew licked his lip and tasted blood. "He tried to rape me."

"I know. Did…?" Harold shook his head and removed a handkerchief from his pants pocket. He tapped above his eyebrow, then pointed at Matthew. "Press this against the cut."

Matthew accepted the handkerchief and applied pressure to his head, which now throbbed with each beat of his heart. His thoughts scrambled as his breaths slowed.

"You got here in time." He looked up at Harold. "Thank you."

Harold's eyes narrowed. "The nurse will be here soon. Let's, um…" He reached for Matthew's ankles and tugged the jumpsuit and boxers up to his knees. "Can you stand?" He helped Matthew to his feet.

With a slight sway, Matthew reached to steady himself and left a bloody handprint on the steel shelf filled with cleaning supplies.

"Not this time," Harold muttered as he dressed him.

Harold was just pulling the jumpsuit over his shoulders when the male nurse arrived.

After examining the gash on Matthew's head, the nurse said, "Let's get him to the infirmary."

The nurse and Harold escorted him out into the group room, which was now empty, and past the nurses' station.

Feeling strangely detached, Matthew watched as if someone else shuffled his feet and hopped him up onto the exam table. Maybe they gave him something before they stitched up his forehead, or maybe he was so numb that he didn't feel the needle. When they stripped him and did a thorough physical exam, he didn't notice the gloved hands roaming over his body. After they'd dressed him in a new jumpsuit and dumped him into a chair in Francine's office, he stared blankly at the painting on her wall.

"What the hell happened to him?" Francine cried.

It wasn't until she clasped his hand, her widened eyes searching his, that he sucked in a breath.

"Justin?" She squeezed his hand.

He blinked as his heart thumped double-time.

"Ezekiel Shaddox tried to assault him," Harold said.

"My God." Francine went to touch the bandage on his head. When he flinched, she stole her hand back. "I should've waited for a guard to return to the group room before I left."

The tears came at once, hot and streaming down Matthew's face. His body shook, and he ducked his head, not wanting her to see his emasculation. Another man had almost owned him, ripped into him, violated his soul.

"Ezekiel's in solitary?" Francine asked.

"Yeah," Harold said.

But not for long. Matthew had to get out of here before Shaddox tried again. Maybe the forensic psychologist would clear him to stand trial before Shaddox got out. But Daniel would likely still be here, unprotected. And once Matthew entered a maximum-security prison, a long line of Shaddox shadows awaited him.

"I want you to focus on your breath. You're safe here," said Francine. "I'm so sorry this happened to you, Justin."

I'm not Justin! he wanted to scream. His brother hadn't visited him once in here, leaving him alone to battle monsters. He closed his eyes, feeling tears run down his cheeks. *You did this. Stop blaming your twin.* Justin had probably killed himself on the outside as the memories consumed him. Hell, Matthew hadn't even been raped and the flashes of asphyxiating force still sparked his synapses.

Harold spoke up. "Maybe I should go. He needs to talk to you after what happened."

"Would you like to talk, Justin?"

Matthew wiped his cheeks with the back of his hand. He looked at Francine, then at Harold. "Thank you. Thank you for saving me."

"You stopped the assault?" Francine asked Harold.

He tensed. "I was in the break room, and I had this feeling. A bad feeling. So I rushed to the group room, but you weren't there. The patients, though, they were crouched around the broom closet, listening in. I knew I had to get in there."

Matthew's eyes closed. If he'd arrived a minute later…

"Your intuition served you well, Harold." Francine swallowed. "You've faced this situation before, perhaps?"

Harold stepped back. After a moment, he spoke. "'Nam. I was in the Marines. The villagers…" He shook his head. "Dr. Pierre." Then he left.

Francine exhaled. "This is my fault. I shouldn't have ended group early."

He tried to even his breathing. She was blaming herself? That didn't sound right. "But you had no idea they'd haul Daniel away and leave you alone with us."

"I should've known. Dr. Majumdar lectures about how important it is to follow the rules in here, about how we shouldn't deviate from protocol."

"You're sure sticking to his rules when it comes to my medication." Wow, he sounded bitter.

She frowned. "I tried to go to bat for you, but I'm not a medical doctor. He's in charge of medication, and I trust his judgment." She shook her head. "Rules are important. I should've known not to alter the schedule without checking first with the officers."

He studied the blush on her cheeks and noticed he wasn't crying anymore. "It was Shaddox's fault, not yours. Stop shoulding all over yourself."

She jumped in her chair, and he realized he'd just used therapist speak. Had he blown his cover?

Then, she gave him a small smile. "Sometimes I think you're not listening to me in therapy. But you take everything in, don't you?"

"Not today." He rubbed his eyes, careful to avoid the bandaged gash above them. "I feel like I'm somewhere else."

She nodded. "You just had something traumatic happen to you. Of course you're in shock."

Shock. That's what he'd been experiencing. Just like when he'd learned about King abusing his twin. At least Matthew had prevented Shaddox from hurting Justin like King had.

"How are you feeling?" she asked.

His hands twisted in his lap. "You have to get Daniel out of here."

She cocked her head. "Why is that?"

Matthew sat back in the chair. The adrenaline rush from the attack had crashed, leaving exhaustion in its wake. "There's a reason Shaddox came after me. I made a deal with him." He let out a breath. "If I let him take me, he'd leave Daniel alone."

She gasped. "Why on Earth did you promise that? Why didn't you tell me or one of the guards?"

"They can't keep Daniel safe. You can't, either. Not from a hunter like Shaddox."

Her lips parted as she stared at him.

"But now the deal's void. I resisted. That's why Daniel needs to be transferred."

"You resisted?"

Matthew looked away. "I wasn't strong enough to keep the deal. I thought only about myself, not Daniel."

"That's ridiculous. Sacrificing yourself like that isn't strength—it's stupidity."

Matthew snapped his gaze toward her.

"I'm not saying you're stupid, more misguided. You don't deserve that. You don't deserved to be raped, Justin."

He never has deserved that. The tears threatened to return.

"I'm not questioning your bravery. I'm trying to say I'm surprised you resisted because I would've expected you to freeze, to be unable to fight back." When he didn't speak, she said, "This has happened to you before. You've been raped?"

Matthew said nothing. It wasn't his memory to tell.

"I've sensed you've been through horrifying trauma, Justin. It's okay to tell me."

So she'd figured out the sexual abuse despite Justin's shamed silence. And Matthew knew his brother's avoidance of the memories had locked in his PTSD symptoms. He wished Justin would finally get the therapy he needed.

Francine's voice sounded strained. "Nobody would make that deal unless he'd been used by someone before. Unless some predator had made him his prey."

She was good. She'd figured out Justin's life story with far less evidence that Matthew had possessed. He'd been so blind to his brother's pain, and he could see his blindness even more vividly after that almost-rape. How had Justin survived years of such horror?

"No wonder you tried to kill yourself."

Matthew looked up.

"Not that suicide is any solution," she added. "But you haven't had anyone to help you with the nightmares and flashbacks. You've been all alone." She sat up in her chair, appearing to have an insight. "The suicide attempts…they got you a one-to-one. They ultimately protected you from Shaddox."

Whoa. She was right. Was saving himself from Shaddox the impetus for Justin to try to kill himself? *No.* He wasn't about self-preservation. He was only about self-sacrifice.

Her eyebrows pulled together. "Have you given up all hope? I thought your recent lack of attempts meant that you'd found the will to live. But maybe you thought Ezekiel would kill you?"

"No. I didn't expect his attack." The trembling in his hands attested to that fact.

"Please don't use this assault as reason to return to suicide. Don't give up, Justin."

She was trying to help him, but the client she needed to talk to hadn't been honest with her and now was long gone. Matthew couldn't be honest with her, either.

The hopeless future stretched before him. Maybe Justin had been right in trying to end his life.

11. Reunion

Justin stared at the looming hospital through the windshield of Matthew's car. With its arched windows and tall brick spires, the exterior appeared almost majestic. He hadn't gotten a good look at the building the first time he'd arrived because an Ohio Department of Corrections van had taken him from the county jail to the rear entrance under the cover of night.

"Gotta sneak you in because you're a terrorist," the guard facing him in the back of the van had said. *"We got a bunch of death threats. People want you dead."*

They'll get their wish soon, Justin had thought then, his chains jangling as he'd shifted in the seat.

But he hadn't succeeded with his plan before Matthew had swooped in and destroyed everything.

Matthew was in there now, instead of him. He'd been stuck in there for three weeks without one visit from his useless brother. Justin's chest vibrated as he gripped the steering wheel. *Get your ass in there*. But he couldn't move.

A guttural roar sounded from the radio. "Friday, May fourth," said the DJ. "May the fourth be with you." Another of Chewbacca's Wookiee roars followed.

Justin remembered endless lightsaber battles with Matthew when they were about seven. After their mother had bought the Star Wars toys for them, their father had scoffed at the inauthenticity of the cheap, white plastic. Despite the twins' protests, their father had whisked the lightsabers off to the basement and emerged an hour later after somehow adding a light source inside the tubes that glowed an incandescent red or blue. After that, Justin and Matthew had become famous in their neighborhood for having the coolest sabers ever.

He turned off the ignition and shoved open the car door. His legs trembled with each step, but he made it past the guard into the lobby. Once his eyes adjusted from sunlight to the dark interior, he headed for the metal detector.

"Hey," a voice snapped.

He stopped breathing as he swiveled toward a guard on his right.

"You need to sign the visitor's log." The officer tapped a clipboard on the desk in front of him.

Justin nodded and attempted to approximate his brother's professional scrawl. When he turned again toward the metal detector, the guard huffed, "Stop."

Justin froze. He felt sweat form under his goddamn wig. As he turned around, the guard's eyes narrowed.

"What's your deal? You know you have to give me your ID."

"Right. Forgot." He removed Matthew's wallet from Matthew's jeans.

The guard frowned at the offered driver's license and took the entire wallet along with it. "Anything else in your pockets?"

Justin swallowed before handing over his keys and phone. When the guard nodded at him, he walked toward the conveyer belt. Another guard seized his arm, and Justin hoped he didn't notice how badly he was shaking.

"Remove your belt and shoes to be scanned first."

He tugged off his running shoes and touched the waistband of his jeans beneath his untucked T-shirt. "Don't got a belt."

On the other side of the detector, he pushed his feet back into his shoes, and yet another guard escorted him through several locked doors. He tried to see the journey toward visitation through Matthew's eyes and imagined his brother's building despair each time a guard buzzed them through the heavy metal doors. There'd been no way to break him out of here, no way to save his life other than switching places with him. A queasy sensation stirred in his gut. Matthew should've let him die in here.

His foot tapped double-time as he waited in the visitation room. The walls were bare, and the same horrid Muzak still played. Was Kenny G really supposed to relax the psychos down the hall? The shitty saxophone had only seemed to agitate the cons—especially that Shaddox lowlife. Justin hadn't thought of him once since the switch, but being back here brought the cretin to mind. His spine prickled as he remembered the man's snaggletoothed grin, along with a fuzzy feeling that he'd forgotten something.

The steel door pushed open and in walked Matthew, weighted down by chains. Right away, Justin noticed the stitched-up cut on his forehead, and then he caught the yellowing bruise across his cheekbone. *Holy fuck.* What had happened to him? He hopped to his feet and looked at Shaw, who held Matthew's elbow.

"He didn't try to hurt himself, did he?"

"Dr. Durante." Shaw had halted Matthew's forward progress. "You need to stay seated."

Justin lowered to his chair, not taking his eyes off his brother.

"His injuries aren't self-inflicted this time, I'm sorry to say." Shaw shook his head as he led Matthew to the chair opposite of Justin. "That didn't come out right. What I meant was that there was an altercation with another patient."

"Who?"

Justin's hostile tone made Matthew look up for the first time. Justin's heart sagged. His brother's eyes looked lifeless.

Shaw crossed the room to lean against the wall. "Can't say. But I can assure you the other patient is being appropriately punished."

"He's in the hole?" asked Justin.

Shaw's eyes creased with apparent suspicion. "He's in solitary."

I should be careful not to use inside lingo. "For how long?"

Shaw paused. "Up to Dr. Majumdar."

Matthew's fists clenched, and Justin wondered if his brother disliked the psychiatrist as much as he did. The short Indian had put off a weird vibe every time Justin had been forced to meet with him.

When Justin reached for Matthew's cuffed wrist, Shaw pushed off the wall. "No touching."

Justin let go and searched for a sign of life in his brother's eyes. "Who did this to you?"

Matthew shrugged. "I'm fine. Nothing happened."

"That's not what I asked." Justin ignored Shaw's frown and pressed again, "Who did this to you?"

After a beat, Matthew sighed. "Ezekiel Shaddox."

Justin's stomach tensed—he'd been afraid that would be the answer. That creep had seemed dangerous. And now he was after Matthew? "Why'd he come after you?"

Matthew glowered at him.

Justin stilled. Why'd he look so mad?

After fuming silently for almost a minute, Matthew seemed to drop his anger. He nodded and relaxed back against his chair. "I made a deal with him a while back, remember? It was time to pay up."

In an instant, Justin felt Shaddox's hot breath on the back of his neck as the man had pressed him into the rec room's concrete wall three months ago.

"Mind your own fucking business," Shaddox had hissed.

Justin had thrust against him but couldn't find traction with the smooth bottoms of his slippers. He didn't hear anyone behind them and hoped Daniel had gotten out of there. "Stay away from the kid."

"Ha-ha." Shaddox's laugh was low and deep. "You can't stop me."

Justin heard the pattering thud of guard boots running down the hall toward them.

"Only way I leave the boy alone?" Shaddox cupped his butt cheek. "You let me have you. No resistance."

Justin felt a weight lift as Shaddox pushed off him. He spun around to see the man fondle the scar on his head just as a guard sprinted into the room, panting. Daniel scampered in behind him, his gaze bouncing back and forth between Justin and Shaddox.

"What's going on here, gentlemen?" the guard demanded.

Shaddox smiled at Justin. "No fighting. No resistance. We have a deal?"

Justin was familiar with this type of deal. He'd swallowed, then nodded. Between him and Daniel, it would be better to offer Shaddox the one who was already destroyed. Daniel might have a chance at a real life one day.

Justin sucked in a breath as he now looked into his twin's eyes. His horror at forgetting to warn him made it hard to think.

"I…" Justin shook his head. "I didn't remember. You have to believe me, Matt—"

"It's okay," Matthew interrupted, wide-eyed. "I know you forgot."

Shaw moved toward them with a questioning look.

Get it together. He'd almost blown their cover.

"Justin!" It was strange to shout his own name. "What the hell were you thinking, making a deal like that? You're going to get yourself killed in here."

When Shaw retreated, Justin exhaled. The guard was used to Matthew talking to Justin that way. A voice crackled over Shaw's radio.

"You'll get yourself killed in here," Justin repeated, sickened by the prospect. Maybe Shaddox hadn't gotten far this time, but he'd be back for more. Justin had to switch back to their rightful places. Maybe he could convince Shaw to take off Matthew's chains? He glanced at the guard, who was now speaking into the radio hooked to his collar.

Justin peered at the cut on his brother's forehead. He'd have to recreate it in order to trade places. Blood had crusted along the black stitches. He wondered if he could smash his head against the corner of his plastic chair to create a similar wound. But he had to move fast—the cut looked a few days old.

Matthew shook his head. "Stop your plotting. You won't be able to pull it off."

Justin flinched. Matthew smirked at him—had he read his mind? Justin pouted, then he looked at Shaw, but the guard was still listening to radio chatter.

Matthew leaned in and whispered, "You get a job yet?"

"Yeah."

He'd appointed himself as a psychologist. Since meeting with Cody, Justin had seen five of Matthew's other clients in two days, and none had seemed the wiser. Nancy Wallace had even offered to help with insurance billing due to his supposedly foggy cancer brain. But he couldn't tell any of that to his brother.

He lowered his voice. "I'm working at your gym. The front desk."

"Perfect." Matthew smiled for the first time. "Looks like you're putting some muscle back on."

Whereas Matthew appeared to be withering away. Guilt flipped Justin's stomach.

"Dr. Durante." Shaw approached. "They need me back on the unit. Visit's over."

"What?" Justin frowned. "No."

"Let's go." Shaw reached for Matthew's elbow.

"No!" Scooting forward in his chair, Justin held up his hand. "I barely got to talk to him. We'll be good here while you take care of things."

"I can't leave the patient unsupervised off the unit."

Justin glared at him. "Like you left him unsupervised with Shaddox? Where *were* you when that psycho attacked my brother, Officer Shaw?"

Shaw stepped back. "I, I feel bad about that."

"Sure, you do," Justin snarled. He recalled how Matthew's threats had worked with Shaw before. "You're determined to kill my brother, aren't you? First you ignore his suicide attempts, then you let the other crazies pop him."

"That's not true." Shaw's radio squawked again.

"We'll see what the courts think when I sue your ass," said Justin. "Just go and do your thing. We'll be fine. My brother's obviously safer with me than with you."

Shaw seemed to hesitate before urgent voices sounded on his radio. He grunted and took long strides to the door.

When Matthew heard Shaw's key lock the door from the outside, he watched Justin bolt to his feet and pace the cracked linoleum. Justin's tirade had impressed him. His brother had seemed authoritative and in control. Not crazy at all.

Justin squatted and yanked the chain extending from Matthew's ankles. "Forgot to ask Shaw to remove these, damn it." He tugged the chain like he was testing its strength.

"Don't even think about trying to switch back," Matthew warned. "I won't go along with it, and they'll put us both behind bars. You can't pull it off like I did. I'm the smarter twin, remember?"

Justin glared up at him. "Fuck you."

His fury made Matthew hold his breath. "I know you're mad." He rubbed his wrist below the cuff. "But you're alive."

"And you'll be dead soon." Justin shot up and seized his shoulders, shoving Matthew back. "I still can't believe you did this to us. These are killers in here, Matty. They're going to get to you. Don't you know that?"

Matthew looked up at him. "But Shaddox didn't rape me. A psych tech — Harold — got there before he could."

Justin's eyebrows pulled together. "The old guy?"

"Harold was a Marine in Vietnam." With a grimace, Matthew continued, "He reported his superior for raping a villager, and he got a discharge as a result. No wonder he's such a bitter old man."

Justin stared at him, then dropped into his chair. He kneaded his forehead. "I see you're still getting people to open up to you, Dr. Durante."

Except for you, thought Matthew. He wondered if they could've avoided this place if Justin had told him about the abuse. Now they'd never know.

Matthew eyed the faded gray Ohio State T-shirt stretched across Justin's chest; his brother must've found that at the bottom of some drawer. "You got to be more convincing, playing me. I wouldn't dress like such a slouch."

"Your clothes are too prissy."

He had to smile at that. In fact, this was probably the most relaxed he'd felt in three weeks. Even though Justin was angry with him, it was such a relief to see him again. "Forgot to tell you there's a box of your clothes in the attic."

"Thanks." Justin closed his eyes. After a beat, he clamped his jaw and looked straight at him. "Sorry I didn't visit you before."

"Why...didn't you?"

Justin blew out a breath. "I wanted to get a job first."

Matthew nodded.

"Actually, that's bullshit." Justin's shoulders hunched. "I didn't come because I can't take this." His hand waved back and forth between them. "I can't sit back and let you take the fall for my mistakes. I can't see you with your face all busted up because of me."

"It's not your fault, Just. I would've tried to kill King, too, if he'd hurt me like that."

"Don't you get it? Shaddox is gonna kill *you!* I got to get you out of here."

"Maybe they'll transfer me back to county before he gets out of the hole," Matthew said.

Justin pursed his lips. "But then Daniel will still be at risk."

"I know. That's why I asked Francine to transfer him, but Majumdar won't do it."

A line formed on Justin's forehead. "That guy's a quack."

So Justin didn't trust the psychiatrist either. Matthew leaned forward. "The meds he has us on — they're not right. They cause memory loss."

Justin's mouth dropped open.

"What?" asked Matthew.

"Makes sense I didn't remember that deal Shaddox forced me into."

Matthew wondered what other hospital memories his brother had suppressed. Would there be another forgotten threat hiding behind door number two?

"And I'm having more memories now…from the past," Justin added.

The chains clanked as Matthew reached for his hand — no guard to stop them this time. "Stopping the meds could help you remember, yeah. Or it could be that you're feeling stronger. Our bodies only let us remember traumatic events when we're ready to deal with the memories."

"I sure as hell ain't ready to deal with them."

Matthew could only imagine what his brother was re-experiencing.

"You're spitting the meds out, right?" Justin asked.

Matthew looked down. "Can't. They have two techs on me at med time."

"Jesus." Justin squeezed his hand. "So your memory sucks, too?"

"Well, on top of the meds, trauma jacks up your memory, but I don't have PTSD. Maybe it's not as bad as it was for you. I just feel a little foggy, that's all."

Justin yanked his hand back. "Dammit. I have to get you out of here."

"Please, Just. I'm okay." Matthew's heart hammered. His brother was the impulsive one, and his unpredictability unnerved him. "They stopped the one-to-one — the forensic psychologist will probably clear me to stand trial soon."

"Awesome," Justin huffed. "Then you'll get locked up with a thousand Shaddoxes once they convict you."

The onion smell of Shaddox's breath flooded Matthew's memory. He wished his heartbeat would settle down. "Truth is, I'll be fine. This is all I wanted — you're alive, with the chance to live a good life. Take it, Justin. Please take this opportunity."

Justin's jaw rippled as he looked away. After a long beat, he asked, "How's Daniel?"

Matthew reflected on the boy's behavior once he got out of solitary. "Clingy."

"Heh." Justin twisted his mouth to one side. "He can't tell the difference between us, huh?" When Matthew shook his head, Justin added, "Bet he likes you more, though. As a psychologist, you're probably a better teacher than I am."

Matthew leaned closer. "What do you mean?"

"You know, teaching Daniel." When Matthew kept staring, Justin asked, "Are the meds making you stupid?"

Matthew tilted his head.

"Oh. Maybe you don't know. Daniel can't read."

Matthew's lips parted. "Ah. You were teaching him how to read?"

"Trying. That boy gets frustrated real quick."

"I could see that."

Justin touched his head, then dropped his hand like the wig disgusted him. "Francine snuck me some paper and a pencil, and I taught Daniel during evening TV time."

"Thanks." Matthew paused. "Anything else I should know?"

Justin frowned. "I've stayed away from Kate, like you asked."

The mention of her name was like an icepick through his heart. "That's good," he forced out.

"Do you think about her?"

"Of course!" Matthew traced the scar inside of his wrist. "I hate myself for what I did. But she's better off now, without me."

Justin's sad smile communicated for him: *You're full of shit.*

Matthew had to change the subject. "Can I ask you a question?"

"Does it matter if I say no?"

"Not really." Matthew braced himself. "Why didn't you tell Francine about the sexual abuse?"

Justin got to his feet and began pacing again. When it was clear he wouldn't respond, Matthew spoke.

"I wish you'd told me, but I get why you didn't. Shame makes people hide. You know it's not your fault, though, right?"

Justin grunted.

"But you can't heal if you don't talk about the abuse. You have to tell a therapist. Please. Go talk to George McCallister."

"But he'll tell the cops about our switch."

"I don't think so." Matthew shook his head. "Psychologists can only breach confidentiality under specific circumstances, and this isn't one of them." When Justin still looked dubious, Matthew shrugged. "Pretend to be me, then, with George. Pretend I was the one abused."

Justin's fists trembled as he paced.

"I'm not bullshitting you, brother. Avoiding the trauma makes it get stuck. You have to tell those memories over and over, and then they have less of a hold on you." Matthew's chest squeezed as he thought about Cody. He hoped he had continued to heal. "I've seen it happen with my clients. It's tough to face what happened, but you start to remember more, and you put the pieces together."

Justin halted.

Matthew hoped he was getting through to him. "Will you think about it?"

Justin returned to his chair and stared at him. "There's a woman... with black hair. And a scarf. She...watched."

Matthew stilled. Cody had mentioned a dark-haired woman as well. His brother seemed to have trouble getting air, and he tried to think of something to say. "That sounds like an important memory. Don't forget to breathe, buddy."

Justin's pained eyes drilled into him. "I don't want to remember, Matty."

"I know." The lump in his throat strengthened his resolve. "I hate that this happened to you. It isn't fair. But the memories are there, asking to be dealt with. Asking to be honored. I know you're strong enough to handle them."

They stared at each other for a minute before Matthew heard the jangle of keys outside the door. "Can I have a hug from my big brother before the po-po hauls me off?"

Justin paused, and Matthew worried he was too mad at him to comply. But right before Shaw returned, Justin wrapped him up in his strong arms. Matthew closed his eyes and let out a long sigh.

12. Rendezvous

"Thanks for meeting with me, especially on a Sunday," Kate said. She tensed as she waited for Pete's response.

His smile looked dejected. "Of course." He closed her office door and sat in the chair across from her. "You lawyers work seven days a week anyway. What do you got?"

It seemed like he was going to ignore her brush-off from over a week ago, after he'd stopped her from buying drugs from that seedy dude at the bar. Once she'd learned Pete had broken up with his girlfriend, Eve, she'd agreed to go to dinner with him. They'd ended up at her place, where Pete had tried to kiss her.

"I want you to see this note that came in the mail yesterday." She reached for the envelope sitting next to her laptop.

"Snail mail, eh? People still use that?" He reached into the pocket of his jacket and extracted a pair of latex gloves. "Your prints are already on there, but should I glove up?"

"Probably a good idea."

He accepted the envelope but didn't open it. "You decided to show me this in your office instead of your apartment?"

So he *wasn't* ignoring what had happened that Friday night. She cringed as she remembered shoving him away. "I'm sorry, Pete."

He looked down.

"I didn't mean to mislead you," she continued. "I thought I was ready to move on, but…" *But I can't let go of Matthew. Even though he threw me overboard, I keep trying to climb back onto his raft.*

He held up his gloved palm. "No need to apologize, Kate. You were with Matthew forever—makes sense it's too soon to move on. I'm just embarrassed I came on so strong, that's all."

"If I wasn't such a fucking mess, I'd reciprocate."

"Hey." He tapped the envelope on the desk. "You're not a fucking mess." He cocked his head. "You're a celibate mess."

She shook her head.

"But good things come to those who wait, right?"

She sure had waited for Matthew a long time, and no good things had come from that. "We'll see," was all she could offer.

"Well, damn." He exhaled. "I've been friend-zoned."

"No—"

"Or investigator-zoned, I should say." He held up the envelope and opened it.

She watched a dent crease his high forehead as he read it.

"Who sent this?"

"No return address." She pointed at the corner of the envelope.

"When'd you get it?"

She sat up taller. His rapid questions echoed her suspicion that the note was somehow significant. "It was in my mailbox when I checked this morning."

"Work mailbox?"

She nodded.

"Your home address isn't listed, right?"

"Yeah, but you can find anything on the internet these days."

"Especially the very public law office address of Justin's attorney," he said.

She chewed on her lip. "You think this is about Justin? But I'm off his case."

He swiveled the handwritten letter and placed it next to her laptop so she could read it. "What do you think?"

The handwriting was shaky and juvenile. She read the poem aloud:

The Lord is with you
Stop him at his sick game
You three are Mighty Warriors
We triumph by my Name

"You think 'you three' refers to Justin, Matthew, and me?" asked Kate.

"Maybe." He studied her. "Or does that bring up any other cases?"

"Hmm." She searched her mind. "Maybe TJ Saxton."

Pete squinted. "The home-invasion guy?"

"Yep." She'd litigated the case before Matthew had dumped her—back when she'd felt invincible in the courtroom. "He and his two buddies got arrested at the same time. Could be the three the poem refers to."

"But you got him acquitted."

She shook her head. "Your *investigation* got him acquitted. Amen for cell phone tower pings."

"And for overwhelming juries with loads of boring technological details, making them vote not guilty just to stop the testimony." He grinned.

His grin was so charming. She wished she felt something for him. But the hole in her heart, formed by Matthew, had to close first. When would she stop thinking about him? She looked back at the poem. "I suppose 'Stop him at his sick game' could refer to King."

"That's what I wondered," Pete said. "Anything else you think it could mean?"

"I hunted around online before you got here. There's a song called 'Mighty Warrior' by Elevation Worship." She clicked on that window and turned her laptop to show him.

He read for a moment. "Do the lyrics suggest anything to you?"

"It's just a bunch of religious crap."

He chuckled. "God, you're cynical. Even for a defense attorney."

He was right. She *was* cynical, specifically when it came to religion. Her mother had embraced Alcoholics Anonymous when Kate turned six, and she'd made Kate pray with her every night until she'd lost her convenience-store job and returned to drugs. Kate looked at the first line of the poem again and frowned. No way the Lord was with her now. If He had been with her, He wouldn't have taken away her two angels.

The twins had always been there for her, softening the blow of losing her mother. Matthew had claimed she was the strongest of the three, but he'd been the one to infuse her with confidence. A memory squeezed her throat.

She'd been having a meltdown while studying for her bar exam four years ago, and Matthew had driven from South Bend, Indiana, to her Evanston apartment. He'd goaded her into a squabble about how five years of graduate school at Notre Dame was far more difficult than three years of law school at Northwestern, and when she'd shot down every one of his arguments, he'd laughed and said, "You're a born litigator. You'll ace this thing."

Her anxiety had diminished, then vanished when they'd made love.

As she drifted off to sleep with him by her side afterwards, he nudged her. "I wanted to show you this news story." He thrust his phone, open to the *Chicago Tribune* suburbs section, at her face.

She moaned as she flung her forearm across her eyes. "Can't we look at it tomorrow?"

"C'mon, read it now."

God, he was annoying. "Read it to me, if you must."

It was a story about a jewelry store in Chicago that had lost a valuable diamond during a renovation. Years later, investigators learned the construction workers had inadvertently thrown away the diamond, and it had been found by a security guard patrolling the grounds. The guard had just been arrested when he'd tried to sell the multi-million dollar stone.

"Why are you telling me this?" she grumbled. "Do you want this shit-for-brains security guard to be my first client or something?"

"I'm telling you this because it reminds me of your mother."

Her eyes opened. "My mother?"

"She was like those construction workers." His blue eyes shone in the faint city lights outside her window. "Your mother threw away the most beautiful diamond." He leaned in to kiss the tip of her nose. *"You."*

She wouldn't let herself cry. "And I suppose you're the security guard in this scenario?"

"But I won't pawn you." He'd kissed the corner of her mouth. "I want to keep this diamond."

"So what's the next step?"

She swallowed her sadness as she looked at Pete. She wasn't a diamond; she was a fake. And Matthew had thrown her away, just like her mother.

Pete rubbed his gloved hands together. "Want me to dust for fingerprints?"

"Would you?"

"You got it." He picked up the envelope and peered at the postmark. "This was processed in Columbus. I'll nose around the Short North post office, see what I can find."

"Thank you." She aimed a grateful smile toward him. "I don't deserve you."

He rose. "Just doing my job. As an investigator, and as…a friend." He looked down. "I'll do anything for you, Kate."

After he left, she closed her eyes. *Will you bring goddamned Matthew back?*

Jefferson wondered if he'd misread Safia's message from Words with Friends. The meet was for Sunday, May sixth, right? But there was no sign of Safia in the park. He'd veered off Lake Trail to the spot near Thoreau Lake where she'd told him to meet her. As he scanned the woods around him, his face felt hot. There wasn't time to waste — not with such an important mission. He thought of Thoreau: "*As if you could kill time without injuring eternity.*"

Feeling beads of sweat at his hairline, he unzipped his jacket but kept the hood in place. The lush greenery reminded him of his West Virginia home. Central Ohio was flat and dull compared to the rolling mounts of his childhood, but at least Blendon Woods featured more varied terrain, including a few knolls and lakes. And solitude. He watched an egret glide to a landing on the far side of the lake.

A sweet melody came from his right, and he turned to see a cardinal perched on a branch. He'd worried about a bird just like that one when he should've been focused on his father's safety. The US government sure as hell hadn't cared about protecting his father when that explosion had killed him and two miners. *Faulty fuses*, the

Federal Mine Safety Commission had written in their report, which Jefferson read after he'd aged out of the foster care system nine years later. It had steamed him that the government blamed his father for the accident. It wasn't possible that a man legendary for meticulous safety precautions would've failed to test the fuses. Jefferson had smelled a rat.

To investigate his suspicions, he'd taken a job at a fertilizer company once he graduated from high school. The company outsold all their competitors when it came to ammonium nitrate supplies for local mines, and Jefferson had used his sleuthing skills to discover why. He'd planted a secret recording device in the boardroom and caught a member of the Mine Safety Commission accepting a bribe from the company CEO—a bribe to ignore the substandard quality of ANFO explosives.

When Jefferson threatened to expose the corruption, the CEO had offered him a bribe as well: tuition and expenses for college and graduate school, and a management position in the company when he returned. He'd accepted the payoff and worked his way through school and up the company ranks before whistleblowing the entire operation, claiming he'd tried to make changes from within, but the government corruption was too deep. The West Virginia senators had been so impressed by his integrity that they'd supported his takeover as company head, thereby starting his weapons-manufacturing empire. He now had plants across the Midwest, but he no longer lived in the West Virginia hills where it had all started. The memories of his father were too raw there.

"You should be more careful."

He wheeled to face the woman who'd materialized on his left. His sudden rage must've shown on his face because she stepped back, her hazel eyes enlarging.

"Calm down. I only meant you should be more aware of your surroundings." She smoothed her hand down the dark-green scarf artfully arranged over her black hair. "Anyone could sneak up on you."

He zipped up his hoodie, and in the process turned on the button mic on his shirt. "What took you so long, Safia?"

"I had to be sure I wasn't tailed."

He wished the government wasn't so damn prejudiced against Middle Easterners like her—they'd stepped up surveillance on everyone from that region. But he was fortunate her Palestinian family had valued higher education. He'd met her in graduate school at Ohio State. She thought he'd simply bumped into her in Thompson Library, when in fact he'd groomed her for a relationship from the moment he'd seen her protesting American support of Israel at a Council on American-Islamic Relations rally. Their shared hatred of the US government had bonded them like epoxy.

"Not many days till *Shaban* moon," she said.

He nodded. Ramadan would begin later in May.

She studied him. "How is your little problem?"

His jaw clenched. "He'll never remember you."

"That's not what I asked, Dr. King."

Bitch. Did she know he was recording their conversation? Scrubbing his name from the footage would complicate the edit of the camera feeds aimed from the tree behind him. He likely wouldn't ever need to reveal the recording, but one could never be too safe. "Do you want the good news or bad news?"

"My country is the holiest of lands yet has been stolen by the Christians, the British, and now the Jews. When has there ever been good news for my people?"

Fuck, her passion was an aphrodisiac. He fought the urge to maul her with a kiss. "There *is* good news, my dear. He will stand in judgment soon."

Her eyes lit up as she inched toward him, and he crept back so the cameras still had a good view of her face.

"But that means he's stopped trying to kill himself." She started to pout. "And the FBI investigation of your company?"

More he'd need to edit out. "That matter will end soon. Or so my contacts say."

She rubbed her chin. "I talked to *my* contact. Our boy. We're go for May twenty-eighth."

"Memorial Day." Jefferson smiled.

She didn't return his smile, but her eyes blazed. "We have much to remember, yes?"

"Much to memorialize." *Like my father.* He studied her for a moment. "We trained him well, but he's young. You think he can pull it off?"

"I already told you, he graduated from the academy and passed his security clearance, no problem. Besides, he knows we will pay him handsomely."

"But it's been a while since I've seen him—are we sure he's well-steeped in the cause?" He nodded toward the lake. "We should heed Thoreau's advice: 'Do not hire a man who does your work for money, but him who does it for love.'"

She shook her head. "You and your nineteenth-century ghosts."

"I like ghosts." He thought about Justin. "I want to create more of them."

"Not ghosts of Christmas past." She tilted her face up to him, and her scarf drew out the green in her hazel eyes. "But ghosts of Christians past. Ghosts of Jews past."

"Now who's quoting nineteenth-century authors?" he teased.

He stepped closer, crowding her space—the cameras be damned—but she made him share precise plans for the transfer of explosives before she said, "Now you can kiss me."

"Why do you think I want to?" he shot back.

"*Please*," she scoffed. "You've been dying to touch me since the second I arrived."

He loved her confidence, so different from Natalia. Safia was married, too, so he'd better act quickly before she flitted away to her husband. When he yanked her close, she gasped, but he knew she liked it rough. Her body lacked the softness of other women and turned him on even more as a result. Though her lips…her lips were soft satin. Every time she let him kiss her, he felt a vicious jealousy toward her husband. She should've been his, not another man's. But they'd known their relationship had to be secret in order to carry out their plans.

As he deepened their kiss, his hands skated beneath her scarf to caress her luxurious hair. Her breathy moan lit a fire within him, and his hand brushed down her face, along her throat, and plunged into her shirt. When she began to push off his hood, he leaped back.

She panted as her eyes tapered. "What's wrong?"

He tugged the hood securely over his ears. She'd left him hard and frustrated, but he couldn't show his bald head to the camera. "Time to go. Someone might see us."

After a long moment, she nodded.

"See you in the game," he said.

"You're on quite the losing streak." She smirked.

He couldn't think as clearly in Words With Friends without a teenage boy to provide release. But once the FBI investigation ended, he'd foster another son. His penis twitched in anticipation.

"Savor the victories now, my darling, because I'll be back to crushing you soon."

Her laugh lilted over her shoulder as she walked away. "In your dreams."

He closed his eyes. *In my dreams.* He turned off the mic and walked to collect the cameras. *My American dream.*

13. Reveal

Justin opened the office door, but there was no one in the waiting room. Nancy hadn't arrived at her office yet either. Only one week into this psychologist gig, he had already learned Nancy wasn't a morning person. She'd said she liked to sleep late. He'd like to sleep, period. He went to rub his buzzed head and touched synthetic wig. When would he get used to the damn Fabio hair?

Cody came in from the outer entrance and stopped when he saw Justin in the doorway. "Sorry I'm late."

Justin checked Matthew's watch and saw it was a couple of minutes before nine. "You're good." He extended his arm into the office and smelled a whiff of chlorine as Cody nudged past him. The boy's dark-blond hair was wet.

Justin's hands trembled as he picked up Cody's chart. Yesterday afternoon, he'd tried to read through Matthew's session notes to gather more background on Cody, but a whopper of a flashback had overtaken him for hours. When he'd returned to reality, nighttime had fallen. And all he could remember of the flashback now was the wooden floor of Dr. King's toolshed. Maybe more would've come to him in dreams, but he hadn't allowed himself to go to bed until after four a.m., thus preventing nightmares.

Cody stared at him as he sat. Was he supposed to say something?

"Last time you said I'm not alone," Cody began. "What'd you mean by that?"

Shit. He'd hoped Cody had forgotten that comment. "I meant you're not the only one who knows what it's like to be a foster kid."

Cody's eyes narrowed.

"That I'm here for you," Justin added.

Cody looked away, and his Adam's apple bobbed as he swallowed. The tense set of his jaw let on that he didn't buy that response.

Justin wondered how to redirect the conversation. "How, uh, how've things been going?"

"Got a paper due tomorrow."

Justin asked, "You're taking classes now?"

"I told you I was taking a Maymester class."

Whatever the hell Maymester is. "Right. Which class?"

"Political science." Cody grunted. "The Quest for Justice—what an absurd course title. As if justice is a real thing. There's absolutely no justice in this world."

Justin sat back. Ever since that fire had engulfed his parents, he'd held the same belief.

"Did you take a poli sci class in college?" Cody asked.

Justin hadn't taken *any* classes in college. "Uh, nope."

"We have to read Nietzche. You know, the guy who said, 'God is dead.'" Cody frowned. "What if he's right?" His voice quivered. "What if we die and we're just bones in the ground?"

Christ. How the hell was he supposed to answer that? Each time he'd tried to kill himself, niggling thoughts about the afterlife had plagued him, but he'd knocked them out of his head in order to get on with business. And now the kid wanted to know his opinion? He couldn't let him know what he really thought. Cody was young, a star swimmer, and apparently intelligent—he still had a chance at making something of himself.

Cody stared at him. "You got nothing for me?"

"Maybe…" Justin cleared his throat. "Maybe you should drop the class."

Cody's chin retracted. "Can't do that. I need it to get my scholarship over the summer."

"Oh." Justin got the sense he'd let him down. Hadn't he given good advice?

Cody pressed his lips together. A few moments later, a small smile cracked through. "And…there's this girl in the class."

Justin watched with fascination as the boy blushed. "Yeah?"

"She's, um…" He shrugged, and a little dimple creased his cheek. "Hot."

"What do you like about her?" That sounded like a good shrink question.

"She plays lacrosse, so she gets the athlete thing—we're both hella busy. And she's got this wicked tattoo."

Justin had been saving up for tattoos before he'd been arrested. He wondered if he could afford one now. No—Matthew didn't have any tattoos, so he couldn't get one. One day he'd come up with a plan to switch back to their rightful places. He just wasn't smart enough to figure it out yet.

"What kind of tattoo?"

"A skull. On her arm." He pointed to the area below his shoulder. "It's badass. She's super smart, too. Our professor said she asks the best questions of any student he's ever taught."

He positively lit up when he talked about her.

"Sounds like God's very much *alive* when she's around?" Justin ventured.

Cody smirked. "Maybe." He took a swig from his water bottle, then scrutinized Justin. "I know what you're gonna ask next."

Justin shifted in his chair. *That makes one of us.*

"And the answer is no, she doesn't drink."

One of the treatment goals Matthew had written in the chart was to help Cody build a sober social network, and this girl seemed to fit the bill. Another goal was encouraging him to retell traumatic memories, which made Justin squirm. He sure didn't want to experience more of his own hellish flashbacks.

"Why doesn't she drink?"

"Her dad's an alcoholic."

Justin nodded.

Cody's smile had long since faded, and his stare was unsettling. "You're not going to say anything about that?"

"Uh, what would you like me to say?"

"Thought for sure you'd say something about my dad. About the parallels of the situation drawing me to Hannah."

Crap. Cody's father had died when he'd driven the wrong way on the circle freeway around Columbus with a blood alcohol concentration three times the legal limit. Cody's mother had been in the passenger seat. He'd read that in Matthew's notes. Cody had been only thirteen when he'd lost his parents.

When Justin didn't say anything, Cody shook his head. "Anyway, you're always on my case to make sober friends, so there."

"So, Hannah is only a friend to you?"

"She...well..." His brown eyes darkened. "I wouldn't mind if she..." He shifted on the sofa. "But what if...?" He scowled. "I don't want to hurt her." He looked away and ran his hands through his hair.

Something was clearly troubling him. "Are you okay?"

"No!" Cody roared. When Justin leaned back, Cody forced out a breath. He clutched his temples as he tilted his head back. "Sorry."

"No problem."

Cody's long, muscular legs extended out and consumed the office floor. After a minute of staring at the ceiling, he blurted, "Sometimes I wonder if I'm gay."

Justin didn't move. "Why?"

Cody glanced at Justin, but then he looked away again. His upper lip trembled. "A couple of times..." His head dipped, and he spoke to his flip-flops. "I got, um, aroused when he..."

When King forced himself on me. If Justin threw up right now, could he play it off as cancer-treatment nausea?

Cody seemed frozen as he rolled his eyes up to meet Justin's. Justin realized he was holding his breath and broke his gaze.

"You're obviously straight," Justin said.

"H-H-How do you know?"

Because the same thing happened to me. Because if you're gay, then I might be gay, too. "You just are. Trust me."

Cody scowled at him. "I think maybe George was right."

"George?"

Cody gave him a strange look. "George McCallister? The guy you referred me to?"

Justin's jaw ticked. "I didn't realize you saw him."

"I tried." Cody let out a breath. "He's nice and all, but he's not you."

Justin tensed. This kid deserved to keep seeing Matthew, not him. He deserved a skilled therapist. Justin was going to screw him up even more, all for the selfish reason of figuring out his past.

"George said you're too impaired to see clients."

Justin smothered a gasp. How dare this George guy judge Matthew like that?

"And I think he might be right. You're different—these drugs make you weird."

Justin licked his lips. "Sorry."

"You're spacey. Out of it. I, I want the old Dr. D back."

Me, too. Justin sighed.

Cody shook his head. "I'm being a dick again." He rubbed his hands over his face. "You said you'd take it—that you're a safe outlet for my rage—but it's still not fair to you. The abuse isn't your fault. I just don't get it. How can God take my parents away—yours, too—and put us in that house with that monster, then give you cancer? What kind of screwed-up God is that?"

Justin nodded. "It's hard to believe in God when so many bad things happen." Like Elyse Frederick dying, or his brother being locked up for a crime he didn't commit.

"But at least he didn't force himself on you like he did me." Cody hung his head low. "I must've provoked him in some way—he had to spend too much on my swim club or something."

Why was Cody blaming himself? Justin wished he could tell him the truth, that he wasn't the only one King had molested.

"And another sign God is dead, I keep having these effing flashbacks." Cody gave a tight smile. "It's the gift that keeps on giving."

Justin's heartbeat kicked up as he braced himself. "More nightmares?"

Cody closed his eyes. "This time I saw her."

Tingles electrified Justin's chest.

"She's beautiful. Even though it was dark, I still got a good look at her." Cody's eyes remained closed. "Black head scarf. Foreign accent, like Middle Eastern. She was talking to King—they were planning something."

Justin couldn't breathe. The scene Cody remembered—he'd experienced it as well. Hazel eyes, lined in charcoal, glaring at him… His heart ricocheted in his chest. *I need air.*

"Not sure what they were planning," Cody continued. "Something about a plane."

The images sparked in Justin's mind like lightning strikes. Moonlight illuminated the woman's face as she smiled up at King.

"Behind the toolshed," Justin panted. "His favorite place." His eyes fluttered shut.

He recoiled at the sound of King's deep chuckle. A pinging noise rang out—his foot must've kicked a rock. The woman's head whipped toward him as he backpedaled to the house.

"Don't let them see you. Run! Get out of there—"

Cody gasped, and Justin opened his eyes to find the boy gaping at him. He wasn't behind the toolshed anymore. He was in Matthew's office. *Fuck.* What had he just done?

"He did it to you, too?"

With unblinking eyes, Justin stared back at Cody. His breaths came fast and shallow.

"You're not denying it." Cody scooted forward on his chair.

Oh God. He'd never told anyone before, and this was hardly the time to do it—when he was supposed to be the damn psychologist, not the crazy patient. But Cody kept gawking at him. Could he lie to the boy after all he'd been through?

"I *knew* it. I knew King did it to you, too." Cody sprang to his feet and paced the small office. "All these months and you never told me?" His eyes tapered. "You let me think I was the only one?" He jabbed his finger toward Justin's face. "You're a sick bastard."

Justin felt an urge to shove him away, but Francine's voice filled his mind: *Breathe.* "I'm sorry. I should've told you."

"Damn right you should've!"

Justin lowered his head. He was ruining Matthew's relationship with Cody. "I'm screwing this all up. Sorry." His head sank lower. "I'm really sorry."

Cody growled as he turned toward the wall. "I can't believe this." He spun back to face Justin. "Your twin brother—Justin? Did King get him, too?"

Justin looked up. Matthew had told Cody about him? What should he say?

"Holy shit—King raped Justin, too. That's why he bombed the warehouse." Cody shook his head. "Smart. I wish I had the balls to bomb him. I'd take a rifle and blow his brains out." His eyes darted to Justin, and he returned to the sofa. "I'm speaking hypothetically, you know. You don't have to report me to the police for threatening King."

Justin nodded. King wouldn't deserve a warning, anyway.

"So you saw that woman with King, behind the toolshed," Cody said.

As Justin's stomach clenched, flashes of that night filled his mind. "Black scarf, yeah. She was asking him about substrates. Stuff about bombs." No wonder he'd developed a curiosity about bomb triggers. "She had a map with Hebrew on it. I was trying to see more, but it was dark, and they were whispering. She must've made a joke, because King started laughing…"

"Wow, bombs?" Cody paused. "King's gotta be the one behind those triggers on that plane that went down. I hope the FBI nails his ass."

Justin shook his head. There was no chance in hell of that happening in a world without justice.

"You overheard a lot," Cody continued. "I only caught a little bit about the cargo hold of a plane before I got out of there."

Justin tried to swallow, but his mouth had run dry. "They didn't see you spying on them?"

"No way. He would've killed me." Cody's eyes widened. "They caught you?"

Justin tried to stem the tide of memories, but they gushed over him…

He ran as fast as he could, but his logy gait confirmed his suspicion that King had drugged him at dinner. He made it only halfway across the lawn when King tackled him. A rough hand clamped over his mouth as he dragged him back to the toolshed.

"They caught you?" Cody repeated. "What happened?"

"King threw me in the toolshed." Justin shuddered. His limbs felt paralyzed. "He smacked me around like he always did, got me on the floor—I couldn't move." He could see the polished grain of the wood. "He wrenched my arms—"

"Behind your back," Cody interjected. "That always got me, too. He's so strong. Where was the woman?"

Justin licked his lips. His heart hammered. "She watched while King…while he did his thing." He clenched his fists as the familiar nausea boiled in his gut. "She laughed." His hands shook. "Then she yanked up my head. She had me by my hair, and it hurt like a bitch. She held a knife to my throat." He felt the sting of the blade beneath his chin. "She said she'd kill me if I told anyone about her. I believed her. She seemed even crazier than King."

"Shit. No wonder you never told me about it." Cody exhaled. "But of course you told a therapist. You 'processed the trauma.'"

Justin blinked at him.

"You didn't?" Cody's mouth dropped open. "How could you force me to tell you *everything* while you keep your secret the whole time?"

He didn't know what to say. He'd screwed up big time.

Cody's eyes darkened. "How're you supposed to help me when you're, you're so fucked-up yourself?"

Good question. Cody was spot on—he was way too destroyed to help anyone. And this therapy charade was so unfair to Matthew. His brother had done everything to help his clients, and here Justin was tearing them down.

"You deserve better, Cody. Better than me."

Cody was quiet for a moment, then shook his head. "Don't say that. I'm surprised, that's all—shocked by what I've learned about you today." He rubbed the back of his neck. "But honestly, you've been a great psychologist. You know how many times I wanted to drink a whole bottle of liquor, but I didn't because of you? You've helped me a lot."

"Yeah?" Justin's eyebrows pinched. "How has therapy helped you?"

Cody chewed the inside of his cheek. "You listened to me. Nobody's cared about me since my parents died. Hell, even my own dad loved alcohol more than he loved me. But you cared. I could tell. Every time you nagged me about drinking, I knew it was because you cared." He jiggled his leg. "And as much as I didn't want to tell you what King did to me, it was what I had to do. I'm better now because you made me tell you."

Justin considered his response.

"It feels like there's a huge weight off my chest," the boy added.

Justin looked at him. "Yeah?"

Cody nodded. "I was pissed at first, but I think finding out about you and King is a big relief. That's how you've helped me the most, I think. I mean, I hate that he did it to you. But now I know it's not me. It's him. *He's* the dickhead. Look at you — you're a psychologist. You have a PhD. You have a gorgeous girlfriend…" He glanced at Matthew's bare desk. "Where'd her photo go?"

Matthew lost her, too. Justin's airway tightened. *Because of me.* "I cleared out my office before," he mumbled.

"Right. Anyway, if you can make something of yourself after what happened, maybe…" He looked at his flip-flops, then back up at Justin. "Maybe I can, too."

Because that session with Cody had made his head spin, Justin decided to use the two-hour break before his next client to jam in a workout. He had to clear his mind, and lifting weights was the only way to do it. He slung his gym bag over his shoulder and slammed his car door. His reflection in the car window stopped him in his tracks.

Mother-effing wig. He glanced around, but there was nobody else in the parking lot. With a gulp, he unlocked the door and flung the wig inside. What if he'd gone into the gym wearing the damn ponytail? He shook his head. He'd already put his brother in enough trouble as it was.

He leaned against the car door and closed his eyes. His heart was racing again. Life on the outside was too stressful. He had to find some way to switch back with Matthew.

As soon as he stepped inside, metal music blasted him, and he could finally breathe.

"Yo, Matthew," the front-desk girl called.

He nodded at the brown-haired girl. "Back on day shift?"

"Yep, they hired a new night guy." She cocked her head. "But you never applied, they said. Why not?"

He tensed. "Business picked up again."

She studied him, then smiled. "Crazy's never on short supply, huh?"

"The crazier people get, the more job security for me."

She laughed as she picked up the ringing phone.

You're the craziest asshole of them all, he reminded himself on the way to the locker room.

After a quick warm-up on the treadmill, he piled weights onto the leg press sled. He didn't recognize any of the meatheads in the free-weight section, and that was how he liked it. He'd just bang out his workout and get the hell out of here.

But his focus was shit because he kept replaying the session with Cody. Admitting he'd been raped had made it more real. Forcing the images out of his brain, he shredded every muscle group in his legs until he could barely walk to the shower. He was shampooing his short hair when his hands stilled on his head.

A quick plan coalesced. Would it work? It would take a while, but Matthew would go for it, he knew. He'd get Matthew to agree to switch places again, and order would restore itself. He dried himself in a flash and shoved his work clothes back on. He had to make a phone call.

14. Caught

Kate scowled as she read the *Columbus Dispatch* story on her office laptop:

When asked why the Yemenia Flight 223 investigation has lasted seven months without producing an indictment, federal agent Kamil Zahran stated, "We make it a point not to discuss an ongoing investigation."

She shook her head. "That's code for saying, 'We don't have enough evidence to go to a grand jury.'" She kept reading.

The attorney for Jefferson King, Barry Reynolds, had more to say about the matter. "This investigation is a witch hunt. Dr. King has worked tirelessly to protect the American people at home and abroad. He has fought corporate corruption and international threats to our safety. To suggest he had anything to do with this tragic plane crash is ridiculous. Dr. King recently received the highest humanitarian award in the state! This investigation has hurt my client's business and excellent reputation, and we demand its swift dismissal."

She exhaled. *Yeah, he's a real saint.* She hadn't seen any of the evidence in the case, but she wouldn't be surprised if her former foster father was up to something untoward. The man was a two-faced creep.

And she wasn't alone in her suspicions. The second anonymous letter she'd received in the mail screamed of King's guilt. It had arrived Saturday, a week after the first.

We will cut down the King
Once the Garden, now the sing
Justice, it must prevail
In a flash drive him to jail

Pete hadn't found fingerprints (besides hers) on either letter. She'd hoped sleeping on it would help, but mystery still obscured the poem. Now that it was Monday, she was supposed to attend to her assigned cases, but she couldn't stop thinking about King. Or Justin.

She clutched her head. *Or Matthew.* She'd almost driven to his condo last night, but had taken a U-turn on High Street instead. Her gut told her to show him the poems, but her heart had stopped her cold. She'd always smacked him down when he'd claimed he was smarter than she was, though she did know he was insightful. He could read people. Could he read between the lines of these poems?

"Knock, knock."

She looked up to find Pete in her doorway. "Hey."

"The garden," he said. "Why's it capitalized?"

She smiled. "You've been thinking about it, too."

He plopped down in the chair on the other side of her desk. "Don't tell Thurman I'm working on this instead of his case."

"Your secret's safe with me." She looked down at the poem. "I was wondering about that as well. Garden of Good and Evil?"

"Going biblical, huh? I'm thinking it means Franklin Conservatory."

She contorted her mouth to one side. "So you think this refers to a location in Columbus?"

"It was mailed in Columbus. The four-three-two-oh-one zip code again. And I visited the Franklin Conservatory website—sometimes they have concerts there. Maybe that's 'the sing.'"

"Hmm…"

"*There* you are, Pete."

Kate looked up and saw one of the firm's partners in the hallway—a gray-haired man of average height.

Pete shot to his feet. "Mr. Thurman."

Neil Thurman smiled at Kate. "Hope your Monday's not as sucky as mine." Before she could reply, he turned to Pete. "Got that security camera feed?"

"I'm headed there now." Pete winked at Kate on his way out. "I'll have it for you *in a flash*."

After the men left her office, her focus returned to the news story about King. He was probably guilty, but he would go free. Unlike Justin.

"My Monday's definitely suckier than yours," she said to herself.

"C'mon, you know this," Matthew said. He sat at a table in the rec room with his student, who had appeared to backtrack on his reading progress.

Daniel squinted at the word. "Preee…" He bit his lip. "Preee…date?"

"It's not predate." Matthew smirked, thinking of the speed-dating company one of his female clients had sworn by: Columbus Pre-Dating. He'd always felt relieved he hadn't needed to deal with dating. His heart sank, thinking of Kate's fiery copper eyes. Was she speed dating now? She'd probably already met another man, one who would marry her like he'd always promised. One who wouldn't abandon her.

"Predate…oar." Daniel's forehead creased as he ground his teeth.

Matthew prompted, "What does that word sound like?"

"I don't know." Daniel's gaze scooted across the room to where Shaddox sat, watching them.

It was then that Matthew noticed how Daniel quivered next to him. He should've known: a clear case of anxiety interfering with cognition. They'd released Shaddox from the hole over a week ago, and Matthew knew that interference well.

"The word is *predator*," he told Daniel.

The boy shirked away as he touched the lump on the back of his head. While Matthew had attended individual therapy with Francine a few days ago, Shaddox had reportedly bludgeoned Daniel and was going in for another punch when the guards restrained him. But they hadn't thrown Shaddox back into solitary. He'd probably need to attempt rape again for that to happen. Matthew feared this time he would finish the job.

When Francine had told Matthew the forensic psychologist would meet with him later that week, possibly to declare him competent to stand trial, he'd had mixed feelings. Getting the hell out of this hellhole would excite him to no end. But Shaddox would rip Daniel apart in seconds without Matthew here to watch over him.

"Why'd you make me read *that* word?" Daniel whined.

"You have to know your enemy."

Daniel stared at his lap.

Matthew wondered when Shaddox would come after him again. The nurse had removed his stitches a while ago, and the scar on his forehead was starting to fade. But the threat had only increased. Matthew wished Justin would visit. He needed his twin's strength to face the monster.

He nudged Daniel. "You know you can't turn your back to him, right?"

"I *know*."

The boy's pronounced eye roll made him seem twelve, not eighteen. "And what should you do when I'm in individual therapy?"

"Stay near the guard," mumbled Daniel.

"Good. So, the next word is *enemy*." Matthew pointed to the paper and handed the nubby pencil to Daniel. "Spell that out for me."

After Daniel wrote the first letter, Matthew shook his head. "It doesn't start with an i."

"Screw this," Daniel huffed.

"You hate him just to punish me!" the sixteen-year-old client screeched at her mother. "You don't want me to be happy."

"Right," the mother scoffed. "I don't want you to be happy. I've only sacrificed my whole life for your happiness."

Justin massaged his temples. Their argument had gone on for thirty minutes, and the session still wasn't over. How did Matthew deal with this shit day in and day out?

"As *if*," the girl, Rachel, sneered. "You don't care about anyone but yourself. That's why Dad left."

"Nice. Yes, he left me. Left me alone to deal with your childish infatuation with this bad boy. Have you told your father about Miles? I'm sure he'd be against this relationship, too."

"Miles is perfect for me," Rachel said.

Her mother glowered. "He's a drug addict."

"No, he's not!"

"Hey!"

Justin's bark echoed in the office, and mother and daughter turned to him, peering as if they'd forgotten he was there.

He looked at Rachel. "You told me last week that Miles takes drugs. You were worried about him, remember?"

She crossed her arms over her chest.

"Maybe you think he's awesome, but bad shit could go down when there're drugs involved." He thought about Daniel back in the hospital, blinking up at him with youthful defiance. "I know a guy the same age as Miles who murdered his mother when he was high."

Rachel reeled. "Miles would never do that!"

"Listen to Dr. Durante, honey," her mother said.

"And *you.*" Justin turned to her. "You realize the more you rail against this Miles, the faster Rachel runs into his arms? You need to calm your shit down. Rachel's got a good head on her shoulders. If this guy's the douchebag you think he is, he'll reveal himself soon enough. And then Rachel will dump his ass."

The mother stared at him like he was a mental patient. She wasn't far off.

Rachel started giggling. "He's right, Mom. You need to calm your shit down."

Justin held his breath, expecting the mother to yell. Instead, the woman started crying.

Rachel looked at him as she chewed her lip, then scooted closer to her mother on the sofa. She patted her mother's leg. "Don't cry, Mom."

"Sorry." She gave her head a quick shake. "It's just hard sometimes. I never dreamed I'd be a single parent." She sniffed. "Mostly I'm sad for you." She scooped up her daughter's hand. "Dr. Durante's more of a father to you than your own dad. I can't believe he doesn't even call to check up on you."

Rachel's mouth turned down. "I don't need Dad. *He's* the douche-bag, not Miles."

The mother cocked an eyebrow at Justin.

Whoops. "Sorry. I got a little heated."

"I didn't realize you swore so much in front of my daughter, but at least you tell it to me straight." The mother wiped under her eyes. "I needed that. So, you think I should back off?"

"Yes," Rachel answered before he had the chance. "I won't use drugs—they're gross. And Miles only uses every now and then to get back at his mom for leaving."

"His mother left the family?"

Rachel scowled at her mother. "I already told you that."

"No, you didn't. That's awful." Her mother paused. "So you've both had a parent abandon you."

"Duh," Rachel said.

"And you support each other through that." Her mother nodded. "It bonds you. I guess that's a reason you're drawn to Miles."

Rachel shrugged, then looked at the clock. "Mom, we gotta go." She popped up.

Her mother looked at Justin as they got to their feet. "Cheerleading practice." She smiled and reached out to shake his hand. "Thank you."

"You're welcome."

"I swear I already told you Miles's mom is a douche," Rachel said as they headed for the door.

"Rachel, you sound like a trucker!"

Justin let out a long breath after they closed his door. He supposed that session had turned out okay in the end. The mother's insight floated in his mind...The kids supported each other after their parents left. Matthew and Kate had done the same thing—found solace in their shared abandonment. As the third wheel, Justin had been forced to hide his jealousy toward them for all these years. And now he'd ruined their relationship, like he ruined everything else.

"That belief is a symptom of PTSD, nothing more," a voice said in his head. *"You're not a bad person—you only think you're bad."*

He grunted. The man who'd told him that obviously didn't know him. They'd only spoken once.

With a yawn, he scrawled the session notes. He wanted to get out of here and grab a coffee.

After he locked his office, he noticed Nancy's door was open.

She looked up from her laptop and waved. "How're you feeling?" she asked.

Typical psychologist question. "Tired." He yanked his thumb over his shoulder, in the direction of his office. "Sorry my last one got loud."

She shrugged. "What're you gonna do? This is why God gave me a son, not a daughter. I probably wouldn't have survived otherwise. Teenage girls are vile."

She had a son? He should've known that. Was she married? He didn't see a wedding band. "How's, uh, how's your son?"

"Good. I miss him."

Matthew probably knew where he lived, and Justin searched for a neutral question. "When will you see him again?"

"His deployment isn't up till February. Maybe you and Kate can come over for Christmas again this year, help a lonely old woman celebrate."

Shit. Matthew hadn't told her they'd broken up? He gave her a plastic smile. "I'd like that."

"How's your brother doing?"

Justin stiffened. *Awful,* he wanted to say. "He's hanging in there." He turned to exit through the waiting room. "Have a good one."

"Take care, Matthew. Get some rest."

Her concern made his nose burn, like he wanted to cry. As he walked to his car, he considered all of the people in Matthew's life — clients, colleagues, friends, ex-lover. Matthew had let them in, showed them his flaws and peccadillos. And they all seemed to care for him. Nobody looked scared when he approached. No one crossed to the other side of the street after spotting him.

It had rained an hour ago, and Matthew's Honda gleamed like it was just whisked through the car wash. Nancy's invitation weighed on his shoulders. No way he'd still be playing this charade when Christmas rolled around in seven months. He needed to find a way to make things right. He'd miss the easy connections in Matthew's life when he resumed his own, but he'd need to build back the wall around his heart to survive in prison.

"Matthew?"

His hand stopped its journey to the car door handle. He knew that voice.

"Please. I know you don't want to see me, but…"

He turned to face her. "Kate."

Her eyes got huge as she backpedaled. "You…" She couldn't seem to form words.

She knows. How'd she know? He'd remembered to wear the wig.

When she backed from the sidewalk onto the wet grass, she stumbled and fell on her ass. He rushed to kneel by her side.

"W-W-Where's Matthew?"

He frowned. "How'd you know I wasn't him?"

Her eyes welled up in tears. "You have that glazed-over look." Her upper lip trembled. "Like you're here, but you're not." She took in a shaky breath. "What's happening? Did you…escape?"

"Um, not really."

Her voice rose. "Where's Matthew?"

"I'm so sorry, Kate." He tried to hug her, but she pushed him away.

"No." She scrambled to her feet, and he stood as well. Her tears had stopped. "Tell me right now what's going on."

A car turned in at the far end of the parking lot, and he glanced at the office building. What if Nancy emerged? What if another client overheard their conversation? He pointed to Matthew's car. "Let's go somewhere to talk."

"I'm not going *anywhere* till you tell me what's going on."

She clearly meant business. He looked up at the cloudy sky as he exhaled. It took a long moment to divulge the truth.

"Matthew switched places with me."

Her jaw unhinged.

"At the Columbus Hospital for the Insane," he added.

"He…he's there now?"

Justin nodded.

She lunged for his arm and peeled down the leather wrist cuff he wore. When she saw the scar from his suicide attempt, she dropped his wrist. Her hand shook as she covered her mouth.

"I told him he was looking more and more like you…" Her eyes tapered. "Wait a minute, you *let* this happen?"

"I…" He inched back.

"How could you let him do this? Why'd you let him?"

He froze.

"Why in the world would he change places with you?"

Dim light slanted across his bedroom carpet just after the door opened with a soft click. He tensed as he felt the mattress dip. He shivered at the man's touch, then whimpered.

"Shh," King said. "You don't want them to hear you. You don't want me visiting their rooms after yours."

Kate's hand slamming into his chest brought him out of the memory.

"Tell me what the hell's going on!" Her eyes blazed.

He blinked down at her as he tried to remember to breathe.

She reached up to cradle his face. "My God, you're shaking."

"Please." His heart thumped in his chest. "Get in the car, and I'll tell you." His peripheral vision caught a man emerging from his car at the end of the row. "Just not out here."

She studied him. "I need to get my briefcase."

He slid into the driver's seat as she hustled to her car. *Crap, crap, crap.* Matthew was going to be furious with him. The air inside of the car felt strangling. He couldn't tell her what had happened to him—she couldn't see how damaged he was. She'd never look at him the same way again.

She brushed the seat of her suede skirt before she climbed into the passenger seat. "My butt's wet from the grass."

He backed out of the space and headed south on High Street.

"Where are we going?"

"Oh." He couldn't think straight, so he'd just started driving in a familiar direction. "Is Matthew's condo okay?"

She stilled. "I guess."

After a few minutes, she asked, "Why were you at his office?"

"Uh…" *Shit.* "Nancy needed help with one of his old charts."

"You shouldn't be in his charts—they're confidential."

He shouldn't have been doing a lot of things.

"Nancy thinks you're Matthew?"

"Yep."

She scowled. "Take off that ridiculous wig."

He peeled it off and tossed it in the backseat.

When she looked at him, both hands covered her mouth and she hunched forward. "I can't believe he did this." She rocked in the seat.

"I can't, I can't…" She dropped her hands. "Your hair's growing out. You look just like you did before they arrested you."

His gaze drifted to the rearview mirror. She was right.

Her hands twisted in her lap. "I never asked you this before, but…"

His shoulders tensed.

"Did you set that bomb, Justin?"

He looked at her, then back at the road as he turned down Matthew's street.

When he didn't answer, she said, "I've always thought you were innocent. But then Matthew told me you were guilty."

He licked his lips. If his twin thought he was guilty, he probably was. Matthew knew him better than anyone.

"Did you confess to Matthew?" asked Kate. "It's okay — I won't tell."

After clicking the garage remote, he waited for the door to lift. "Honestly, I can't remember. That night's real cloudy. But they found ammonium nitrate in my apartment, fuel residue on my hands — I must've done it."

As he pulled the car into the garage, Kate shook her head. "That's bullshit, Justin. Nobody forgets murder."

He flinched at the reminder of Elyse. "I know it sounds like bullshit. But my memory really does suck — I'm not making that up."

"Why are you having memory problems?"

His breath caught in his throat. He turned off the engine and looked into her eyes. "Matthew says that's what happens with trauma."

She blinked. "The fire."

His stomach dropped, and his face got hot. "No." His hand curled into a fist as he stared at his lap. He couldn't look at her anymore. "Matthew found out something about me." He closed his eyes. *You can do this. Just get it over with.* "He had this patient — Cody — who was King's foster kid years after us."

"What a weird coincidence."

"It wasn't." Justin forced out a breath. "When I got arrested, Cody looked Matthew up. He sought Matthew out after learning we'd also been King's foster sons." His entire body vibrated, but he'd started the story, and now he had to finish it. It was hard to get air. "King did bad things to Cody."

Kate had been rubbing her skirt, but her hand stopped on her knee.

His breath quickened. "King…abused him. For years." His full-on body shakes made his voice uneven. "H-H-He drugged Cody. Told him if he didn't take it, he'd rape Cody's foster sister."

The car was quiet except for the sound of his labored breaths. When Kate gasped, he knew she'd put the pieces together.

She clasped his hand and tugged him to face her. "He did it to you, too." When he dared to meet her eyes, she added, "To protect Matthew and me?"

He'd stopped breathing but managed a slight nod.

She burst into tears. "Oh, Justin." She leaned across the car to engulf him in a hug. "I'm so sorry."

He closed his eyes as she wept in his ear. He wondered why she'd want to hug him, to be close to him. Matthew had chosen him over her—she should've hated him. But embracing her as she cried felt right. He was probably the one holding on the tightest. She smelled like cocoa butter and more innocent times.

"I need tissues." She ducked as she pushed away from him. Grabbing her briefcase, she flew out of the car and scurried through the door from the garage into the condo.

He didn't remember getting out of the car or walking into the condo. He was surprised that revealing the abuse hadn't flattened him. Somehow, he was still on his feet. But this was the third time he'd confessed his sordid past—first to Cody, then to George McCallister. Last week he'd pretended to be Matthew in his appointment with the psychologist. And hell if he hadn't sobbed through the whole thing. He wasn't crying now, though. Kate was crying enough for both of them.

She emerged from the first-floor bathroom, sniffing, and cocked her head at the sound of Slim's meows. She followed the cries to the small kitchen, where Slim yowled by her food bowl.

"Is Slim sick?" she asked as he came up behind her.

He furrowed his brow. "No."

"She's lost weight—are you sure?"

"I have her on a diet." He wiggled his finger in his ear. "You can hear she's not too happy about it."

Kate opened the cupboard and pulled out a bag of treats. Slim rushed her, going apeshit by her feet until she poured a few treats onto the floor.

Justin frowned. "You're as bad as Matthew, indulging her."

"Ah." She splayed her hands to the side, drawing attention to the quietness of the condo now that the cat was hoovering treats instead of meowing. "How do you sleep with all that caterwauling?"

He looked away. "I don't sleep much."

She nodded with a frown. "You're in Matthew's bed?"

"Yeah."

She started, then her eyes widened. "No way. He *planted* that black bra under his pillow."

"What?" Justin peered at her.

"To get me off the scent before he switched with you! There is no other woman."

He swallowed. "You're right."

"Son of a bitch. I'm going to kill him."

Not if Shaddox gets to him first.

After a beat, she asked, "So Matthew told you about Cody, his client?"

"Uh, yeah."

"He told you his name? That doesn't sound like him, violating confidentiality like that."

He paused.

"How'd you find out about Cody?" She nailed him with her stare. He was on the witness stand, and she was the prosecutor.

"Holy hell." She glared at him. "Please tell me you're not seeing Matthew's clients."

His shoulders hunched. He waited as long as he could before admitting, "I am."

"Matthew will lose his shit when he hears this. You're lucky he'll be in chains."

Justin's eyes widened. "No — he can't find out."

"Oh, he'll find out. We're going there tomorrow, buster."

"Don't screw this up, Kate!" Justin took long strides into the family room. "So far he won't let me switch back with him — he says he'll tell the guards and we'll both be in jail — but I have a plan now to make him agree. You're gonna mess it up."

"A *plan?* Just like Matthew's ridiculous plan to switch with you in the first place?" She stepped over Slim and marched up to him with her hands on her hips. "You two are freaking imbeciles."

A stab of anger pierced his chest. "He had to do it before I killed myself."

Her hands lowered to her sides as the anger slipped from her face. "Do you know what that was like for us? Knowing we would lose you?" She paced the carpet. "It was killing Matthew, watching you attempt suicide over and over. We both felt so damn helpless."

"Sorry." He swallowed, thinking of his failure to save King's last foster son, Gideon. "I couldn't live with myself."

"And now you can?"

"I can't let Matthew rot in there."

"So what's this plan of yours?"

"Matthew begged me to go to therapy, to talk about what happened. He said it's the only way to heal. So I went."

She stopped pacing. "Once?"

"I'm going again, of course. And when Matthew sees that I'm better, he'll let me switch back."

She unclasped her briefcase and withdrew some envelopes. "Maybe neither of you will have to be in there. Let me show you these notes I got in the mail."

15. Conjoined

The next day, Matthew flinched as Officer Shaw led him into the visitation room. He couldn't believe Justin had forgotten to wear the wig.

"You cut your hair, Dr. Durante," Shaw said.

Justin looked up at him. "That I did, Ginja Ninja."

Shaw laughed and ran his hand through his flame of red hair after he pushed Matthew onto his chair. "Looks good on you."

Matthew relaxed and couldn't help but notice the shift in his twin — beyond the surprising smile. He seemed less miserable, less on edge — less on the verge of detonating. He wore a white button-down shirt with thin navy stripes and dark gray pants that showcased his lean waist. At least he'd dressed more like a psychologist this visit.

"That cut on your forehead's healing well," Justin said.

Matthew nodded. "Nice duds."

When Justin shifted in his chair, Matthew wondered if he was nervous about how his new hairstyle would go over. But Justin's next revelation went way beyond the shock of a new haircut.

"Kate dressed me."

Matthew blinked once, then his mouth dropped open. "You told her? How could you—?"

"She came to me yesterday." Justin's fidgeting increased. "She figured it out right away."

Kate knows? Matthew's heart pulsated. Shaw was somewhere behind him, and Matthew knew he was listening. "Where'd she, uh, visit you?"

Justin looked away.

Matthew's gaze remained riveted on him. *What's he hiding?*

"At my office," Justin said.

"Your office?"

"My counseling office." Justin licked his lips. "I had, uh, just finished with a patient."

Matthew stilled. Justin was saying that for Shaw's benefit, right? He hadn't actually met with clients. But why would Justin be at his office? "You finished with a client…you've been spending some time in the office?"

"Y-Y-Yeah." Justin's eyes filled with guilt. "Nancy Wallace was holding onto my charts, but I took some of them back. It just sort of happened." He seemed to hold his breath. "Trying to make a living, you know? Turns out I'm not bad at it."

What had his brother done? "No." His chains jangled as he shook his head, each word more forceful than the last. "No, no, no, no, *no*."

"Durante," Shaw warned.

Matthew ignored him. "You said you were at the *gym*."

"I was. I am. Working out, I mean."

"You have no idea what you're doing," Matthew seethed. "These are people's *lives* you're messing with. You don't have the training—"

Shaw had sidled up to his chair, and Matthew started as he looked up at him.

"Please," Matthew said.

Shaw eyed him.

"I'm, I'm calm." Matthew clenched his teeth. *Get your shit together.* "I just got some disturbing news, but I'll calm down. Please let me keep talking to my brother." He needed to find out exactly what kind of shitstorm Justin had brought them into this time.

"It's my fault for riling him up, Officer," said Justin.

Shaw tucked his thumbs into his belt. "Why would talking about your patients disturb him?"

Justin scrubbed his fingers down the side of his mouth as he looked at Matthew. "Justin knows I treat people for trauma, and he gets upset when he's reminded of his own childhood sexual abuse."

Matthew's eyes widened. His brother was admitting to being abused?

"It's a textbook PTSD response," Justin continued. "Just like with the college student I've been seeing. The guy's foster father raped him, destroyed him. The kid begged me to meet with him. He needed my help."

Oh. That made a little more sense. Cody had reached out to Justin, and his brother hadn't been able to turn him away. Matthew knew how desperate Cody could get. Still, Justin pretending to be a therapist could be a disaster.

Over his shoulder, Matthew watched Shaw retreat to lean against the wall, keeping his eyes trained on him. Turning back to Justin, he asked, "So, the college kid—he's the only client you've been meeting with, right?"

Justin's tongue darted to the corner of his mouth.

As silence stretched between them, Matthew felt bile at the back of his throat.

"Not really…" Justin squirmed.

You're a goddamn nightmare to the helping profession.

"But last night, my attorney made me realize I should downsize my practice," Justin added.

Thank God for Kate. But Matthew still wanted to pummel his twin. Just how many of his former clients had fallen for this charade? What damage had Justin done?

"Your attorney sounds smart."

"She is." Justin nodded. "Just like your attorney. She's in the parking lot, by the way."

"Here?" Matthew's chains clanked as he sat up.

"She might have some information about Gargamel, and she wants to be on your case again. You need to let her."

Matthew leaned back in his chair. Kate had information about King? The fact that she still wanted to speak to him was a small miracle, but he had no idea how she'd act when she saw him. His betrayal was so deep—he didn't know if they could climb out of the chasm.

"You'll take her back as your attorney, won't you?" Justin's eyes begged. "She's gonna beat me up if you don't."

Matthew hid a smile, and Justin's mouth twitched, as well. They'd both endured Kate's smacks and punches as teenagers, though they'd learned how to exact revenge—Justin had held her while Matthew tickled the hell out of her. Her shrieks and their laughs echoed in his mind.

As they'd progressed through high school, Justin had started refusing to participate in their games. He'd become sullen and shoved them away, one time pushing Matthew against the bookshelf so hard his ribcage had bruised. The initial warmth of Matthew's memories turned cold—like the chains weighing him down as he sat across from Justin.

"She wants to come back, even though I fired her?" Matthew ventured.

Justin winced. "Yeah. Especially when she heard the reason you fired her." His gaze drifted toward Shaw, then zoomed back on Matthew. "The reason, uh, you made a switch in your life."

He'd told Kate about the abuse? "You told her the reason?"

"Uh-huh." He lowered his voice. "Also told Cody."

Matthew stiffened. Would Shaw know what they were talking about? He blinked as he considered the risk, wishing his brain wasn't so damn slow. But no, Shaw should've had no idea who Cody was.

He pictured the tall swimmer. Cody had asked if King had abused Matthew as well, and at first Matthew had followed guidelines to avoid self-disclosure by declining to answer. But with the boy's continued anguish, Matthew had caved and admitted that King had left him alone. Now Cody would believe he'd lied to him, destroying all the trust he'd carefully built.

"Was he angry?"

"At first, yeah." Justin rubbed his head. "But then he was grateful."

Matthew retracted his chin. *"Grateful?"*

"That he wasn't alone."

Whoa. He hadn't thought of that, but of course…A major advantage of group therapy was decreasing feelings of being alone and misunderstood. Justin's admission would also help challenge Cody's belief that his inherent badness had caused the abuse. *Challenges Justin's trauma beliefs, too.* Just like Cody benefitted from knowing he wasn't alone, so would Justin.

"I'm proud of you, Matty," said Matthew. "You see? You're still standing after telling Kate and Cody."

"And George."

Matthew looked up. "You met with George?" When Justin nodded, Matthew exhaled. "Thank you."

"I'm, uh, talking about the past. Trying to heal, you know? Working toward making some big changes in my life. Switching…around. Switching back. Making it up to people, to those I've hurt."

Ah. Matthew now had a better grasp of what had motivated Justin to see George after a lifetime of avoiding the past. "And you believe going to therapy will motivate that switch in your life?"

"I really hope it will. I can't sit back and do nothing."

Justin's eyes pleaded with him, and Matthew had to look away. No wonder Justin was acting more like a man and less like a wounded, impulsive boy—he'd started to shed the shackles of childhood trauma by processing it.

But now that he was getting his life back, there was no way Matthew would allow Justin to switch places with him. Justin deserved to live the life Matthew had enjoyed, the life Justin had given him through his sacrifice.

Enough about Justin manning up and facing the past. Matthew shook his head. He had to do the same himself.

He swiveled to look at the guard. "Officer Shaw, would you pass along my request to reinstate Kate Summers as my attorney?"

Shaw palmed his billy stick. "You sure you want that?" He eyed Justin. "Sounds like you're brother's kind of bullying you into it."

Justin smirked at Matthew. They both knew the bully in this scenario was female, not male.

"I'm sure. Ms. Summers is on the property, actually. May I meet with her after my brother leaves?"

"I should be in that meeting, too," Justin added. "There're some urgent matters we need to discuss."

Matthew angled his head. *What urgent matters?*

"Nobody's in the room with a patient and his attorney," Shaw snapped. He seemed to soften as he looked at Matthew. "No guarantees you can see her, but I'll ask."

"You're a credit to all ninjas, sir." Matthew turned back to Justin as Shaw spoke into his radio. "What're you maxing on bench press these days?"

"More than you ever did."

A few minutes later, Shaw pulled him up by the elbow. "I'm taking you to a conference room."

"Will they let me see Kate?" asked Matthew.

Shaw grunted. "Maybe." He looked at Justin. "Stay put, Dr. Durante. I'll be back to escort you out, and then you can tell the lawyer to come in to be processed."

"Okay," Justin said. "Good luck, Justin."

Matthew would *need* luck during the meeting with Kate and every moment on the unit after that.

As Shaw led him out of the visitation room, he nodded at his twin. "Thank you...for everything." He was almost out the door when he added, "And listen to your attorney about your practice."

Shaw guided him to another room, this one smaller, with a table and two chairs. Amid his nervousness about seeing Kate, he realized something. "Uh, Officer?"

"What?"

Could this be more demeaning? "I need to pee."

Shaw sighed. "After I get back from escorting your brother."

"Thank you."

The wait for Shaw seemed endless. He was already on edge about Kate's arrival—would he have to greet her with a pee stain on his jumpsuit? He couldn't even take a piss by himself in here, and prison would probably be even more controlling. Still, he couldn't let Justin take his place.

Once Shaw returned and let him do his business, Matthew let out a long breath on the way back to the conference room.

But he frowned when Shaw locked his y-chain to a hook screwed into the floor beneath his chair. "Why the extra security?"

"Meetings with attorneys are private—I have to stay outside the door." Shaw tugged at the chain and stood. "This is protocol for a maximum-security patient with a female attorney."

He was glad Shaw wouldn't be eavesdropping.

"It'll probably be a while before they clear her." Shaw sat in the seat across the table from him, and they stared at each other. "So, your brother knows your attorney?"

Matthew gave a wary nod.

"Why'd you fire her?"

How could he answer that? "Truth is…I didn't want to bring her into this. I've already burdened my brother enough—I don't want to bring her down, too."

"But you're letting her back on your case now?"

Matthew speculated how she'd react to seeing him in chains. "Seems she won't stay away."

"How does your brother know her?"

He wondered why Shaw was asking, and whether he should be honest. But Shaw's questions seemed more conversational than investigative, and the guard had been good to him. "They're dating." Or, *were* dating. "We three grew up in foster care together."

Shaw pondered his response. "You're on the fringe, huh? The third wheel."

Was that how Justin saw it? Matthew had often felt guilty for excluding him from his intimate connection with Kate. He and Kate had wanted Justin to find a girlfriend, but he'd never seemed interested in dating.

"I know the feeling," Shaw said. "Used to hang out with my sister all the time till she met her husband." He lounged back in the chair and let his knees sag to the side. "Now I don't get to see her much."

"That sounds rough. Does she live in Columbus?"

"Cincinnati."

"Do they have kids?"

"Got a bun in the oven." Shaw smiled, but then frowned. "Forget I said that. I'm not supposed to talk about my personal life with patients."

"Don't worry, the meds make me forget everything, anyway."

Shaw studied him for a long moment. "What your brother said? Is that true?" His cheeks reddened as he fidgeted.

Channeling his twin, he answered, "I don't like to talk about it."

"Yeah. Just wanted to say…sorry I wasn't there in time when that patient came after you."

Unsure of how to respond, Matthew shrugged. "It's okay."

"I'm glad, uh, you stopped trying to off yourself."

The guard's kindness bowled him over.

"I don't want to face your brother's wrath after another attempt."

Shaw's smile vanished when his radio squawked: *"Durante's attorney's ready for escort."*

"Be right back. Don't go anywhere, you hear?"

A long time later, Matthew tensed as Kate came into the room, carrying her briefcase. God, she was beautiful. Her auburn hair tousled over the shoulders of her navy business suit, and her heels added to her elegant height. He wanted to touch her so badly his chains stirred.

She gulped as she scanned the metal around his wrists, waist, and ankles.

"I'll be right outside, Ms. Summers," Shaw said. "Just knock on the door if there's trouble."

She didn't take her eyes off of Matthew. "Thank you, Officer."

Once Shaw left, Kate took slow steps toward Matthew, like a panther stalking its prey.

Matthew held his breath.

She hovered over him, making him look up to meet her fierce gaze. He hoped she could read the apology in his eyes. He hoped she could see his love for her.

Whap. Her slap across his cheek made his eyes water. *Damn.*

Her eyes zipped toward the door, but Shaw didn't barge in. He probably hadn't heard a thing.

Then her lips were all over him, desperate kisses that made his heart ache. When her hungry mouth pressed into his, he returned her fervor. She curled herself into his lap, and he responded in a heartbeat. With his wrists locked, he couldn't skim his hands through her hair or pull her close. He longed to stroke the length of her legs draped over his lap, but he couldn't do that, either. He just accepted her kisses, her touch, her soothing scent; gratitude welled in his chest for her presence when he'd thought he'd never see her again.

Her lips lingered at the corner of his mouth, then skated up his jaw. The guards didn't allow him to handle razors, and he hoped Harold had given him a smooth shave this morning. As she pressed a kiss close to his ear, she breathed, "Matthew."

He inhaled her scent of cocoa butter. "God, I've missed you."

She bent her forehead to his, their eyes centimeters apart. "What the hell have you done?"

"I'm so sorry." He blinked. "I couldn't tell you."

She leaned back. "You *should've* told me."

He shook his head. "You would've never let me do this."

"Because it's the most absurd, outrageous, nonsensical —"

"Justin's still alive, though."

"But *your* life's ruined!" She exploded off his lap and paced the floor. "I can't believe I started birth control pills for you."

She clearly wanted to hit him again. He tried to slow his heartbeat to match the click of her heels on the tile.

She knelt by his chair and touched the scar on his forehead. "What's this?"

"Nothing, just a scratch."

Her lips thinned. His chains clinked as she took his hand, stroked his fingers, and rotated his palm to face up. She pushed the handcuff toward the heel of his hand. The scar inside his wrist was still tender when she feathered her fingers across it. As she sniffed, her hair fell across her face. "I should've known what you were up to." Her voice shook. When she leaned in to brush her lips across his scar, he felt wetness on his wrist from her tears.

"Kate." He curled down to kiss the back of her head. "Please forgive me."

They stayed huddled in a ball for some time.

"I hate crying," she said, lifting her head. She wiped under her eyes as she rose to her feet.

Guilt tattered his heart. "But you've seen the change in Just, right? Now that he's talking about the abuse?"

Her eyes narrowed, stopping her tears. "I want to shred King's balls in a Cuisinart."

Matthew shuddered.

"How could he…" A strangled sound came from her throat, and she began to pace again. "Did Justin tell you about the poems?"

Poems? Matthew shook his head. "We can't say much. There's a guard in the visitation room."

"There is? That doesn't sound right." She scowled at his chains. "Just like this overkill, with you trussed up like that." Her pacing stopped. "You're chained during visits, right? How'd you make the switch?"

He paused. "I got the guard to unlock the chains. Then I acted crazy so he'd go get the psychologist and leave us alone."

"*Acted* crazy?" She perched a hand on her hip. "Then what happened?"

Matthew swallowed.

"Matthew?"

His face warmed, and he ducked his head. "I told Justin I knew King had raped him — repeatedly. I made him dissociate by dredging up some details of the abuse…" He forced himself to look up. "He became a rag doll in my arms."

She stared at him as the horror of his behavior vibrated between them. No way she'd forgive him now.

She slid into the seat across from him. "I represented a client last year — he was seventeen."

Her non sequitur left him confused.

"He was accused of raping a girl from his high school."

Oh.

"I watched a recording of the girl's police interview. She kept blaming herself for drinking too much that night." Kate's jaw flexed. "Of course I used that against her in the trial, and of course I got my client off. And when that poor girl looked straight at me after the verdict, before she left the courtroom, I wanted to talk to her so bad. I wanted to tell her something."

Matthew waited.

She jutted her chin forward. "You're not the one who did this. *He* did. He's the perpetrator." Her gaze nailed him to his chair. "Got that?"

When he didn't answer, she opened her briefcase and slid out a manila folder. She pushed the folder in front of him, open to a poem. The words swam before his eyes.

"Where'd this come from?"

"It was mailed to me at work a little over a week ago." She turned the page to reveal another poem. "This one came on Saturday."

His muddled brain tried to process her words. "What day is today?"

She frowned. "It's Tuesday. Tuesday, May fifteenth." She leaned toward him. "They have you on something?"

"A lot of something, I'd say. The psychiatrist, Majumdar, believes in prescribing a heavy arsenal. I told Francine all of the meds interfere with memory."

"Who's Francine?"

"Francine Pierre, my psychologist."

Kate's eyebrow quirked. "You have a female psychologist? Who lets you call her by her first name?"

"Insists on it, actually." He smiled as a storm passed over her face. "I think she's got a crush on Justin."

"Who she thinks is *you*."

He shrugged.

She brightened. "If she can't even tell you two apart, she obviously doesn't know you. She's no threat." She tapped on the second paper. "Does this mean anything to you?"

He read it. "Who sent these poems?"

"Justin thinks they come from a boy named Gideon. Gideon—"

"Hall," Matthew finished with her. "King's latest foster son." When Kate's head tilted, he explained. "I made a CPS report when, uh, one of my clients told me he had been abused."

"I know about Cody, Matthew."

"How?" He blew out a breath as realization dawned. "From his fake-ass psychologist." He growled. "Justin has done some harebrained things in his life, but this trumps them all. I can't *believe* he did that. You have to make him stop seeing my clients."

"I already have. I chewed his butt for all of the legal risks before I made him call Nancy Wallace to take over his caseload again."

Matthew looked at the stained ceiling and appreciated the quiet of the conference room. If only he could get out of the damn chains, he might feel a little like himself again. "How *is* Cody? Do you know?"

Kate tucked a strand of hair behind her ear. "Justin's worried about how he'll take the news that their therapy has to end. He proposed calling Cody to tell him he had a cancer relapse, but I told him to wait. I wanted to ask you what we should do."

"So you were sure I'd take you back as my attorney?"

She tossed her hair over her shoulder with a challenge in her eyes. She'd known it would be impossible to resist her.

"I'm worried about Cody, too," he said. He wanted to run his hand through his hair as he considered what to do, but his hands were cuffed, and he didn't have much hair now, anyway. "He's in a fragile place. Justin has us, but Cody's alone. His foster sister wants nothing to do with him. She's in school in Washington State, probably to get as far away as she can from King. Cody got lumped into her feelings about foster care, and she won't talk to him."

"Bitch. So Cody sacrifices himself for her, and she acts like he's not alive?"

"She doesn't know he did that for her."

Kate's chin quivered, and Matthew guessed what she was thinking: *Just like we didn't know.* But he couldn't wallow in emotion, not when he had limited time with her. "The only family Cody has is his swim team, and they've turned on him since he got a popular teammate in trouble."

"What happened?"

"A drinking issue." Matthew shook his head. "I referred him to a psychologist with experience in PTSD and substance-use disorders, but I doubt Cody took me up on it. Especially since it looks like he tried to see me again." He tapped his finger on his thigh. "Have Justin take Cody with him to his next appointment with George McCallister. Tell George what's been going on."

"Tell George the truth? Won't he go to the authorities?"

"Justin might've already told him about the switch. I think it'll be okay, as long as Justin stops masquerading as a damn therapist. Hopefully George can fix any damage my brother has done." Matthew swallowed. "The damage I've done."

She didn't rebut his statement, which made him feel even guiltier. He reread the poems and willed his underperforming brain to accelerate. "So you, Just, and I are supposed to take down King, I gather."

"But how?" she asked.

His thumbs rubbed together. "How do we 'cut down the King'? There's something about driving here — maybe a hit and run?"

Kate's eyebrows scrunched.

"Why does Justin think Gideon sent these?" asked Matthew.

"It might be wishful thinking. Before he was arrested, he said he staked out King's house after he discovered he had more foster kids. Justin tailed King when he drove the kids to school. Once King dropped them off, Justin talked to Gideon, told him to resist King's advances. Then Gideon disappeared, and this whole time Justin's been thinking King killed him, and it's his fault. But now he's hoping these notes mean Gideon's still alive."

"Christ." Matthew shook his head. "Even more motive for Justin to bomb King. The prosecution can't find out about this."

"They will if they find Gideon before we do. We have to locate him, if he's really behind these poems. Maybe he can exonerate Justin somehow." Kate exhaled and studied him for a moment. "Justin's determined to switch back with you."

"You need to talk him down from whatever he's got cooking. Doesn't he understand I've accepted this? He can't stop me just because of his misdirected guilt. I made a decision, and he can't change it."

"You're so full of shit. You know Justin. He won't sit back and let his twin go to prison. He'll keep fighting to get back here, where he thinks he belongs. Even though he's innocent."

"You *still* think he's innocent?" Matthew huffed. "Maybe you're the one who's full of shit."

Her eyes flared. "Why do you think he's guilty?"

Matthew's chin dipped. "He told you what King did to him, right? How could he *not* be guilty? Of course he tried to blow his abuser to pieces. Anyone would do that."

"Would you?" she prodded. "If King had raped you instead of Justin, would you try to kill him?"

He paused and tried to slow his breathing. Would he kill King? He wanted to, after what the man had done to Justin — and to Cody — but could he pull the trigger? "No."

"Then how could you think Justin would take a life like that? He's your twin. He's a good person."

"I know that." His voice sounded sharper than he'd intended. He sighed. "But he's never denied it. He's never claimed he's innocent."

"That's because he doesn't remember that night. He assumes he did it because he thinks he's an awful person."

Matthew closed his eyes. How could he be so obtuse? He'd known in an instant that Justin had forgotten the deal he'd made with Shaddox. He knew his twin's heart, and it wasn't that of a murderer, no matter what had happened to him. "Will you tell Justin I'm sorry for doubting him?"

"So you agree he's innocent?"

His thoughts jumbled. "I don't know. I don't know anything anymore."

She shook her head. "You thought he was guilty because of the abuse, when I think the abuse means he's innocent."

His head tilted.

"If King is that depraved, what's to stop him from framing Justin for the bombing?"

A chill bloomed up his spine. *Jesus.* What if Justin had been framed? "How do we prove that?"

She gestured to the poems. "We have to find this Gideon."

A jangle of keys in the hallway turned them both to the door.

"...need to be notified—"

Dr. Majumdar's harsh voice halted once he burst in the door, trailed by Shaw. The psychiatrist seemed flushed as he glared at them.

"What's the meaning of this?" demanded Majumdar. "You have a court-appointed attorney now, not her."

Kate stood and slung the strap of her briefcase over her shoulder. Matthew realized she'd shoved the folder back inside and clasped the briefcase without him noticing.

"Wrong." She towered over the short man. "Kate Summers. I'm representing Mr. Durante again."

Dr. Majumdar tugged the lapels of his white doctor's coat. "I didn't approve that. All changes need to go through me."

"And who are you?" Kate peered down at him.

"Director of this hospital, Dr. Majumdar."

"You're the psychiatrist?" Kate breathed out through her nose. "A real bang-up job you've done treating my client's depression. Your medications do more harm than good. How many times have you let him try to kill himself in here?"

Matthew tensed as he watched the man's fists clench. She didn't know how much power he wielded in this place.

"How dare you question our care? My staff does everything possible to help these men…" His lips curled down as he looked at Matthew. "…no matter how undeserving they may be."

"Wow. Nice to know how you truly feel about your patients—"

"Kate?"

She looked over at him after he interrupted her. "How about you let Officer Shaw escort you out?"

She glanced back and forth between him and the psychiatrist.

"I can't thank you enough for being here," Matthew added. "And I know you'll find what you're looking for. *Justice will prevail.*"

Her lip trembled as she studied him. Did she want to kiss him goodbye as much as he wanted her to? She set her jaw, then walked out.

Majumdar stepped toward him after they left. "You telling your attorney tall tales, Durante?"

Even standing, the man's head wasn't much higher than Matthew's—what would he know about tall tales? Still, Matthew's chest seized at being left alone with him. "No."

"Just remember, I'm often asked to speak at sentencing hearings about how patients behaved when they were in my care. You want a glowing report, you shut the fuck up about your medications."

Matthew swallowed and found his throat to be dry. *Maybe I won't have a sentencing hearing. Maybe I'll be found not guilty.* That hope felt like a delusion, a symptom treated by the very medications Majumdar referenced.

The psychiatrist leaned closer. "Make sure to tell everyone how good you've had it here. If you don't see that now, you will in prison." One side of his mouth arched. "Men like Shaddox are a dime a dozen there, with no psych techs to protect you."

16. Flash

The constant vibration of Cody's knee shook the waiting room sofa. Justin rested his hand on the bouncing knee to still it and said, "I already told you I'd write you an excuse for your coach."

"He won't like it. You just don't miss afternoon practice like this."

Justin eyed the woman seated nearby and lowered his voice. "It's the middle of May. I thought you're in the off-season."

"There *is* no off-season," Cody huffed. "Coach is gonna be pissed."

Justin sighed. "Sorry. This is the only time George could get us in."

"Why are you dragging me in there?"

"I'll tell you inside."

Cody groaned.

Justin closed his eyes. He wasn't looking forward to this session either. But on the ride home from the hospital yesterday, Kate had relayed that Matthew wanted him to take Cody to see George. After Matthew had lit into him for seeing his patients, Justin owed it to his brother to do what he asked. He just wished he didn't have to reveal what a dumbshit he'd been to two more people.

All smiles, George entered the waiting room. "It's a pleasure to see you both." He extended his arm toward the hallway, and Justin waited for Cody to grab his backpack before he led the way to the office.

Once they sat, George spoke. "Cody, when Matthew called me to set up this appointment, he gave me permission to tell you about my sessions with him. But I haven't had the chance to ask *your* permission. How comfortable are you with me disclosing the content of our individual sessions to Matthew?"

"Seriously?" Cody scowled. "Dr. D. knows me better than anyone. You can tell him whatever you want."

"Good to clear that up." George winked at Justin and looked back at Cody. "Do you know why we're here?"

Cody frowned as he gestured to Justin seated next to him on the sofa. "So I won't freak out when he tells me he can't meet with me anymore."

Justin froze. Cody already knew that?

George's eyebrows lifted. "Very perceptive. And you know the reason Matthew can't meet with you anymore?"

"Of course." Cody slumped. "He's sick again."

George gaped at Justin. "You *are?* You didn't tell me that."

Justin fidgeted. *Here we go.* "Cody, it's true that I have to stop meeting with you. And I wanted to tell you in Dr. McCallister's office because I was nervous about how you'd react." He rubbed his chest. "But it's not because my cancer has returned."

Cody turned to him. "I thought that's why you cut your hair— 'cause it would fall out from treatment."

Justin shook his head. *Kate hates the wig so much that she let Slim shred it.*

Cody seemed to exhale with relief.

"I think the shorter hair looks great," said George. "Of course, I'm a bit old fashioned." He nodded at Justin. "Go ahead, Matthew. You can tell him the real reason why."

Justin knew what George expected him to say. "Dr. McCallister and I talked on the phone about how wrong it is for me to keep seeing you, Cody, when I have my own, uh, 'unresolved' issues from the abuse." He waited a beat. "But that's not why we're here, either."

Both Cody and George tilted their heads— Justin had their full attention. His palms felt clammy, and he wiped them on his jeans. *Just say it.*

"I've been misleading you both, and I'm sorry." He let out a breath. "My name is Justin Durante."

Cody's jaw dropped, but George's only acknowledgment of the bombshell was a slight pinch of his eyes.

The heat of deceit made Justin's head sweat, even without the wig.

George asked, "Where's Matthew?"

"Columbus Hospital for the Insane," answered Justin.

Cody leaned away from him on the sofa. "You made him trade places with you?"

"He made *me* trade places…to save my life." Justin looked down. "I kept trying to kill myself in there."

Cody pressed his lips together. He scooted closer and fidgeted a moment before placing his hand on Justin's shoulder. "Because of what King did to you."

Justin fought the urge to shake him off. He wasn't deserving of such kindness.

"Do you still want to kill yourself?" George eyed him.

"No." Justin sighed. "Even if I did, Matthew told me he'd commit suicide right after I did."

Cody's nose scrunched. "You two are twisted."

That's what Kate said.

"When did Matthew trade places with you?" George asked.

Justin swallowed. "April thirteenth."

"Over a month ago." George shook his head. "That's why he wanted to refer his clients to me. Oh!" He sat up and pointed at Matthew's watch. "Let me see underneath that." When Justin showed him the scar, George nodded. "Matthew had to give himself the same scars to switch with you. I *knew* he wasn't suicidal."

"Dr. D slit his wrists?" Cody dropped his hand from Justin's shoulder and shrank back. "But, wait—if he stopped seeing me so he could switch with you, this means he doesn't have cancer, right? He's not gonna die."

Justin's shoulders hunched. "As long as the other cons don't get to him in there."

"Matthew's in danger?" asked George.

Justin held his breath. "There's a psychopath in there—he came after Matty, but a guard saved him." *It's your fault, asshole.*

"Can I visit him?" Cody asked.

Justin blanched. "No! Nobody can know, or we'll both be in jail."

"But I might have to report this," George said.

"Matthew said you wouldn't." Justin's heart rate kicked up a notch. "There's no imminent threat of harm to self or others, and no current abuse."

George stroked his beard. "That we know of." He looked at Cody. "You said Matthew already made a report to CPS?"

"Yep." The college student scowled. "It did jack shit."

"That's because Gideon was gone before they investigated," Justin said.

Cody and George stared at him, and George asked, "Who's Gideon?"

Justin thought about the boy's black hair and green eyes, the slouch of his skinny body. "Another of King's victims."

"Son of a bitch." George's eyes narrowed. "How many are there?"

"I only know about the three of us."

George stroked his beard as he looked at Justin. "How old is Gideon?"

"Uh, fifteen or sixteen?" *Looks younger, though.*

"Hmm."

Cody leaned toward George. "What?"

"The timeline seems off," George said. "King started abusing Justin about sixteen years ago, then Cody about six years ago, right?"

Cody nodded.

"And then you think King started abusing Gideon around a year ago, Justin?"

"Maybe. So what?"

"What was King up to between you and Cody?" George asked. "Pedophiles tend to exhibit a pattern of behavior, but the pattern doesn't fit here."

Justin's stomach turned. "Maybe he couldn't find a foster son who would take the abuse."

"That's not it," George chided. "The abuse is about the perpetrator, not the victim. It wasn't your fault, either of you."

Cody blinked. "So King abused Gideon, you, and me...but not Dr. D.?"

Muted hallway light across his bedroom floor. Approaching footsteps on the thick carpet. Nausea stirred in his gut. "I made sure Matty was safe. Kate, too."

"I hope you're right." George's jaw flexed. "But this King sounds like an opportunist. He may have abused Matthew without you knowing."

"No. Matthew knew nothing about the abuse." Justin swallowed as he looked at Cody. "Until you became his patient."

Cody sucked in a breath.

"You had a foster sister," Justin said.

Cody's head bobbed. "How'd you know? We haven't talked about Brooke."

"Because that's King's MO. He threatens to rape the other foster kids if you don't submit to him."

George made a sound of disgust, and Cody froze.

"When you revealed the abuse, Matthew figured out the same thing had happened to me." Justin's airway seemed to close. "He said I sacrificed myself for him, and it was his turn to do the same for me."

Cody's wobbly hand floated up to cover his mouth. "It's my fault he switched with you?"

"No, Cody," George said. "You had every right to seek therapy, to try to heal. Of course you went to see a psychologist who would understand what you'd been through. You wanted someone you could trust." He swiveled to Justin. "And you went and obliterated that trust with the stunt you pulled."

Justin licked his lips. "Sorry." He turned to Cody. "I'm really sorry. I wanted to help, but I made things worse. I just keep destroying things."

Cody frowned. "I should've known you weren't Dr. D."

"You did know. You kept saying I was different, but I blamed it on the cancer drugs."

George scratched his gray beard. "This conversation makes me uncomfortable on multiple levels. Pretending to be a licensed psychologist is a big deal—a major abuse of power, staggering exploitation. But then I'm wondering how you pulled this off at all. Does the extensive training Matthew and I went through mean nothing? Could any guy off the street play psychologist without his clients knowing?"

Justin shrugged. "It seemed to work with all of my patients."

"Come again?" George's chin lowered.

Shit. Had he just said that out loud?

"You saw clients besides Cody?" The man's face reddened. "You took their money?" He scooted forward and thumped the armrest. "What the *hell* were you thinking?" His shouts echoed in the office.

Justin winced. Matthew's anger seemed to pale against this psychologist's, though that was probably only because his brother had been chained with a guard listening in at the time.

"I'm calling the state psychology board when we get done here," George spat. "I'm reporting you."

"Great." Justin's chest squeezed. "Ruin the rest of Matthew's career."

"Matthew's not the one who broke the law, son. *You* did. I'm reporting you."

Justin's heart thumped as his face got hot. "Go for it—they won't care. Pretending to be a shrink is nothing compared to murdering Elyse Frederick."

Cody's head whipped up, and Justin read the question in his eyes: *Did you murder her?* He couldn't go there right now. He turned back to George. "Don't make Matthew pay for my mistakes. He needs a career to return to when I get him out of there."

"You're getting him out of there?" asked Cody. "How?"

"I'm going to make him switch back with me."

Justin thought Cody would feel relief at that, but the boy's face fell.

George's glare faded as he shifted his focus from Justin to Cody. "That upsets you, Cody? Justin switching back with Matthew?"

Cody's breath seemed shaky. "I don't want either of them to be in there."

Justin stilled. Cody cared about *him?*

George sat back in his chair and seemed to consider Cody's words. "I don't either."

That makes three of us. Justin shook his head. He deserved to be in prison, not outside and free.

"But a woman was murdered," George added. "Did you set off the bomb that killed her, Justin?"

He pictured Elyse's long hair and brown eyes, the curve of her mouth as she smiled up at him. *"Okay, Dad, I'm going home now..."* Then those eyes had narrowed with seeming suspicion. She was mad at him? He tried to grasp the memory, but it was like clutching a cloud.

"I probably did."

George stared at him. "You don't remember?"

Justin blew out a breath. "Sorry."

The clock ticked as silence settled over them.

"I bet this is somehow King's fault," Cody said.

"Kate thinks he framed me, actually."

"Holy shit." Cody's eyes widened.

George angled his head. "Kate is Matthew's girlfriend?"

"Yeah. My foster sister, too. She was with us at King's house."

"Dr. D's girlfriend was his foster sister?" Cody grimaced. "I mean, they're not related, but that's a little creepy, isn't it?"

"Tell me about it," Justin agreed. "They were all over each other when we were teenagers."

George sighed. "So you sacrificed yourself to protect Matthew and Kate."

Justin swallowed.

"Just like you sacrificed yourself for Brooke," George told Cody.

Cody's fist clenched.

"I don't know either of you well, but what you went through…" George looked at Cody, then at Justin. "It would destroy most boys. You need some counseling to process this."

Justin nodded. "That's why we're here. It's what Matthew wants: for both of us to see you individually."

"It is?" Cody asked.

"Yeah. He was really mad at me when he found out I'd pretended to be him—he was worried you'd feel betrayed. Your trust means a lot to him, Cody. He wants you to keep going to counseling."

"And what do you want, Justin?" George cocked his head. "Do you want to be in counseling with me?"

No. "It's not a matter of want—it's about need. If I have any chance of Matty switching back with me, I need to show him I'm in a better place."

George shook his head. "You need to engage in therapy for yourself, not for others. It needs to be self-motivated."

"I knew you'd say that." Justin grunted. "I have to admit, therapy seems to be working for Cody. He told me his nightmares have decreased, and he's doing well in school."

Cody shrugged. "Yeah, and I...I asked out that girl in my class yesterday."

"Way to go, dude!" Justin beamed.

"Hey, *I'm* the psychologist here," George said.

Contrite, Justin's smile faded.

George looked at Cody for a few seconds, wrinkled his forehead, then sighed. "I can't think of anything else to say. Way to go, dude."

Cody laughed.

"Maybe you didn't do a horrible job playing psychologist," George told Justin. "Fact is, you have a lot of empathy for emotional pain."

No kidding.

"The abuse *didn't* destroy either of you," George continued. "You two are survivors, stronger than you know. The choice you made to protect others...it's a beautiful thing."

Justin frowned. It hadn't been a choice. No way would he have let King hurt Matty or Kate.

"It wasn't beautiful," whispered Cody.

George nodded. "What happened to you wasn't beautiful, you're right. I meant the care you showed for loved ones was...*transcendent*. You gave yourselves to help others. You tried to do something good and honorable in the midst of all the pain. Your hearts are pure. Please know how much I admire your strength and sacrifice, your huge hearts."

Cody looked at Justin with a line creasing his forehead, like he doubted George's words. Justin wished Cody would listen. George was dead wrong about *him*, but he was right about Cody being a good man. Cody hadn't murdered Elyse or abandoned Gideon.

"I can tell neither of you believes me." George let out a breath. "And this is why I'm furious at this Jefferson King. I don't care if the CPS report didn't work the first time. We have to take down the bastard."

Justin stared at George. He hadn't expected him to be so spirited.

"How do we do that when everyone thinks he's freaking humanitarian of the year?" asked Cody.

George looked at Cody, then at Justin. "You both go to the police and report what happened to you."

Justin's breath caught in his throat, and he saw a flash of fear in Cody's eyes. "I should've gone to the cops a long time ago. But I was too chickenshit."

"No, you weren't," George said. "You were *traumatized*. You were trying to pretend the abuse never happened, trying to deny the pain. That's where the suicide attempts came in."

Justin trembled.

"But now you're talking about the abuse. You're no longer alone—you have Cody on your side. There's power in two."

Justin thought about Gideon. Maybe even more power in three?

"Many survivors don't report their abuse to the authorities," George continued. "If you accuse a powerful man like King of this crime, your life will change—in some ways for the worse. Yours too, Cody. People will question you, accuse you of making it all up. I'm only saying that reporting is an option to explore."

Justin nodded. "Look, Doc, I never thought I could tell *anyone* what happened. I thought I'd die if anyone found out my secret. Then Matty tore that to shreds, and Cody got me to break my silence." He rubbed his jaw. "I'm just not ready to go public. Even if I wanted to, I can't blow the lid off this with Matthew still in there." His phone buzzed in his jeans pocket, and he removed it.

It was a text from Kate:

Pete thinks you should show the poems to Cody.

Justin typed:

Who's Pete?

The firm's PI.

"What is it, Justin?" George asked.

Justin tensed—he didn't like involving more people. Was this Pete guy trustworthy?

"Kate got some poems in the mail. Whoever wrote them wants to take down King, too." He scrolled through his photos. "She wants me to show the poems to Cody. Is that okay?"

George nodded.

"Here's the first one." He read:

The Lord is with you
Stop him at his sick game
You three are Mighty Warriors
We triumph by my Name

Cody fell back on the sofa. "Ugh. This is like literature class—I hate poems. Just come out and say what you mean."

"Sounds religious," George said. "Like from the Bible or another holy text. Who do you believe sent this?"

Justin huffed out a breath. "I was thinking Gideon, but now I'm not sure."

"Why not?" Cody studied him.

"Gideon went through the same thing we did. If you had a way to take down King, you wouldn't be all cagey with these stupid poems, would you? You'd come to us direct. No messing around."

Cody nodded. "Good point."

"Maybe there's another of King's victims out there," offered George. "The average pedophile molests over two hundred children in his lifetime."

Cody looked green. "I need to barf."

"Me, too." Justin shuddered. How many more boys had King destroyed because he hadn't come forward?

"There's another poem?" George asked.

"Yeah." Justin tried to steady his hand to read it from his phone.

After the anonymous writer's words sank in, Cody bolted up from the sofa. "Flash drive!"

George looked up at him. "What?"

"In a flash, drive him to jail," Cody answered. He knelt to rummage through his backpack, then held up a USB drive. "Flash drive, jump drive, whatever you call it. The person who wrote this has one for us. Maybe it can destroy King."

George beckoned for Justin's phone. "Let me see that poem—I'm a visual learner."

As Justin handed him the phone, his chest rattled with a hint of excitement. But he tried to tamp it down. There was no justice in this world.

"Great, so maybe there's this flash drive out there. Where do we find it?"

A smile stretched George's beard as he removed his reading glasses. "The Short North Stage."

"Huh?" Justin peered at him.

"Once the Garden, now the sing." George jabbed his finger at the phone's screen. "There's a theater in the Short North—you know, the area between downtown and campus—that used to be called The Garden. It fell into disrepair, but they opened it as Short North Stage recently. They have musicals and concerts there."

"So whoever sent these poems…" Cody's eyes lit up. "They're at this theater. What do we do next?"

"We go find them," Justin said.

17. Warrior

A few hours later, Justin pulled Matthew's Honda into a surface parking lot in the Short North. He trolled the lot for a few minutes, squinting against the setting sun, before waiting to take a space from another car pulling out.

"I finally get to meet Dr. D's girlfriend," Cody said from the passenger seat. "This should be good."

"Watch yourself. She punches hard if you say something she doesn't like." Justin climbed out of the car and locked it. After he looked at his phone's GPS, he cocked his head to the left. "Theater's this way."

Cody fell into step next to him, heading south, with the noisy High Street traffic on their left. Justin had to look up to see Cody's Buckeyes ball cap. How unusual it was to spend time with someone taller than him.

"So, Dr. McCallister thinks we should go to the police," Cody said.

Justin tensed as he gave him a sideways glance. The psychologist's advice had plagued him since they'd left his office and eaten dinner at Matthew's condo.

"He's right."

"But you can't do it with Dr. D locked up."

Justin sighed. "And once we switch back, nobody will believe me about King. They'll think I'm making it up to avoid prosecution."

He was talking about switching places with Matthew like it was a done deal. But even if Matthew were willing, how the hell would he pull it off? The jail where he'd stayed for two months had tighter security than the hospital, and Matthew had told Kate they might restore him to competence soon since he hadn't attempted suicide in weeks.

Cody nodded. "Sucks."

"But *you* could go to the cops," Justin suggested.

Cody chewed on his lip. "I don't know if I could do it. Alone, I mean. I…" He puffed out a breath. "I'm too much of a wuss."

They approached a homeless man with a dirty cardboard sign by his feet that said something about being an Army veteran. Justin looked away, but Cody stopped.

"Hey, man." Cody dug a folded twenty-dollar bill out of his jeans pocket and pitched forward to toss it into the bowl next to the sign. "Stay strong."

The man's eyes crinkled. "You're a beautiful soul."

Cody grinned. "You too, man."

Justin studied Cody as they continued to the theater. "How'd you afford that?"

"Well, I got two-hundred Gs in my pocket now."

Justin smirked. He'd returned Cody's therapy payments back at the condo. Once he'd discovered Cody was surviving only on his scholarship, without accepting any of King's blood money, he'd planned to return them, but George McCallister had forced the issue. George had wanted him to return money to the other patients as well, but Justin had almost depleted the money Matthew had left for him, and he didn't know how to return the payments without outing himself as fake. He was still nervous that George would report him to the state board of psychology.

After a beat, Cody said, "I was homeless once."

"Yeah?"

Cody looked at his feet. "I ran away when I was fifteen."

Justin gritted his teeth.

"King kept showing me videos of all the awful stuff America has done—invading countries, stealing oil, rigging elections…He wanted me to see the evil, the corruption. He wanted me to hate this country." Cody's jaw clenched. "But ever since I started swimming, my goal has been to make Team USA. My dad wanted that for me, too. It was our dream." He tugged at the bill of his cap. "On top of what King was already doing to me, it was just too much, I guess. I left school early one day and ended up sleeping on the streets. I had to give up swimming to get away from him."

Justin closed his eyes.

"But the police found me, and they returned me to King." A disgusted sound rumbled from his throat. "Would've been the perfect time to tell them what he was doing to me. But I missed swimming too much, and I chickened out. Then King started fostering Brooke…"

Hot rage pulsed up Justin's spine. "…And he threatened to rape her if you ran away again."

Cody stared straight ahead.

"I never even tried to run away." Justin shook his head. "You're not a wuss, Cody."

A woman carrying a shopping bag walked toward them, and when Justin met her eyes, she froze. She looked to the right at the busy street, then back at Justin. She zipped between parked cars and scooted across the street like a frog jumping through traffic. One driver had to slam on the brakes to avoid hitting her, and the car's honk echoed long after the woman had reached the opposite side.

"She recognized you?" Cody asked.

His heart beat double time, and he looked behind him, but there were no police officers thundering toward him. He'd had quite a few nightmares about police coming for him since his arrest. "Give me your hat."

He slid the ball cap on, feeling the transferred warmth from Cody's head. The sunny spring day had cooled as night approached.

"It's May sixteenth," Cody said. "We're here in the Short North a little before eight p.m. See that arch over the street?"

Justin gaped at him. "What're you talking about?"

"You look freaked. I'm using grounding skills."

As his heart started to settle, Justin kept watching Cody. "Matthew taught you those?"

"Yeah." Cody shrugged. "They don't stop the flashbacks, but they give you something to focus on…till you can breathe again. Dr. D always harped on me to ground myself in the present when my mind was flashing back to the past."

Was this why Matthew had been on Justin's case to disclose the abuse in therapy? To learn skills for dealing with trauma? Matthew had tried to talk to him before about breathing and some other bullshit, but Justin had pushed him away, thinking he'd never understand. He'd told his brother to stop psychoanalyzing him—to stick to his patients. And now Matthew was in a place where his talents rotted away, where he couldn't help anyone, including Cody.

The enormity of his screw-ups crushed his chest. "Sorry I took him away from you."

Cody frowned as he started walking again. "Sounds like you had no choice. Dr. D can be really stubborn."

Justin grunted as he fell into step with him. Cody knew his brother well.

A hundred feet from the theater, Justin paused. Who was that guy leaning against the wall next to Kate? The guy said something to her, and she grinned as she elbowed him.

"What's wrong?" asked Cody.

"Nothing." Justin looked around, but no one seemed to notice him. He took a breath and approached the theater.

Kate's smile faded when she saw them. She pushed off the wall and looked up at Cody. "Whoa. How tall are you?"

"Six-seven."

The unknown man chuckled. "Didn't know we had a varsity athlete on our side."

The guy must've noticed Cody's Ohio State T-shirt. Justin leaned back. He hardly wanted this stranger on his "side."

"Football or basketball?" the guy asked.

Justin felt Cody stiffen next to him.

"Swimming," came the terse reply.

Kate said, "Justin, this is—"

"Let's get away from the street." Justin pointed around the corner of the building.

"Sure." As Kate turned and headed for the alley, the guy placed his hand at the small of her back.

Oh, hell no. Who'd this cat think he was? Justin hustled after them.

Once they stood in the shadow of the rusty fire escape, with the rank odor of garbage floating over them, Justin and Cody faced Kate and the man.

"You're Dr. D's girlfriend," Cody said.

"Kate. And you're Cody." Her attempt at a smile only ended up making her look sad. She stepped toward Cody and wrapped him in a hug.

As she embraced him, Justin sized up the stranger, who had his eyes glued on Kate. The guy was shorter than him, with a high forehead and suspicious hazel eyes Justin didn't trust.

"You've been through a lot," Kate told Cody as she let him go.

Cody ducked his head like he wanted to be invisible, so Justin removed the hat and returned it. Cody slipped it on.

"Pete Dixon," the stranger said as he offered his hand to Justin. "I'm the firm's investigator. Your secret's safe with me."

Justin hoped Kate's apparent trust in this guy wasn't foolhardy. After an excessively forceful handshake, Justin introduced himself, adding, "My twin is Kate's boyfriend."

"I thought he broke up with her."

The boldness in the jerk's eyes made Justin want to punch him.

"Justin?" Kate's voice drew his attention. "You told us to meet you here. Why?"

Cody pointed at Justin's jeans, where he'd pocketed his phone. "The poems say this is the place."

Kate tilted her head. "How'd you figure that out?"

"George McCallister figured it out," said Justin. "He's old. He knows things." He pulled out his phone, but Kate had removed copies of the poems from her purse and unfolded them before he had a chance to open his photos.

"May I?" Cody asked, and Kate handed them over. Pointing to the last line of the second poem, Cody said, "We think this guy has a flash drive for us."

Pete took the paper from his grasp and examined it. "Damn, that's so obvious. Why didn't I see that?"

"And the poet's supposedly here at the Short North Stage?" Kate asked. "Who're we looking for? Do we still think it's Gideon?"

Pete frowned. "Who's Gideon?"

Justin looked at Cody, who answered, "King's foster kid after me. We're not sure it's him, though."

Pete shuffled the papers so the first poem was on top. After reading for a moment, he removed his phone from his pocket. His fingers flew over the screen as he typed.

Justin scowled. The dude seemed strange, and he was a lousy investigator to boot. He'd better not be making moves on Matthew's future wife.

The drumbeat coming through the theater walls competed with Justin's thumping heart. He wondered if George had identified the wrong location. They didn't even know who wrote the freaking poems.

"The more I think about it, we're probably looking for someone else," he said. "If Gideon's still alive, he's hell and gone from Columbus."

"Oh, we're looking for Gideon." Pete looked up from his phone with a smug grin.

"What?" Kate leaned in to see. "Why?"

Pete held up his phone and showed them a website. "Judges six, verses eleven to twenty-two. 'The angel of the Lord greeted Gideon: The Lord is with you, mighty warrior.'"

"Mighty warrior?" Kate grabbed the poems, scanned the first one, and jumped. "You three are mighty warriors!"

The skin of Justin's back tingled.

Pete scrolled down his phone screen. "Listen to this: 'In the Bible, Gideon was a hero of Israel who won battles through faith and skill instead of physical strength alone.'"

Kate's nodded frantically. "And the poem says, 'We triumph by my name.' The name Gideon. This *has* to be it."

"Wait—let me look at Gideon on a baby name site." After a moment, Pete grinned. "The meaning of the name Gideon is *he who cuts down.*"

Kate stabbed the paper before her arm shot up, her index finger pointed to the sky. "'We will cut down the King.'"

"Holy hell." Butterflies dive-bombed Justin's gut. Could they cut down that miserable piece of shit with Gideon's help? He looked at Cody, whose wide eyes stared back at him. "So where do we find Gideon?"

Cody glanced around the darkening alley. "I…I'm not sure."

"You know what he looks like, Just?" Kate asked.

"Skinny, black hair, green eyes. Not much of a mighty warrior." He placed his hand on the exterior wall of the theater. "But why the Short North Stage?"

"Maybe he's an actor in one of their shows," Pete suggested.

Justin frowned. "He's just a teenager."

Kate took off in the direction of the street. "Let's see if we can get in the front entrance."

Pete followed Kate, but Cody stayed put.

"What is it?" asked Justin.

Cody shook his head. "We shouldn't barge in there. Writing those poems the way he did…It's like Gideon's not sure he wants to be found. He's gotta be scared."

Justin slipped his hands in his pockets. "You know what it's like to be on the run from King."

Cody nodded.

"I had Matthew and Kate, but you didn't have anyone."

Cody exhaled. "When I found out about the warehouse bombing, and then I discovered Dr. D…it was such a relief. To tell him what it was like to be King's foster kid…" He blushed as he looked at Justin. "Thanks for getting arrested, in such a spectacular, public-enemy-number-one kind of way, I guess."

Justin smirked. "Hey, go big or go home."

"Gideon needs us." Cody set his jaw. "Even if he can't help us take down King, we need to find him. Help him."

"Agreed." Justin heard the drumbeat increase in volume, almost vibrating the wall.

"Locked," Kate said as she returned to the alley with Pete trailing her. "Why didn't you guys come with?"

Cody headed for a side door marked *Employees Only* below the fire escape, and he grinned when it swung open. The drumbeat became louder, joined by strains of piano and guitar through the open door.

Pete stuck his head inside, then beckoned for them to join him before the darkness inside the building swallowed his body. Cody followed, leaving Justin to stare at Kate as he held the door open for her.

Her smile seemed nervous. "How old is this theater?"

"C'mon." He took her hand and led her inside. "Can't be scarier than Columbus Hospital for the Insane."

They followed the sound of the music to the foyer, where Pete and Cody peeked through an open door near the sign, *Green Room*. Justin came up behind Cody and looked around him to see a few musicians playing on a small stage. A shout came from their left, and Cody backed straight into him. Justin tensed, but let out a breath when another voice responded — the dialogue sounded like scripted lines, like a rehearsal of some sort. He tiptoed toward the larger opening off the foyer and peered around a drawn red velvet curtain to find a larger theater where several actors performed.

"Booth," called a gray-haired man from the seats facing the stage. "Maybe less aggressive? You're trying to *inspire* Oswald, not attack him."

On the stage, a man with curly black hair and a ruffled tie and vest befitting the nineteenth century placed his hand on his hip. "But I'm angry he's having second thoughts." He gestured toward the man in a nerdy white shirt and khakis.

"Play it more subtly. You're cleverer than that. Save your anger for the theater scene," the director ordered.

Even from outside, Justin could see the actor roll his eyes.

Pete had sidled up to him. "Any of those actors look like our man?"

"Nope."

The band in the Green Room stopped playing, and someone said, "Take ten." Footsteps approached the foyer.

Standing across the theater entrance from Justin, Kate's eyes widened.

"Relax," Pete said. "What're they gonna do, beat us with their drumsticks?" He gestured to the main theater. "Soliloquize us to death?"

"Guys!" Cody stage-whispered. He pointed down a stairwell on the left side of the foyer. "C'mon."

Following Cody, Justin hustled down the stairs and felt Kate behind him. Despite Pete's scoffing, he came down the stairs after them. The lighting was brighter and the decor more modern in the basement, like it had been recently renovated. Doors with stars on them lined the hallway. While Justin listened for footsteps on the stairs, Pete nudged ahead and strolled by each door.

He returned to the base of the stairs with a headshake. "None of the doors says Gideon."

After a brief scan of the lower level, Justin determined the hallway was the only accessible area. When he pressed his ear against the first door and heard nothing, he tried the doorknob. *Locked.* He proceeded to the next door, and Kate followed his lead, trying the doors on the opposite side of the hallway.

The third doorknob unexpectedly gave way, and Justin almost fell inside the room. He righted himself and looked around: a black silk robe draped over a coatrack, and a lighted mirror hung above a dresser littered with makeup.

"What's a bed doing in a dressing room?" Pete asked from behind him.

Justin turned to see his three companions crowding the doorway. He swiveled back around. The twin bed jammed next to the wall did seem out of place in the small quarters.

"Wonder who Eric Lopez is," Kate said, tapping the star on the open door.

Pete pointed at the ceiling. "One of those actors up there looked Latino. I bet it's his dressing room."

Justin wished Pete would shut up. He glanced at Cody. "What do you think? Dead end?"

Cody pursed his lips as he weaved around Justin and picked up a notepad from the dresser. After thumbing through a few pages, he leaned back. "These are good drawings." He turned the page. "Really good."

"Yeah." Justin had come up next to him to take a look. Though he didn't know much about art, the drawing of a girl holding an umbrella was so detailed that he knew right away it was from Schiller Park in nearby German Village.

When Cody turned the page, he and Justin gasped.

"What is it?" asked Kate.

Justin's heart hammered as he stared at the perfectly drawn tool shed, complete with bricks, ivy creeping up the windows, and evil.

Cody touched his shoulder. "Breathe."

Justin inhaled and tried to think straight as he looked at the mussed sheets on the bed. Gideon *had* to be nearby. He knelt and lifted the floral dust ruffle, then flattened his cheek against the floor. Peering back at him from the darkness were two wary eyes, narrowed like a cat's. A Converse high top swept out from under the bed and cracked into his shin.

"Fuck." He grabbed his throbbing leg and wiggled back, still holding up the dust ruffle. "Gideon, it's me—Justin Durante. We're not King or the cops, I swear."

"Then who's with you?" a scared voice hissed.

Kate told Pete, "Close the door." She leaned toward the bed. "Gideon, it's Kate Summers, Justin's attorney. Come out and talk to us."

When the boy didn't emerge, Cody lowered his body next to Justin's. On his hands and knees, he peered below the bed. "I was King's foster son right before you." But the boy stayed put. Cody scoffed, "*You're* the one who sent the dumbass poems and lured us here, right?"

After a moment of silence, Gideon whispered, "Yes."

"Then start acting like the mighty warrior you say you are, or we're leaving."

Cody's threat spurred action, and soon the three former foster sons stood by the bed, staring at each other. Gideon's dyed blond hair washed out his pale complexion, but Justin knew those eyes. Thank God King hadn't killed him.

Cody stuck out his hand and introduced himself.

As Justin reached to pull a dust bunny out of Gideon's hair, Gideon flinched. "It's okay, buddy." Justin showed him the piece of fuzz. "We're not gonna hurt you."

"How'd you get out of jail?" Gideon asked.

Justin glanced at Kate. "That's a long story. You can't tell anyone you saw me, okay?"

"And the same thing goes for you." Gideon angled his head toward Pete. "Who's he?"

"My firm's investigator. He helped us find you." Kate inched toward Gideon. "You have something for us? Something to 'take down King'?"

A blast rang out from above, and Justin jumped. "Christ, what was that?"

"*Assassins,*" Gideon said with a shrug.

"Here?" Cody's eyes expanded. "Coming after us?"

Gideon shook his head. "The musical they're rehearsing upstairs—it's called *Assassins*. By Stephen Sondheim." He looked at his cheap watch. "That was probably John Wilkes Booth shooting Lincoln. Doesn't the recording sound just like a gunshot?"

Justin stuck his shaking hands inside his pockets. "Very authentic."

Gideon crossed over to the mirror and studied his reflection. He brushed a finger through his hair. "Eric will be done with rehearsal soon. You guys have to leave."

Cody's mouth opened as his eyes went to Justin, and Justin shook his head. No way they'd leave without getting more information. He was about to suggest they take the skinny boy out for food when Pete butted in.

"Eric's the actor playing John Wilkes Booth?"

One corner of Gideon's mouth quirked. "He's got top billing. The show opens in two weeks."

Pete stepped closer. "And he's your lover."

Gideon stiffened, looking like he wanted to bolt from the room.

"Back off, Pete," Justin warned.

Gideon shrugged. "We're not…in a relationship. Eric says he has enough drama in his life already." He pointed at the stage above. "He doesn't want the burden of emotional attachments." His eyes shifted to the floor. "That's why he likes me."

Justin's throat constricted. Was this Eric guy providing the boy shelter just so he could be his sex slave or something?

Kate wore that sad smile again. "Sounds like Eric takes good care of you."

Gideon's head bobbed. "He keeps me safe. But you guys have to go. He won't like all these strangers near his stuff. I'm not even supposed to be here, really."

Justin tried to relax his voice. "How 'bout we buy you some dinner, Gid?"

"No!" The boy's eyes got big. "I don't go outside—King has spies all over. They almost got me once at Schiller Park."

Cody chewed on his lip, then gestured to the notebook. "Your drawings are amazing. That girl with the umbrella statue? Just like at the park. Spot on, dude."

Gideon's frightened eyes bounced from one person to another.

"This drawing…" Cody studied Gideon as his hand inched toward the notebook. When Gideon didn't protest, Cody tilted up the notebook so that the toolshed drawing was visible. "Maybe this is something you see in nightmares?"

Gideon backed up a step. He brushed against Justin then boomeranged away.

Justin splayed his hands. "It's okay, buddy." He eyed Cody. "Cody and I have nightmares, too. You're not alone."

The boy's tortured breaths filled the room.

"Thank you for sending the poems to me, Gideon," said Kate. "You want to tell us why you sent them?"

Gideon swallowed as he looked at the opposite wall. "I didn't want him to get away with it."

"King?" Kate asked. "Get away with what, sweetie?"

Justin frowned at Kate. He'd never heard her call anyone *sweetie* before.

"Setting up Justin for the bombing," Gideon answered in a flat voice.

Justin's spine snapped straight, and he stepped into Gideon's line of vision. "He set me up? How do you know?"

"H-H-He told me he would. After I tried to resist him…"

After Justin had told Gideon to stand up to the bully. *Idiot.* "King didn't like you resisting him."

Green eyes pleaded with Justin. "Sorry."

"Why're you sorry?" Justin asked. He was the one who should've apologized.

"He beat it out of me…made me tell him why I started fighting him, even when he threatened to hurt Julie. Sorry, I didn't want to tell him, I…"

Justin's gut roiled. "You told him I talked to you, at, at your school. That I said to resist his advances?"

Gideon's eyes brimmed with tears. "Sorry, I screwed up. I didn't want to tell him it was you—he made me."

Justin imagined the fear Gideon must've felt. King's callous pale eyes would've drilled into him as he'd leaned close, threatening. "After he beat it out of you, King said he'd show me not to interfere in his affairs?" Justin asked.

Wide-eyed, Gideon nodded.

Justin wished he didn't know King so well. He didn't want any part of being inside that monster's head. "And he threatened to do the same to you—ruin your life—if you didn't submit to him."

Gideon scrubbed his wet cheek. "That's when I knew I had to get away. Get away and never be found, so he couldn't set me up for murder, too."

Justin flexed his shaking hands as Gideon's words sank in. *King set me up!* He knew it. Part of him had always known.

Kate clasped Justin's wrist. "We have a witness." She tilted her head toward Gideon. "A *distressed* witness. But not much evidence. This won't clear you or Matthew."

Fuck. He closed his eyes, but opened them to the sound of a drawer scraping against the dresser. He watched Gideon wrench it all the way out, then reach into the opening. His hand emerged, clutching an object. He unfurled his fingers to reveal a flash drive in his open palm.

"Holy shit," Cody said. "King's secrets?"

Gideon sighed. "It may be nothing. The files are all encrypted—I can't open them."

"How'd you get them?" Kate asked.

Gideon lowered to the bed. "King took us to a hotel when the media found out it was his triggers that blasted that Yemeni plane. The next night—the night the warehouse got bombed—police showed up at our hotel suite. I overhead them talking to King in the next room. When the cops said Justin was the prime suspect, I knew what had happened. I knew what King had done. He went with them to the precinct, and I had my chance to run away. But first I downloaded everything I could find on his laptop. He'd left himself logged in—I don't think he expected the police to show up at the hotel."

In a fog, Justin felt a hand clasp his elbow. He looked up to see Cody staring at him.

"How 'bout you sit next to Gideon?" Cody suggested.

Justin frowned but allowed Cody to guide him to the bed. He didn't feel his feet.

"I'll crack those files," Pete said, thrusting his hand toward the boy. "Give me the flash drive."

Gideon shied away from Pete as he clutched the device.

Cody crossed over to sit on the other side of Gideon. "It's okay. King did the same thing to me—there's no shame in it. Nobody wants to take down King more than Justin and me. Justin's twin brother, Dr. D, too."

Gideon turned to look at Cody.

"That's right," said Cody. "Dr. D's in jail now—he switched places with Justin to save his life. We gotta get him out, okay? You did real good getting those files, and maybe they can help us. Can we have them?"

After a long moment, Gideon handed the flash drive to Cody.

"Gideon, is it okay if I ask you a question?" Kate knelt before him and waited for him to give a shaky nod. "You ran away from King in October, right? The night of the bombing?"

"Yeah."

"Why wait till now to send me the poems?"

Gideon pressed his lips together. "Ramadan's coming."

"Ramadan?" Kate asked.

"King and the lady with the scarf—they're planning something for Ramadan. I heard them." Gideon's voice trembled. "Something bad."

Kate's face went white as she looked at Justin.

Pete looked up from his phone. "Ramadan started today."

Kate stood, nodding at Justin, Gideon, and Cody. "Sounds like we need some mighty warriors then. You three up to it?"

18. Decode

A sharp noise jarred Matthew awake. He gulped for air — his dream of Shaddox suffocating him with a pillow had felt so real that it took several seconds to realize where he was. When he saw the harsh hallway light seeping through the metal door's Plexiglas window, his heart sank.

Locked up in a psychiatric unit — it wasn't a dream.

He shook the sleep from his head, but the meds put him right back into a stupor. With a groan, he sat up. The thin mattress dipped, and he could feel the concrete block of his bed frame press into his bottom.

A muffled scream shot him to his feet. Was that the sound that had woken him?

He zoomed to the door and strained to see into the hallway. Two men rushed past his door — a guard and the psych tech that usually worked nights. The scream became louder and more recognizable. Matthew took a step back.

Daniel.

A few shouts and grunts later, a shadow approached his door. Matthew pressed his nose to the glass and gasped as he stared straight into Shaddox's crazy eyes. Shaddox reeled back, and Matthew could see the guard behind yanking him away from the door. The guard shoved him down the hall via his grip on the naked patient's hand-cuffed wrists. Shaddox maintained his leering grin until the guard pushed him out of sight, toward the solitary cells.

What had Shaddox done to Daniel before they'd stopped him? Matthew had trouble swallowing.

The guard returned after a minute or two, alone this time. When he passed Matthew's window, he glared over at him. "Back in bed, Durante. It's the middle of the night."

Matthew shrank back but stayed near the window. He had to see if Daniel was okay.

His heart beat erratically as he waited. How had Shaddox gotten into Daniel's room? All of their small rooms were on lockdown starting at nine p.m. That's when Matthew would do calisthenics and meditation, followed by unsuccessful efforts to ward off memories of Kate.

A moan drew his attention back to the hallway, which was still empty. Had Shaddox used the trusty gum-on-the-door-strike technique again? Matthew had tried to sneak a look at the interior of his door every time a guard or tech escorted him in at night, and he'd told Daniel to do the same. But had the boy forgotten?

Another moan announced Daniel's presence before Matthew could see him. When he came into view, dragged along by the guard and tech, Matthew wished he'd stayed out of sight. Mottled bruises covered one side of his face, and his pronounced limp sent shivers up Matthew's spine. Daniel's jumpsuit prevented Matthew from seeing if there was blood running down his legs.

"Stop," the guard barked. He glared at Matthew again through the cloudy window. "Do I need to come in there and cuff you to the bed?"

Matthew backpedaled. He didn't know which was worse: his guilt or his helplessness. He climbed back onto the thin mattress and closed his eyes. This time the images assaulting his brain weren't of Kate. They weren't about tender love or longing. Trembling, he knew there'd be no way for him to sleep.

$$\textcircled{\text{II}}$$

"What time is it?" Gideon asked from his seat at the dining table in Matthew's condo. His pencil scratched against his sketchbook, and Justin wished he could see what he was drawing.

From Matthew's sofa, Justin yawned as he looked at his watch. "A little before five a.m."

"Shit," Kate muttered to her laptop. With her legs propped on the ottoman, she rested the back of her head on the loveseat cushion and stared at the ceiling.

Pete scowled at Matthew's desktop computer across the room. "So King's wife's name isn't the password, evidently."

"Not a surprise." Kate slouched. "He always seemed to hate her."

Pete nodded. "Plus, men are less likely to use people's names for passwords."

Justin deflated. Their initial excitement at the idea of cracking into King's files had long ago vanished. Pete had determined that they could access the encrypted files with a password. "No problem," he'd said. "We'll blast through this asswipe's security."

Eight hours after beginning their decoding attempts, they still had nothing.

Justin squinted at Pete, who scrolled through websites on the desktop. How did Kate's firm win *any* cases with this guy as their investigator?

Slim purred from the carpet where she'd curled up near Cody's hip. The swimmer's long body swallowed the floor space. At first, Cody had worked with Justin to tell Pete and Kate everything they could remember about King in order to guess the password. After countless fails, he'd succumbed to sleep an hour ago.

Justin got up from the sofa and nudged Cody's knee with his foot. "C'mon."

Cody groaned.

"Cody."

His eyelids fluttered open. When he saw Justin, his torso jolted up. "Did you get the password?"

Slim meowed as she rearranged herself, clearly pissed off by the interruption.

"Nope." Justin offered his hand and pulled the swimmer to his feet. "I'm putting you in Matthew's bed."

Cody slipped his phone out of his pocket and shook his head after he looked at it. "I have to be at the pool in an hour."

"I'll write you another note. You can't swim on zero sleep."

His hands perched on his hips. "I can't miss two practices in a row!"

"Just get some sleep, Cody, then you'll be back in the game. We need you." Justin licked his upper lip. "Matthew needs you."

When Cody still hesitated, Justin folded his arms across his chest. "Doctor's orders. Dr. D says go to bed."

Cody rolled his eyes but headed for the stairs.

Gideon watched them leave.

"You didn't hear me call myself doctor," Justin told him.

As he followed Cody up the stairs, he wondered about getting Gideon into counseling. They'd had to coax him to leave the theater before that actor, Eric, had finished rehearsal. When Gideon had gathered up his belongings, Justin's heart had sunk. All Gideon appeared to own was a sketchbook, a cell phone, and a pair of winter gloves—an odd clothing item for mid-May. The boy hadn't said much all night.

Despite Cody's earlier protests, he climbed right into bed.

"Hey, I just washed the sheets." Justin yanked off the swimmer's gargantuan gym shoes.

"Sorry." Now shoeless, Cody slid underneath the covers. "I never have time to wash mine."

Justin nodded. "It's easier when you don't have to go to the Laundromat. Matthew has a washer and dryer in his basement."

Resting the back of his head on the pillow, Cody stared up at him for a long moment. "We'll get him back."

Justin swallowed. He wished he could feel as optimistic.

"Will Slim come up on the bed with me?" Cody yawned. "I liked sleeping with her."

Justin shook his head. "She won't stray far from her food bowl if there are people downstairs." He looked around the room and snatched Azrael from the bookshelf. "Here, sleep with him."

Cody accepted the stuffed orange cat with a drop of his chin. "What the fuck's this?"

Matthew's tears when they'd first come to live with King had killed Justin. He'd known it was his fault they'd lost their parents and cats.

"Azrael helps you sleep." Justin waited for an eye roll, but Cody turned onto his side and hugged the stuffed animal as his eyes closed.

As Justin pulled the comforter over him, his throat ached. How could King have hurt him like he did? Gideon, too, for that matter—two boys who had done nothing wrong other than enter the foster system. His shoulders squeezed. They *had* to cut down King.

"Justin!" Kate called.

He hustled down the stairs, only to find Kate glaring at him from the kitchen.

She gestured to the almost-empty cabinet. "Who doesn't have coffee?"

"McCallister told me not to drink caffeine." Justin shrugged. "It jacks up my sympathetic nervous system."

She huffed out a breath, then stormed back to her laptop. "Ridiculous."

"I'll go get some, if you give me money," offered Gideon.

Justin worried they'd never see him again if they let him leave. "Don't worry about it," he told the boy. "My brother's got a guest bedroom upstairs, if you want to get some sleep?"

Gideon shook his head.

He probably fought sleep as much as Justin did.

"I'll, uh, run out for some coffee," Justin said.

"Forget about it." Kate angled her head to the blinds covering the sliding glass doors. Faint morning light had started to filter through. "I'll grab some on my way to court."

Justin crossed over to sit on the sofa. "You can't leave until we figure out the password."

"What?" She ran her hands through her hair. "We've been at it all night—we've got zilch. I think we should take a break, come at this again more clear-headed."

"We gotta get Matty out of there. Now."

She squinted at him. "He's been in there a month already. Why the rush?"

Justin scrubbed his head. "There's a sicko in there. I made a deal with him, and he came at Matthew because of it."

Kate's eyes widened.

"The guy will try again, I know it. You saw that scar on Matty's forehead?"

"He said that scar was nothing!"

"It's my fault." Justin looked down. "Sorry. But we have to keep pushing—"

"I can't do this anymore." Kate popped to her feet. "This Middle Eastern woman you and Cody talk about—King's mistress or whatever—she *has* to be part of this." She pointed at the computer screen and walked toward Pete. "But we can't find anything tying them together."

Pete reached up to caress her shoulder. "King's not stupid enough to be seen with her in public."

"You said passwords tend to personally meaningful, right?" Kate asked.

Pete nodded.

Justin felt a rumble at the base of his throat as he eyed Pete's hand on Kate's shoulder.

"Maybe she *is* the password, but we don't even know her damn name!" Kate shrugged off Pete's hand and clutched her head. "This is hopeless."

Justin closed his eyes. Had King ever called that woman by name? All he could remember was her light laughter as King pressed into him, subduing him, hurting him—all as that lilting laugh rolled over him...

The dip of the sofa cushion forced his eyes open, and he rocked back when he saw Gideon sitting right next to him. Gideon's wide eyes blinked at him, and then he handed over his sketchbook.

Justin froze as he looked at the drawing. "Holy fuck."

"What is it?" Kate stepped closer.

Staring back at Justin was a face with symmetrical eyes, flawless skin, and a Mona Lisa smile, framed by an artfully arranged scarf. The drawing was in charcoal, but Justin could see the hazel of her eyes, her olive skin, and her shiny black hair. The image began to shake, and it wasn't until Kate clutched his wrist that he realized the tremor in his arm was responsible.

Kate slid the sketchbook from his grasp. "This looks like her?"

Justin panted for a breath. "It *is* her."

"We can use this." She nodded at Gideon. "Good job. We can give this drawing to the prosecutor." She paused and scrunched her mouth. "But it's still not enough. So what if there's some woman King's bonking on the side. It doesn't make him a terrorist." She scowled at the computer. "Or give us a password."

As she handed the sketchbook to Pete, she asked, "Maybe you could search for this image online or something?"

Pete looked at the drawing, then returned it to Kate. "I'll do it later, when I talk to my police contact. We'll search mug shots. But right now I want to persevere with this password. Something personally meaningful, like I said. Let's keep digging into his background, keep brainstorming."

Kate groaned. "We already did this."

Pete ignored her as he pulled up King's Wikipedia page again. "Guys often turn to sports for passwords. What's his favorite sports team?"

"Columbus Blue Jackets?" Kate suggested.

"He's not into sports," said Justin.

His heartbeat had slowed after the adrenaline party started by Gideon's drawing, and he could breathe again. Slim waltzed by, rubbing against his legs, then hopped up onto Gideon's lap. The plus-sized cat dwarfed his skinny legs.

"Slim…" Justin warned, studying Gideon. "Is she bothering you?"

Slim lifted onto her hind legs and began kneading Gideon's chest. He leaned back against the cushions. "She's okay. But why's she named *Slim?*"

Justin blew out a breath. "Matthew's into irony, apparently."

"That's not why." Kate scratched Slim's ears. "She only weighed a pound when we got her from the shelter. Such a tiny little thing. Her mother had abandoned her, and the vet told Matthew to make sure she got enough food."

"Mission accomplished." Pete smirked.

Justin wondered where he'd been when Matthew had adopted Slim. Probably on an alcohol bender, trying to avoid memories of the past.

"She actually weighed more before Justin put her on a diet, if you can believe that." Kate smiled at Gideon. "She likes you. She doesn't take to strangers well."

"Back to work, people." Pete scrolled down the webpage. "So what *is* King into?"

"He's all proud of his library," Gideon offered. "And he likes to show off his big vocabulary. He plays Words with Friends."

Kate cocked her head. "Really? That online Scrabble game?"

Pete typed a few words into the password field but grimaced. "Nope."

Justin tensed. "He's also into bombs."

Pete shook his head. "We already tried the password *bombs*, with various number combinations, as well as explode, detonate, explosion…" He peered at the website and read aloud. *"King grew up in Farmington, West Virginia, the only child of Alexander and Betty King."*

Kate collapsed on the loveseat with a sigh. "And we know Betty bit it giving birth to her evil spawn."

"Correct," Pete said. "King's mother died from an infection the day he was born."

Justin thought about his mother, Isabel Garcia Durante. She'd often shared the memory about how he and Matthew had arrived a month before their due date, when their father had been out of town at a weapons conference in Pittsburgh. She'd been with a psychotherapy patient when her water had broken, and her patient had driven her to the hospital. Justin's father had missed his birth but had made it to the hospital just as Matthew had come into the world, squalling. As children, Matthew had often claimed he was their dad's favorite, though he'd stopped saying that after the fire — the one Justin had caused by playing with chemicals. The fire that had killed the parents who'd created him.

"You tried Betty, right?" Justin asked.

Kate replied, "Yes, and Elizabeth, Betsy, Bitsy, Beth, Liz, Betty Boop —"

"It won't be his mom's name," Gideon interrupted.

Justin, Kate, and Pete all stared at him as he petted the cat that had curled up in his lap.

"Why not?" asked Justin.

"Because he's inhuman." Gideon's chin trembled. "He doesn't love people. He, he doesn't know how."

Justin lowered his voice. "You lived with him most recently. Got any more password suggestions?"

Gideon rubbed his elbow, exposing the underside of his forearm and giving Justin a good look at scars crossing his pale skin. When Gideon noticed his stare, he pulled his arm flush to his body. "Don't know."

"You said you heard King and Scarf Bitch planning something." Justin gestured to the drawing. "What'd you hear?"

Gideon swallowed. "I…" He closed his eyes, and his long eyelashes drew Justin's attention to the smudged hollows beneath them. Gideon pulled his other arm across his waist, hugging himself.

Justin felt guilty for leading him back to a dark place.

"Soldiers," Gideon muttered. His eyes opened. "Something about soft targets."

Pete shook his head. "That doesn't make sense. Soft targets are civilian, not military."

"Try soldier anyway," said Kate.

Pete typed into the password field, but as usual, nothing happened. He tried some more words to no avail.

Kate rubbed her temples. "I need coffee."

Clicking back to the Wikipedia page, Pete kept reading. "Says here that after the death of King's mother, his father went from mine supervisor to explosives manager."

"Where King learned his sick craft," Kate said.

As he exhaled, Justin wished his father had chosen another place to work as a chemist. But he did recall his dad's excitement after coming home most days. *It's rare for the CEO to be a chemical engineer,* his father had told his mother. *Usually it's all about money, not science. But Jefferson gets it—he really gets it. He loves chemistry almost more than I do.*

What would his father say if he knew what King had done to Justin after he died? Everyone had thought King was magnanimous to take in the twin sons of his deceased employee. But Justin had a sense that his father, wherever he was, knew the score.

"So, a mining explosives manager," Kate said. "What is that, exactly? Is it the same thing King does now?"

"King's more advanced than that," Justin said. "He got a PhD in chemical engineering, like my dad." His mother and father had met in graduate school at Ohio State. Justin was the only Durante without a doctorate. Hell, he didn't even have a bachelor's degree. "King's dad probably used more primitive explosives, like ANFO."

Pete cocked his head. "Don't they still use that now?"

"Yeah." Justin nodded. "Ammonium nitrate fuel oil—it's some good shit, a potent combination. The fertilizer oxidizes the fuel. Pretty cheap, and safer than a primary explosive."

Kate stared at him. "How'd you know that?"

Elyse catching him with that text on explosives filled his mind. Her surprised smile...He looked up to see Kate's mouth in a tight line, nothing like a smile.

"You picked that up working at King's warehouse?" Kate asked after a moment.

Justin swallowed.

"ANFO wasn't so safe for King's father," Pete interjected, then turned back to the monitor and read, *"Alexander King died in a mine explosion when Jefferson was only nine. The Federal Mine Safety Commission's report concluded that he'd used faulty fuses."*

"Wait." Kate sat up. "Both of King's parents died when he was young? Who raised him?"

Pete read further. "Huh. Says here he was in foster care."

Kate's lips parted as she looked at Justin. King had never made that known. Why?

"Did you know how King got his start in weapons manufacturing?" Pete's excited voice cut in. "He blew the lid off a corruption scandal between a fertilizer company and the Mine Safety Commission."

"No way." Kate crossed the room to read the webpage over Pete's shoulder.

Pete continued. "He caught the company offering a bribe to the safety commission to overlook substandard ANFO, maybe the same faulty explosives that killed his father." He harrumphed. "Government corruption, what a shocker." He leaned closer to the computer. "Wow, he bugged the company's conference room to uncover the scandal." With a glance around him, he rubbed his sizeable forehead. "Any chance King's bugged this condo?"

Gideon's eyes widened as he stopped petting the cat.

Justin's stomach churned. Or maybe it growled from hunger. He eyed the empty box of cookies on the ottoman. "King's not after Matty—he's after me. Matthew didn't interfere with his little plans."

"I doubt there's a listening device in this condo." Pete shuddered. "Hearing about this creep has made me paranoid. Maybe his mind's too evil for us to get inside of."

"Try this." Justin stood and approached the desk. "Capital C, N, H…" When Pete kept staring at him instead of typing, Justin pointed at the keyboard.

"What is it?" Kate asked.

Justin pointed again. "Just try it."

Pete shrugged but began typing.

"C, N, H," Justin repeated, "two, N, plus sign, two."

The three near the computer gasped when a folder full of files appeared on the screen.

"Oh my God!" Kate shoved Justin's shoulder. "You did it."

Pete wheeled to face him. "What did I just type?"

Justin's heart raced as he turned to see Gideon approach with the cat spilling over his arms. "You said King doesn't love people," he told Gideon. "And you're right. But he does love chemistry, especially explosions." His memory sucked, but damn if he didn't remember that formula from the textbook: C_nH_{2n+2}. He looked at Kate and Pete. "It's the chemical formula for ANFO."

"Brilliant, Just." Kate beamed, then jabbed her finger at a folder. "Combatics. Try that first."

Pete clicked on the folder, and hundreds of video files filled the screen. "Shit. This USB drive must have a lot of memory."

"I needed it for videos of my installations," Gideon said.

"Art installations, sweetie?" Kate touched his shoulder.

A video image snapped Justin's attention to the screen. He froze when he saw her long, brown hair fall across her face as she bent over a device on the worktable.

Kate squeezed his elbow. "Elyse Frederick?"

Justin trembled as he watched himself come into view, rolling a large garbage can.

On the screen, Elyse glanced over her shoulder, then turned back to the device with a grin.

"*Working late again, young lady?*" Justin smirked and sidled up next to her at the table.

She looked up at him. "*I'm hoping this guy I know will walk me to my car.*"

It was hard to get air. This was the night after she'd kissed him for the first time.

She extended her hand. On screen, he peeled off his work gloves and accepted her touch.

He remembered how her skin had felt—so soft in his calloused hand. She'd stared at him like nobody else ever had, like she'd waited all night to see him, like she'd *wanted* him by her side.

He watched himself nudge closer to her. His hand cradled hers, and she stroked the inside of his palm with the lightest of touches.

"Breathe, Justin."

He looked up to find Cody standing behind the group, watching him.

"We got the password!" Gideon said.

"No shit, Sherlock." Cody nodded at Pete as he skimmed a hand through his bedhead. "Play another one."

As the next clip began, King sat in his plush office at the front of the warehouse, frowning at the computer. He straightened when there was a knock. "*Enter!*"

"*Dr. King.*" Elyse blew in. "*Thanks for calling me—I've been worried sick. You saw what they're saying about the bomb triggers on that downed flight? They're ours!*"

"*Dr. Frederick, please.*" King pointed to the chair, but she remained standing. "*I wanted to assure you that those triggers were obviously stolen.*"

She leaned back. "*They were? How would Sharik al-Islam accomplish that? Security's too tight here.*"

"*Speaking of security…*" He again pointed to the chair facing his desk. "*Please, sit. I have something unpleasant to tell you.*"

Elyse seemed to hesitate before complying with his request.

"*We monitor employee computing activity, of course.*" He rustled through some papers on his desk and plucked one from a pile. "*These websites came up on your search history. That's your IP address, correct?*"

After accepting the paper he'd handed to her, she gasped. *"Disgusting."* She leaned forward. *"But this wasn't me! I'm not into child pornography or, or whatever these sites are."*

King studied her for a long moment.

"Jefferson! You know me. You know I'd never get involved in something as abhorrent as this."

He beckoned for the paper, and she gave it back. Then he smiled. *"I do know you, despite you questioning the way I run this company. I had security watch the camera feed from your office—"*

"There's a camera in my office?" She angled away from him.

"We just discussed how important security is in weapons manufacturing. What if the enemy got hold of our drone-defense blueprints?" He gave a self-righteous frown. *"Back to the camera feed—we know who used your computer to access those sites."*

"Who?"

King waited a beat. *"Justin Durante."*

Justin's jaw dropped as he looked wildly around the living room. "I did not!"

"The charges against you didn't include sexual exploitation of children," Kate said.

"That's because King's full of shit!"

Elyse's voice turned their attention back to the video.

"That doesn't sound like Justin."

"It doesn't? Security also showed me countless times of him stalking you."

"What? No, it's not like that—"

"And I have video to prove he was the one on your computer, jacking off to kiddie porn."

She stood. *"Let me see it."*

"What?"

Her arms folded across her chest. *"I want to see the video."*

"Well, I've turned it over to the feds, of course."

Her arms dropped to her sides. *"Why?"*

"How stupid are you?" King got to his feet. *"If Durante's deviant enough to get into child porn, what's to stop him from stealing triggers for terrorists? The feds will nail his ass, then we'll get back to business. And watch who you spend time with in the future."*

Elyse stood motionless. *"Something's off about this whole thing."*

"Durante's the one who's off. Getting off, I mean." He paused. *"How's the drone coming?"*

"Getting there."

"Good. I need it tomorrow morning for the DoD."

"It'll take me all night!"

He nodded. *"Don't let me down."*

"Please keep me informed of the investigation." Elyse turned and left the office.

Silence enveloped Matthew's living room.

"What's the date on that video?" Kate asked.

"October third, last year," Pete answered.

Kate inhaled. "The date of the bombing. Do you know what happened next, Justin?" She searched his eyes. "Did Elyse act differently toward you that night?"

He blinked. "I…don't remember." Could she have believed those awful things about him?

"Here's another file with the same date." Pete pressed play.

King stared at his computer as a smile grew on his face. *"Gotcha."*

"This is a few minutes later, according to the time stamp," Pete said.

Kate leaned in. "What's he watching on his computer?"

Sharp voices came from the video King was watching. Justin couldn't make out what they said until he heard, *"How could you?"* Elyse's voice.

"What the hell are you talking about?" His voice.

That memory of Elyse hating him—it was real. She'd confronted him that night. She'd told him never to talk to her again.

"Shh, King's calling somebody on his cell phone!" Cody said.

Justin's legs felt paralyzed.

"It's working," King said. *"She went straight to him, and now she's telling him to stay the fuck away from her."* He listened for a moment. *"Don't lecture me—your guy's the reason we're in this mess in the first place. What the hell happened with that flight plan?"* He shook his head. *"You're right, not the time to discuss—I have to get rid of this burner first. But we're doing this my way next time. Soft target, US soil. Someone we know and trust."* He nodded. *"Everything set up at his apartment? Good, meet me at the loading dock with his car."*

He ended the call and unzipped a laptop from a case.

"That's the laptop he had at the hotel," Gideon said.

Pete scratched the back of his neck. "He must've transferred the files from his desktop to his laptop, knowing the blast would obliterate everything in his office."

"So he kept these incriminating files while the FBI investigated him?" Kate asked. "Why would he take such a risk?"

When no one spoke up, Pete clicked on another video. "Here's the last one from that date."

The footage showed Justin slumped in a chair in the messy maintenance office of the warehouse. An open bottle of vodka sat within arm's reach.

Kate peered at the screen. "How much did you drink that night? Your BAC was only point oh nine—hardly enough to make you unconscious."

As King and a woman wearing a scarf entered the office, Gideon narrowed his eyes. "King drugged him."

Justin clenched his teeth as his heart hammered in his chest. Why had he been stupid enough to drink from the bottle he'd kept at work? It was like he'd begged King to drug him. He should've gone home and gotten drunk there. But he hadn't wanted to leave Elyse, even though she wanted nothing to do with him.

"Interesting." Kate stroked her chin. "I think they took Justin's blood at the hospital. Maybe we can get it tested."

King and the woman from Gideon's drawing appeared in the frame and stepped to either side of Justin's chair. They dragged him to his feet. They then worked together to push him toward the room's exit.

The woman's voice sounded strained. *"He is so heavy."*

"Why do you think I like the young ones?" Despite struggling to maneuver Justin toward the door, King looked up at the camera and grinned.

"So revolting." Kate stepped back from the computer as the camera feed stopped. "I bet he kept these so he can watch them on repeat. His greatest hits."

Justin looked at Cody, then at Gideon. He bet he wasn't the only one wanting to vomit.

Kate stumbled to the loveseat and sank onto it. She massaged her cheeks, then looked at Pete. "Do we have enough to go to the prosecutor?"

Justin didn't hear his response because Cody grabbed his shoulder.

"Hey." Cody looked down on him. "You're gonna be okay. Come over here and have a seat."

Justin let Cody lead him to the sofa. Gideon sat down next to him. When a weight thumped on his thighs, Justin looked down to see that Gideon had shoveled Slim into his lap. He closed his eyes and stroked her fur as images from the warehouse filled his brain. He'd wanted to drink that entire bottle of vodka that night. The woman he'd loved had thought he was a monster—there was no coming back from that.

Cody told him to open his eyes, breathe, and focus on Slim's soft fur.

The sound of Pete thundering up the stairs interrupted Slim's purrs.

Kate sat on the ottoman and clasped Justin's hand. "Are you with me, Just?" After he managed a nod, she continued, "Okay, here's the plan. Pete's taking a shower while I search King's files, then I'll go shower." She reached for her phone, plugged into the charger. "It's almost six-thirty. We're meeting with the prosecutor at seven-thirty before he goes to court."

"He agreed to meet with you already?" asked Cody.

"Oh no, but he will."

Justin made to get up. "I'll shower after you."

Kate pushed him back onto the sofa. "Uh-uh, you're not going."

"What?"

"Look at you. No way you'll pull off pretending to be Matthew. You haven't slept all night, and it doesn't take a psychologist to see you're in a PTSD meltdown."

He opened his mouth to object, but Kate cut him off.

"All three of you are a mess, actually. And we don't think you're safe here, especially when King gets wind of us coming after him. Pete will book a hotel room for you."

Cody smacked his thigh. "This is nuts! I can't miss more practice. I've got class today, too."

Justin scowled. "You need us at the prosecutor's, Kate. You need Gideon to tell them about the Ramadan threat."

"We'll probably go to the FBI next, but you have to realize that none of this is admissible in court. Gideon stole those files." When

Gideon's shoulders slumped, Kate tapped his knee. "You did good, though. We wouldn't have a shot to free Matthew without you."

"How do we get Matthew out of there if it's all inadmissible?" Justin yelled.

"Calm down." Kate stood. "The rules of evidence work differently when it comes to freeing Matthew versus indicting King. One thing at a time. Our only goal right now is to convince the prosecutor not to move forward with the case."

"Do you think you can do that?" asked Cody.

"I'm sure as hell going to try. Listen, Gideon." She looked up at Cody. "Cody, too. We'll try to keep you guys out of it, but I'm afraid that'll be tough. If the only way to get Matthew out of there is for the DA's office to know about your abuse, do I have your permission to tell them? I need to know where you are on this before I go in there."

"Absolutely." Cody nodded. "I should've come forward a long time ago." His cheeks colored. "Maybe Gideon would've been safe if I had."

Justin closed his eyes.

"Thank you, Cody." Kate turned to Gideon. "What do you think? Can I tell them you drew the woman in the scarf?"

Gideon seemed to stop breathing as he stared at her.

"It may be a way for us to keep you safe," Kate told him. "But no pressure, sweetie. I'm asking a lot here. They'll want to interview you, talk about what happened, dredge up the past."

When Gideon remained silent, Cody offered, "I know it's hard, but it helps to talk about it."

"It does." Justin couldn't believe he'd admitted that.

Gideon's mouth trembled, but his eyes flared. "Whatever it takes to stop him. Cut down the King."

Justin marveled. *He's got balls.*

Pete hollered from the top of the stairs. "Shower's all yours, Kate!"

Justin sprang to his feet. "Make sure he's dressed before you go up there."

Kate tilted her head as she smiled. "Jealous, Durante?"

"Just looking out for my brother."

Her copper eyes shifted from amused to determined. "Let's get our boy back."

19. Truth

*I*t was difficult for Justin to hear the TV over the rumble of Gideon's snores. Cody's rapid breaths only added to the noise.

Justin rubbed his eyes as he tapped the crown of his head against the hotel bed's headboard. He and Cody had woken up a few minutes ago, a little before six p.m. They had arrived at the hotel that morning, inhaled Wendy's cheeseburgers, then agreed to stay awake until Kate returned. That plan hadn't lasted long — Justin had crashed around nine a.m., shortly after his younger companions had succumbed to sleep.

It sickened him that Kate hadn't texted once. *No news is bad news.* Matthew was rotting in the hospital while Justin had slept away the day, oblivious to his brother's pain. He rolled off the mattress, dressed only in his jeans, and looked down at Cody as the swimmer pumped out pushups.

"You're making me feel guilty." Justin frowned.

Between breaths, Cody said, "So join me."

Justin shrugged, then lowered to the thin carpet. It was dark purple with a gold diamond pattern — a real high-end establishment Pete had brought them to. At least a hotel clerk had delivered a cot for Gideon so they didn't have to share a bed.

"Four sets of forty," Cody panted, "with twenty lunges between each set."

Justin's joints felt stiff from his recent sleep coma, but once he got going, the exercise quieted his anxious mind.

As Justin lowered to one knee in a lunge, Gideon's sharp snort almost made him lose balance. "Who knew such a skinny guy could snore so loud?"

Cody's smile seemed sad. "Probably the best sleep he's gotten in years." He dropped to resume pushups.

No doubt it had been Justin's best sleep in a long time.

A few minutes later, beads of sweat had collected at the nape of Justin's neck. Gideon's cry echoed through the room. Justin looked up from his plank to meet Cody's eyes. Together they hopped to their feet and approached Gideon's cot.

"Hey." Justin cupped the boy's shoulder to contain his thrashing limbs.

From the opposite side of the cot, Cody nudged closer. "Gideon?"

"*Houughhh.*" Justin's breath whooshed out when Gideon sent a slashing jab to his solar plexus.

A second later, Gideon shot up from the pillow, blinking madly.

"Who knew such a skinny guy could punch like that," said Cody. "You all right?"

Justin watched Gideon's eyes fill with guilt and ignored the burn below his lungs. "Yeah."

Cody stepped back from the cot. "Nightmares suck, huh?"

Gideon's gaze darted from Cody to Justin as he panted. After a beat, he zoomed off of the cot and jammed his socked feet into his scuffed shoes. He grabbed his sketchbook and was heading for the door when Justin blocked his path.

"Hey, don't go, Gid. I'm okay."

Gideon's chest heaved as he tried to weave around Justin.

Justin seized his arm. "Settle *down.*"

"Get off me!" Wiggling, Gideon tried to escape his hold.

Cody came up behind him. "Please don't leave, Gideon. You were just having a nightmare—it's okay. Justin probably deserved that for waking you up."

Gideon's fists clenched, and his arm vibrated under Justin's hand.

"No big deal." Cody's voice softened. "We get nightmares, too. Right, Just?"

Justin released the boy's arm. "Yeah." He was surprised he hadn't had nightmares last night after watching King's videos.

"But you don't…hit people." Gideon's voice was uneven.

"That's because I sleep alone." Cody dropped on his bed with a scowl. "If I could get a honey to spend the night with me, I'd have to be careful during a nightmare, too."

Justin tried to remember if he was as girl-crazy as Cody at that age. But he hadn't really thought about romance or anything else, other than survival, until he'd met Elyse.

The revelations from last night were still too shocking to sink in. King had killed Elyse and led everyone to believe Justin was responsible? It was too sick to believe.

Gideon sniffed. "I hit Eric once, when we were asleep."

Justin looked at Cody, then back at Gideon. "He didn't like that, huh?"

"He threw me out."

No wonder the kid had bolted for the door. "Well, nobody's kicking you out."

Gideon still clutched his sketchbook and phone.

"Want to take a seat?" Justin gestured to the cot.

"Promise me?" Gideon swallowed. "Promise me you won't put me back there, back in the system."

Justin's thoughts jumbled. Of course they wouldn't let Gideon return to King's funhouse, but what would they do with him? The boy was still a minor.

At the click of the door unlocking, Justin spun around to find Kate standing there.

"Where've you been?" he snapped. "You didn't call all day."

She should've looked exhausted, but her smile made her face shine. "Taking care of business." She lifted her chin. "Accomplishing something you never could." She held the door open as she came into the room.

When Matthew filled the doorway, Justin's jaw went slack. "Motherfucker."

Matthew flew into his arms, and Justin closed his eyes as he clutched him. A lump lodged in his throat as he tightened his hold. Despite his schemes to switch places, he'd never imagined Matthew would survive long enough to make it happen. And now they'd both made it out. His nose burned as he melted into his brother.

Somewhere behind him, Justin heard Cody ask, "He's free? Dr. D's free?"

"The prosecutor's going to drop the charges," a male voice said.

Justin let his brother go and watched Pete enter the room.

"He's not free yet," Kate amended as she closed the door. "But they agreed to release 'Justin' from CHI due to safety concerns." Her nose wrinkled as she set her briefcase next to the TV. "God, it smells in here. You boys are stinky."

Matthew wore an old T-shirt and too-short khakis along with his white hospital slippers. He tilted his head as he watched Justin.

"You're crying?" he asked. He reached out to stroke his face. "It's okay, buddy, I'm here. You did it. You got me out, like you said you would."

As Justin sniffed, Matthew turned to approach Gideon, seeming cautious. "Hey, you must be Gideon. Kate told me you were here." He offered his hand. "I'm Matthew." When Gideon didn't move, Matthew put his hand in his pocket. "Thank you. Thanks for saving my life."

"I…I didn't do that."

"You did," Kate said. She looked around at King's foster sons. "All three of you saved Matthew."

Matthew stepped toward Cody. "I'm sorry." He cleared his throat. "Sorry I had to lie to you."

Cody nodded, seeming dazed.

"How are you feeling?"

Cody smirked. "Such a psychologist question." He chewed his lip. "I'm doing good. But how'd you get out of there?"

"The prosecutor agreed Matty was in danger?" Justin asked.

Kate lowered onto a bed and kicked off her heels. "The assistant DA was tough. He kept asking where the videos came from, and when we wouldn't tell him, he refused to watch. But then Pete played the one where King and Scarf Bitch dragged Justin out of the maintenance office, and he got interested. There's a treasure trove of naughty King behavior on there. We found a folder with recordings from years ago…" She glanced up at Justin, then studied Matthew.

Justin scrutinized her. What was that look in her eyes? Guilt? Sympathy?

Kate swallowed. "Anyway, we convinced the assistant DA to test Justin's blood sample from the night of the bombing."

"I can't believe they tested it in mere hours," said Pete from across the room.

"Never seen the government move that fast," Kate agreed. She stroked her neck as she looked up at Justin. "And yes, there was a sedative in your system."

It wasn't until Justin sucked in a breath that he realized he'd stopped breathing.

"But the DA argued that didn't mean anything—that Justin could've taken the sedative himself—until we got to more videos showing King and Scarfita in the toolshed one night years ago. She was freaking out about Justin seeing her face, but King told her the boy was too drugged to remember anything. So the DA could see this was a pattern with King. But it wasn't until we watched video from ten minutes earlier, that same night, that I knew we had the DA convinced King's a monster."

The pity in her eyes shriveled Justin's heart. "Do you remember what happened that night, Justin?"

He wished he didn't. "King caught me eavesdropping, and he… raped me." He couldn't breathe. "While she watched."

Justin hadn't seen Matthew approach, but in a flash his twin's arm rested across his shoulders. "You didn't tell me that in the car," Matthew said to Kate.

"I don't want to tell you now." She shook her head as her chin trembled. "I'm so sorry, Justin. Sorry I didn't help you."

"Me, too." Matthew squeezed his shoulder. "Sorry I wasn't there for you."

Justin shrugged out of Matthew's hold. "Stop it, both of you!" Their eyes widened at his shout, but he couldn't contain his fury. "You didn't know! You would've done the same thing for me—hell, you *are* doing the same thing for me, but you didn't know, because I never told anyone." He pointed at Cody, then Gideon. "And now they're hurting—their lives are ruined—because of me."

"Because of King," Matthew countered, his voice matching his twin's in volume and intensity. "*King* did this, not you, dickwad."

Justin glared at him, and Matthew glared right back as he continued, "And you not telling anyone about the abuse? It's textbook. Survivors are too ashamed to talk. Do you know how rare it is for survivors of childhood sexual abuse to disclose what happened, especially male survivors?"

"Yeah, well, Cody told you," Justin harrumphed.

"The only reason Cody came forward was your arrest, idiot."

Justin pursed his lips.

Matthew shook his head. "Another reason it was near impossible for you three to come forward? King threatened your life if you did!"

As Matthew's chest rose and fell with each agitated breath, Cody spoke up. "How'd you know that? I never told you he threatened to kill me."

Matthew's shoulders sagged. "Because that's textbook, too. The abuser tries to keep it secret. Cover his tracks."

Kate stood and leaned into Matthew. He tucked her into his side. "Thanks to Gideon, King's tracks are now uncovered. Blown apart, actually. Once we told the DA that another patient had almost raped 'Justin' in CHI—and the DA checked with hospital staff to confirm it—we convinced him to get Justin out of there."

"And that took all day?" asked Justin.

"No." Kate leaned her cheek against Matthew's chest as he stroked her hair. "We agreed they needed to obtain warrants to search King before releasing Justin, or King would be tipped off. So again, the justice system moved more efficiently that I've ever seen—I'm going to remember this when they use stall tactics on my future cases—and got a judge to grant search warrants for King's cameras and computer files at home and work. The feds must've helped. They've wanted the search ever since that plane went down, but King's government connections must've blocked judges from allowing it."

Gideon's small voice asked, "Did they arrest him?"

Kate paused, then grinned. "They're questioning him as we speak."

"And searching for Scarfface," Pete quipped.

Justin flinched as Cody attacked him with a hug. Cody thumped him on the back and said, "The bastard's going down!"

Over Cody's shoulder, Justin watched Matthew shake his head.

"Guess you two bonded as therapist and client." Matthew looked at the ceiling.

Cody let Justin go and bounded over to hug Gideon. When Gideon's eyes widened as he backed to the wall, Cody halted. After a moment, Cody lifted his hand. "High five?"

Gideon seemed to exhale, then slapped Cody's palm in the best celebratory gesture he could manage.

"Justin?"

He turned to Kate to find her studying him and tensed when he noted that her smile had vanished.

"What's wrong?" Matthew asked, tilting his head to see her face.

She let go of her boyfriend and unclasped her briefcase. Without a word, she removed her laptop, sat on the edge of the bed, and powered it up.

As silence spread throughout the room, Justin met Matthew's eyes. He felt his forehead scrunch.

"We found an old video in King's files," Kate told him, "from seventeen years ago."

Justin squinted as he calculated back in time. He and Matthew had been twelve years old then.

"What does it show, Kate?" asked Matthew.

"Here." She thumped the mattress. "Sit and I'll show you both."

Justin looked at Matthew again, and his twin seemed to hesitate along with him. Dread coiled in Justin's belly. But his butt found the mattress next to Kate after Matthew lowered to the bed on the other side of her.

A grainy video started playing, showing King at the Combatics plant, but his office looked different. The walls were yellow instead of taupe, and the wooden desk appeared stuffy compared to the sleek, modern desk King had used before the explosion. Someone knocked on the door, and when a man entered the office, Justin stopped breathing.

Kate must've heard his gasp because she paused the video and clasped his hand. "That's your father, right?"

Justin couldn't speak. The sight of the tall, black-haired man had closed his throat.

Matthew answered, "Yes. Resume play, Kate."

Justin braced himself.

"Who was that woman here last night?" Marco Durante demanded.

King scowled. *"Marco, have a seat."*

"Who was she?" Their father remained standing.

King leaned back in his chair. *"What woman?"*

"Don't play dumb with me, Jefferson. We ran into each other in the parking lot, for chrissake."

"Calm down." King rose from his chair. *"She's a friend from graduate school, that's all. I wanted to show her the plant."*

Their father crossed his arms. One hand held an elbow while the other elevated to rub his chin. *"She's Palestinian."*

King recoiled. *"Why do you say that?"*

Their father dropped his arms. *"Because she wore a PLO scarf!"* When King didn't say anything, he added, *"Her scarf's pattern means she supports the goals of the Palestinian Liberation Organization—namely, violence against Israelis."*

"I know what the PLO is," King spat as he rounded his desk. *"And their only goal is to get their land back, plain and simple."*

A slack jaw was their father's only response.

"So what if she's Palestinian?" King challenged. *"You're sounding racist, Marco. There are countless peaceful Arab-Americans among us."*

"Racist? That's ridiculous. We're bidding for the biggest government contract in history, and you're associating with enemies of the state? I'm only thinking about your company."

"My company is just fine, and we'll win that contract." His smile was smug.

"Not if the NSA sees you with that woman."

King's eyes narrowed. *"Have you told anyone about her?"*

"Of course not."

"Good. This meeting's over." King shooed him out of his office, then leaned against the closed door.

Justin's heart thudded as his father left the screen. "Play it again?"

Kate obliged him, and he touched the screen when his father entered the office. The conversation between his father and King was a blur as his focus zeroed in only on the sharp lines of his father's suspicious face.

"What's the date on this?" asked Matthew after the recording had ended a second time.

A buzzing in Justin's ears prevented him from hearing the date, but he couldn't help but hear his brother's next words.

"My God. That's the day before the house fire."

Justin froze. "What?"

Matthew backed away from the bed. "My God," he repeated. His eyes locked on Justin's. "King set that fire."

"No." Justin got to his feet. "I did. I was doing an experiment."

"What experiment?" Matthew took his wrist and drew him closer.

Justin tried to swallow, but his throat was dry. "Simple distillation."

"For what purpose?" Kate asked.

Matthew answered, "Separating liquids with different boiling points."

"You *were* listening to Dad," Justin said.

"I listened enough to know not to play with volatile chemicals on my own."

"Dad showed me how." Justin's defensive voice sounded twelve again.

"Sorry." Matthew shook his head. "That was uncalled for. So what happened when you attempted distillation?"

Justin clutched his head as he tried to remember. "I put boiling chips in the distillation apparatus, like Dad taught me, to prevent superheating of the liquid."

"But a fire started anyway?"

Justin nodded. "And it spread like crazy…"

"Had that ever happened before?" Kate searched his eyes.

"No." Justin rubbed his tongue against the front of his teeth. "Dad made sure I was safe. The chips were supposed to control the boil."

"But they didn't?" Matthew stroked his chin. "Is it possible King sabotaged the materials for the experiment? Like substituted something for water, or — ?"

Justin inhaled. "Calcium carbide!"

Matthew squinted.

"Remember when Dad showed it to us?"

Matthew shook his head.

"It kind of looks like boiling chips," Justin said. "What if King threw some calcium carbide pieces in with the chips?"

"Holy shit," Matthew breathed.

"What?" Cody had come up next to Kate, and both of them wore confused expressions. "Dumb it down for us, chemistry nerds," he demanded.

"The Bunsen burner heating the water…" Justin's face flamed as anger overtook him. "Add calcium carbide to the mix, and you come up with acetylene real fast." When Cody still stared at him, Justin added. "Fuel. Fuel for a fire."

"The fire that took your parents," Kate added.

Matthew paced the small space. "I can't believe King did that to you. To us. Making you think you killed our parents?" He threw his arms in the air. "So pathological." His pacing halted. "But why do I continue to be shocked by his behavior? Once Cody told me what King did to him…" He shook his head and turned to Justin. "I should've known he'd framed you for murder. Not once, but twice."

"He killed our dad." Justin swallowed. "I want to kill *him*."

"Me, too," Cody said.

Gideon piped in, "Me three."

"You'll have to hold off on that execution," said Kate. "You can't get to King in police custody. And hopefully he'll stay there for some time."

Justin watched Matthew sway on his feet. "Hey." He clasped his twin's shoulders. "You okay?"

Matthew gave his head a quick shake. "Feeling kind of woozy. Shaky. Maybe it's withdrawal from the meds."

Justin guided him to a bed and propped him up against the headboard. Kate curled next to him.

"We need to get some food in him." She took Matthew's hand between hers.

"Let's order pizza," Cody said. "Gideon, help me decide which kind."

Justin tried to process all that had gone down in the past twenty-four hours, but it was too much to take in. He backed into the wall near the door, where Pete still stood, and looked over at his twin.

Matthew pressed kisses into Kate's hair, and Justin exhaled a long breath. It was right for them to be together. He had to make sure he didn't pull any more stupid shit to keep them apart.

Pete held his phone, but he wasn't looking at the screen. Instead he stared at the reunited couple with a slight frown. When Pete noticed Justin's eyes on him, he looked down and tapped on his phone.

Justin kept his voice low so Matthew couldn't hear. "You hoped for a different outcome with Kate."

"No." Pete's mouth tightened. "She's happy with him. I want her to be happy."

"Spoken like a man in love."

Pete breathed out through his nose. Fatigue seemed to deepen the creases around his eyes. He tapped his forehead. "It's my forehead's fault. Too high. Turns off the ladies."

Justin was about to protest when Pete added, "I don't look at it so much as a receding hairline…more like an expanding facial frontier. I'm gaining face."

Justin grinned. He watched Cody and Gideon huddle over one of their phones as they selected pizza toppings, then turned back to Pete. "Thank you for helping us. You didn't have to do that."

"Well, it's not over. King's going to assemble an expert legal team to fight this."

"Mushrooms?" Across the room, Gideon shoved Cody's shoulder. "Gross."

"Mushrooms are fire," Cody replied. "You have no taste, little man."

Justin nodded at Pete. "You're right. King won't go down without a fight."

20. Ticking

*M*atthew eyed the scar Kate had drawn on Justin's forehead and hoped it looked authentic enough. He had to remember not to touch his own forehead, lest he wipe away the makeup hiding his real scar—and have to answer questions about how he'd gotten it. Avoiding anxious behaviors like rubbing his face would be a challenge during this upcoming meeting. Only ten days removed from imprisonment, Matthew had resumed his real identity, but still tensed around law enforcement.

As Kate and Justin joined him, taking their seats at a round table in the assistant DA's office, Matthew noticed Justin chewing on his lip. Maybe he felt nervous around prosecutors, too. Or maybe the presence of Jefferson King—held without bond somewhere below them in the Franklin County Courthouse—rattled his twin. Justin had been hiding out in Pete's apartment since King's arrest.

"Thank you for being here on a Sunday night," said a thin, blond-haired man who looked like he might be Ray Donovan, the assistant DA Kate and Justin had described. "On a holiday weekend, nonetheless."

"*Why* are we here, Ray?" Kate demanded.

Matthew had the same question, but Kate had told him and Justin to shut up and let her do the talking. The prosecutor had yet to drop the charges against Justin, and she worried they would endanger that prospect by saying something stupid.

"We have an update for you about that patient you keep asking about," Ray replied.

Kate tossed her hair over her shoulder. "About time."

"And more questions about King," said the man seated next to Ray.

"SAC Kamil Zahran," Ray supplied as he pointed to the FBI agent.

Agent Zahran shook Kate's hand, then extended his hand toward Justin. "Good to see you again, Mr. Durante." Next, he shook Matthew's hand. "Dr. Durante."

Matthew noted the hardness in the agent's dark eyes and hoped he'd given King hell in his interrogations.

Ray turned to Zahran. "How can you tell the twins apart?"

"Easy." Zahran nodded at Justin. "Justin has a scar on his forehead from the assault at CHI."

Matthew's heart banged a staccato beat, but he kept his face neutral.

"Speaking of assaults," Kate butted in. "What's the status of Daniel Vanderkay?"

Ray smiled. "He's back on the unit at CHI."

Matthew shared a scowl with Justin. Why was the assistant DA smiling at that?

"And that's because Ezekiel Shaddox has begun serving a long sentence at the state pen," Ray continued. "His attorney convinced him to take the plea bargain when we threatened to push an attempted murder charge."

Kate narrowed her eyes. "That man never should've been allowed to stay at CHI once he assaulted Justin."

"You're right."

Her eyes expanded at Ray's instant agreement.

Agent Zahran cleared his throat. "We've combed through the accumulating evidence against King."

Matthew held his breath. According to Kate, the FBI had scoured King's various hard drives and phones, at first coming up short in finding anything incriminating. The camera apps on his phones were scheduled to delete files every twenty-four hours. But the DA's office had managed to hold King on sexual abuse charges after they'd interviewed Justin, Cody, and Gideon.

Even with Gideon's drawing of the woman in the scarf, the FBI couldn't find her, nor confirm any terrorist activity. However, Gideon's mention of King's obsession with Words with Friends had given investigators the break they'd needed.

King's private messages in his game with MinivanMom had revealed a suspicious discussion — a plan for some sort of attack on US soil. A message from King months ago had included a reference to a secret website where he'd hidden videos he liked to re-watch. Investigators had found the website in his phone's search history, then used the same password Justin had discovered to crack into it. There they'd obtained all the evidence they needed to confirm the sexual abuse, as well as terrorism plans. The last Kate had known, the feds were trying to track down MinivanMom using her mobile network signal.

"We also found some immigration documents on King's hidden website," Agent Zahran added.

"Okay?" Kate retracted her chin.

"Immigration involving the Majumdar family," the agent said.

Matthew sat up.

"We believe King was blackmailing Dr. Majumdar," said Ray with a shake of his head.

"How?" huffed Kate. "I *knew* that midget was shady from the get-go."

"Looks like members of Majumdar's family are here illegally." Zahran folded his hands on top of the table next to a manila folder. "King likely threatened to expose them to INS unless the doctor did his bidding."

Kate's eyes tapered. "Like keeping Shaddox at CHI."

Matthew's face felt hot. "Or prescribing meds to mess with Justin's memory."

"Wow." Zahran's eyebrows flew up. "Yes, we suspect both of those as possibilities. However, King's not talking, Majumdar lawyered up, and Dr. Pierre refused to speak to us without her client's permission."

"Is Francine in trouble?" Justin's spine straightened.

"We don't think she's involved."

"She's not," Justin said firmly. "She was good to me. She tried to help me."

Zahran opened a folder and slid a paper toward Justin. "Do you give permission for her to talk to us about your treatment?" When Justin paused, Zahran pushed the paper closer to him. "It's the only way to clear her."

"No, it's not." Kate glared at him, then turned to Justin. "You don't have to sign a release if you don't want to. If Dr. Pierre is innocent, that will come to light." When she arched an eyebrow at Matthew, he recalled her earlier jealousy toward Francine.

Justin signed the release and returned it to Zahran.

"Also…" Zahran looked at Justin. "We located the records from the house fire investigation, but they're inconclusive."

Justin nodded, like he'd expected to hear that. But Matthew knew King had sabotaged his brother's chemical experiment—just like he'd sabotaged the rest of their lives.

"My client has cooperated with state and federal investigations," Kate said. "We've waited long enough—when will you clear him of charges?"

Ⅱ

"Thanks for patrolling this zone with me, Lee," Sebastian told the officer next to him as they looked down at the field. Other than sound techs on the stage, Soldier Field was empty.

"No prob, Smalls."

Sebastian bristled at the nickname. Lee had started calling him Smalls within five minutes of meeting him at the security briefing earlier this evening. His last name was *Smoll*, not Smalls. But when the older, taller officer had found out Sebastian was only twenty-four, and brand new to the job, Lee had ruffled his curly brown hair like he was a schoolchild.

Sebastian patted his pants pocket and heard the rustle of the suicide note inside. His shoulders relaxed.

"I like this side of the stadium better anyway," Lee said. The sixty-four-year-old police officer gestured toward the field as he took a drag on his cigarette. Years of smoking had turned his face sallow, but his short, gray hair lent him a distinguished air. "Closer to the stage."

A glance down at the field revealed a smaller stage jutting out from a walkway connected to the main stage, and it was indeed closer to the west side of the stadium where they now stood.

"I can't believe I'm here." Sebastian bounced on his feet. "They're the best band in the world."

Lee looked down on him. "Settle down, little man. We're here for security, not for music."

"Sorry." Sebastian gave an innocent shrug and tried not to cough as secondhand smoke filled his nostrils.

"Just showing you the ropes on your first concert detail. You picked a good one—sold out, first night of a two-show set."

Sebastian nodded. "And the crowd will be rocking the night before Memorial Day." *The energy will be explosive.*

"Yep." Lee flicked the cigarette butt to the concrete floor and ground it under his shoe. "C'mon, let's head to the lower level, supervise any last-minute concession deliveries."

Sebastian suppressed a smile. He'd already supervised the best delivery of them all, tucked away in a corner of a west-side concessions stand. Though they stood on the club level, he swore he could hear the ticking from the package three floors below.

ADA Ray looked over at Special Agent Zahran with Kate's question about Justin's charges still hanging in the air, but Matthew couldn't decipher his expression.

"Are any of the videos from our USB drive on King's website?" Kate asked.

"Yes." Ray clenched his jaw. "Including the one of an unconscious Justin being dragged out of the office by King and Shaheen."

"Who?" Kate leaned forward.

"Right—haven't gotten to that part yet. Safia Shaheen, aka the woman in the scarf, aka MinivanMom, is in our custody." Ray patted his chest proudly. "We tracked her down through her phone. Her prints match a mystery set we found in Justin's apartment after the bombing."

As Kate's excited gaze met Justin's, Matthew's muscles tingled. Would his brother actually go free?

"But the real kicker?" Ray exhaled through his nose. "We found ketamine in King's medicine cabinet, prescribed to his wife." He looked at Justin. "The same drug found in your system that night."

Justin looked like he had difficulty processing the DA's words. But Kate had no such trouble.

"So you've dropped all charges against Justin Durante."

After a beat, Ray nodded. "We have."

Matthew shot to his feet and yanked his twin up as well. When Justin continued to frown with apparent confusion, Matthew shook him by the shoulders. "You're free, buddy! You're free."

The second Justin's eyes lit up, he engulfed Matthew in a hug.

"Hot damn." Justin's voice shook.

His twin's strong hold nearly crushed Matthew, but he could breathe again when Justin let him go and scooped up Kate from her chair.

"You did it, Kate," he said.

She laughed as she shoved his shoulder. "*You* did it, Durante." Justin ricocheted from her shove and pulled her into a hug.

Matthew studied her flushed cheeks and satisfied smile after Justin released her. He'd never seen a woman so beautiful. His breath caught in his throat when she met his eyes.

"So let's get the hell out of here." Justin turned to leave.

Agent Zahran stood next to the assistant DA. "Hold on."

Justin swiveled back around. "You said I was free."

"You are." Zahran gestured to the table. "But will you stay and help us? Help us take down King?"

"That sicko's already going to hell." Justin gripped the back of the chair he'd occupied. "You said you have everything you need to take him there."

Zahran clenched his teeth. "We still haven't proven his connection to the Yemenia flight crash that killed seven Americans. And we think King's trying to take down more innocents in a bombing he and Shaheen have planned for tomorrow."

"Tomorrow?" Kate paled.

"Memorial Day." Zahran pulled out his chair. "Please, sit, and I'll tell you."

Once they'd resumed their places, the agent said, "It's the middle of Ramadan, and we've picked up chatter encouraging attacks on the West during the holy month—which fits the video we found of King and Shaheen talking in the woods somewhere, plotting an attack for May twenty-eighth…something involving a conspirator who graduated from an academy—probably a police officer."

"Jesus." Kate covered her mouth.

Matthew wanted to hold her hand, but Justin sat between them.

"How'd you pick up audio if they were in the woods?" Justin asked the agent.

"King wore a mic, as far as we can tell. A hidden mic. We showed the recording to Shaheen, and she looked furious, like she hadn't known about the camera. Still, she won't talk."

Zahran sighed. "We've searched King's bank records, but we don't know the location of the attack. In the past six months, he's traveled to DC, New York, Chicago, and San Diego. To the best of our knowledge, he hasn't been out of the country, which would've gotten him in more trouble since we told him not to leave the US while the Yemenia investigation was ongoing." He looked at his phone. "We're hunting down Shaheen's records, but the damn holiday weekend's causing delays."

Kate shook her head. "This is top-secret stuff in the midst of an investigation. Why're you telling us?"

Zahran glanced at Ray, then back at Kate. "Because we want Justin to talk to King."

Kate's mouth dropped open.

"Get King to divulge his secrets," added the agent. "He agreed to meet with Justin without his lawyer present."

When Justin didn't move, Matthew started rubbing his back.

"That's freaking insane," Kate spat. "No. No way."

Zahran shrugged. "We considered having Mr. Keystone or Mr. Hall speak to the suspect."

"No!" Matthew lowered his jaw. Cody had returned to classes and practices at OSU, and he'd resumed therapy with George. Gideon was in a nearby psychiatric residential facility due to repeated self-injury attempts in the days after King's arrest. Matthew was horrified by the idea of subjecting either of them to King, but he felt the same way about sending his brother.

"Look, I wish I didn't need your help," Zahran said. "But I can't get that smug narcissist to cough up his plans. All he says is he hates the US government, and I represent the very thing he hates. But you, Justin, he has a more complicated relationship with you."

A shudder traced Matthew's spine.

"Abuse is about power." Zahran emphasized his words with a karate chop. "King wants to dominate and humiliate you. If he feels like he's in power, he might reveal his secrets to show you how smart he is, how helpless you are to stop him from hurting you and everyone else."

Queasiness rose in Matthew's throat, and he could only imagine how his twin felt. Justin still seemed frozen beneath the circles Matthew rubbed on his back.

The room was silent for a few moments before Justin spoke. "I'll do it."

"What?" Matthew dropped his hand and leaned back in his chair. "No, you won't."

Justin glowered at him as he stood. "All your bullshit about avoidance locking in PTSD—I thought you'd want me to confront my abuser."

"You've just started therapy!" Matthew got to his feet and shook his head. "You're not ready."

"Do you think King's victims tomorrow will care if I'm *ready?* I've already got Cody and Gideon and God knows who else on my conscience, and now you want me to add more to the list?"

Matthew skimmed his hands through his short hair. He missed his ponytail—he wanted to tug on something, hit something. Hit King. God, he wanted to smack that smug smile off the monster's mug.

"Only way I let you do this is if I'm in there with you," Matthew said.

"I don't need your effing protection," Justin fumed. "I'm the older twin."

"Not protection, backup. Another set of ears. As a psychologist, I'll try to disarm him, put him at ease."

Kate's eyes blazed as she stood. "Attorneys are way better than psychologists at interrogations. I should be there, too."

"No," Matthew and Justin said at the same time.

"King hates you," Matthew told her. "You'll piss him off, and he won't talk."

She glared at him.

Matthew lowered his voice. "Kate, you're the only one of us who stood up to him. And I love you for it. But he won't let his guard down if you're there."

When her lips pursed, Matthew knew she was searching for another argument.

Agent Zahran stood. "It's settled, then. The Durante twins will talk to the suspect. Ray, will you call down there and get him ready?"

The assistant DA crossed over to his desk and picked up the phone.

"Let's go." Zahran pointed at the door. "I'll brief you on the way."

Kate's eyes burned as she watched them leave. On a whim, Matthew reached for her and pulled her in for a kiss.

She whispered, "You're an asshole."

He smiled against her lips. "Love you, too."

Sebastian delighted in the irony of the band's opening song: "Sunday, Bloody Sunday." But he squinted as the next song began — those lyrics weren't in the original version of "Bad," were they?

"All come to look for America," the lead singer crooned, and he didn't have to repeat the line because the sold-out crowd did it for him. The energy was electric, lighting Sebastian up inside. Lighting his way to the big finale of the evening.

Thank God he didn't have to wait until tomorrow, like they'd originally planned. The beautiful lady told him something had gone wrong with his father, so they needed to bump up the attack. Then she'd gone radio silent. But he didn't need her or his father — he was ready. For years they'd prepared him well for Sunday, bloody Sunday.

Lee kept his eyes trained on the crowd as he cocked his head toward Sebastian and shouted, "Where you from, Smalls?"

"Columbus, Ohio," Sebastian yelled back as the cheers amplified at the end of the song.

"Thank you for supporting us all these years," said the lead singer. "America's been good to us!"

Sebastian's face flushed as he palmed the butt of his weapon in its holster. The singer had just told a big, fat lie, intended only to sell

CDs and concert tickets. America had *not* been good to anyone — especially not Sebastian or those he loved. But tonight, America would learn. Tonight, the evil would be punished.

Ⅱ

Why did I agree to this meeting?

Just as Justin's racing heart told him to get the hell out of the interrogation room, the door opened and a uniformed man led in a shackled King, clad in an orange jumpsuit. The overhead lights gleamed on his bald head.

What had his pulse climbed to now — one ninety? Justin was grateful that Matthew had insisted on being here with him, and that Zahran was allowing Kate to observe the meeting through the one-way mirror on a side wall.

"Establish rapport with him," Zahran had told them as they'd walked down the stairs to the holding cells. *"Don't challenge him. Let him feel in control."*

But as Justin felt those cool eyes slide down his body like two ice cubes dripping over his skin, the agent's advice melted away.

"You killed our mom and dad," he blurted after the guard had left the room.

King's eyebrows elevated as a soft smile overtook his thin lips. "You think you're a clever boy, don't you, Justin? But everyone knows *you* set that fire."

Justin was about to respond when Matthew spoke.

"How are you, Dr. King?"

The accused appraised Matthew with a look of disinterest. "How nice of you to ask, Matthew. I am well. And you? I see you've cut your hair."

Justin felt Matthew tense. Like him, he'd probably been unaware King had kept tabs on them as adults.

But Matthew's voice was smooth. "I'm relieved they've dropped all charges against my brother."

A slight tightening of King's eyes let Justin know the news was a surprise. "So that's why you've come to see me." He shot daggers at Justin. "To gloat."

"No." Matthew shook his head. "There is no winner here."

Justin pictured Gideon curled up on some psychiatric hospital bed. *Truer words have never been spoken.* He had to calm his shit down to fight for Gideon, Cody, Elyse, and all the miserable fucks about to be blasted by King's bombs.

Justin let out a long breath and nudged his foot against Matthew's. Matthew leaned into his leg, and he felt bolstered by his support.

Justin met King's eyes. "They know about your sexual abuse now. No more pretending to be humanitarian of the year."

"They know nothing about me." King's words were crisp. He turned to Matthew. "And how did you feel when you heard about me and Justin, Mr. Psychologist?"

"There is no *you and me*, you demented fu—"

"It's a fair question, Just," Matthew interrupted.

Justin felt his fingers furl into his palm. *Just give me one punch.* But Zahran had warned them not to touch the prick, or King's lawyers would use it against them.

"I felt…" Matthew waited until King looked at him. "Devastated. My life, and especially my brother's life, will never be the same because of your choices."

King stared like he was trying to discern Matthew's angle. Justin attempted to do the same. Why let this cretin know how much he'd hurt them?

"You're obviously a genius, Dr. King." Matthew sat back in his chair.

And now he was complimenting the beast?

"So why'd you keep those incriminating videos around?" Matthew peered at him. "That demeans your intelligence."

The chains jingled as King shifted in his chair.

When he didn't respond, Justin smirked. "Kate thinks he kept the videos to watch over and over. To get off. 'His greatest hits,' she called them."

King's jaw muscle rippled.

"I bet he's hard right now, sitting across from me." Justin leaned forward. "But you can't have me now, can you?" He locked his gaze on those cold eyes. "Or maybe you don't want me anymore. You only like the young ones."

"Fuck you," King jeered.

"You wish. Just how many boys have you raped?"

King chuckled.

"You think this is *funny?*" Justin railed.

Justin felt Matthew's hand on his knee and almost yelped at the fingers digging into his flesh.

He turned to look at Matthew, who wore a shut-the-hell-up glare. Tamping down his rage, he forced himself to exhale.

Matthew's voice was conciliatory. "Dr. King can't help his sexual preferences."

Justin's eyes widened.

"Not after he himself was raped in foster care," Matthew added.

King stilled.

Justin and Kate had told Matthew about King's stint in foster care, which had surprised him, too. None of them had read up on King's history after they'd left his home.

"That's why you never told us you were in foster care, too, right?" Matthew tilted his head. "Avoidance of traumatic memories, a classic response. You never wanted to think about foster care again, but then you found yourself fostering twins—messed-up boys who were grieving their parents, who rejected your attempts to care for them. You tried to block the memories, yet there you were with foster kids, the *parent* this time, and it all came flooding back."

King couldn't take his eyes off of Matthew, and Justin couldn't look away from King. The man didn't move.

"In the midst of your loveless marriage, overwhelmed by hate for the government that had ripped your father from you, you didn't know what else to do but turn to someone weaker than you for comfort," Matthew continued. "Someone who was already destroyed by thinking he'd killed his parents. You turned to him for reassurance that you were still in control, still in power. Your foster father stole almost everything from you, but you exacted revenge. You got back at the man who'd hurt you by hurting someone else. By abusing Justin, *you* became the powerful one."

Shadows darkened King's eyes. "You don't know me," he repeated, though he sounded less certain this time.

Justin's foggy mind tried to catch up with his brother's case study on the perpetrator across from them. King had been sexually abused as well? How did Matthew know?

"It wasn't my foster father," King said after a long silence. For once, he didn't look at them as he spoke.

"Oh." Matthew tapped his fingers on his thigh. "Foster brother, then. He's the one who raped you, owned you. Snatched your childhood away in one fell swoop."

King continued to look at the floor at the side of his chair.

Bingo, thought Justin. *He doesn't deny it.*

"Your foster brother taught you well, didn't he?" Matthew leaned in. "He threatened to hurt the other foster kids if you didn't keep quiet."

King's head snapped up. "You. Don't. Fucking. Know. Me."

Justin trembled, his lungs shaking with each labored breath.

"I don't?" Matthew blinked. "Correct my understanding, then. Tell me how I'm wrong."

"You're one-hundred-percent wrong!" King roared. "The past is in the past—it doesn't matter, doesn't affect me now. *I'm* in charge of my destiny. I'm always in control."

Acid swirled in Justin's stomach. Disgusted by his fear of this pathetic man, he shook his head. He eyed the county-issued jumpsuit and shackles encircling his waist—King didn't even wear his own clothing.

"You don't look so in control now," Justin noted.

King's stare immobilized him immediately. "You think you're so righteous? You haven't heard a word your brother said. He claims that what happened to me as a child made me do what I did. Don't you get it? The exact same thing will happen to you. You won't be able to stop yourself from diddling little boys."

Justin inhaled. Was he right? Did that same evil live within him?

"Wrong, Dr. King." Matthew eyed him with contempt. "Justin's different from you. Maybe you both were violated, but you forget an essential element: free will. Justin chooses to protect, not assault. He would never hurt anyone. Not everyone who's abused repeats the pattern."

"Keep telling yourself that. Won't be long before you're back in jail for another fuck-up, Justin. You and I, we're not different at all. Fire took my father, too."

Justin felt bile in his throat—the familiar surge of badness through his bloodstream. King was right. They'd both lost their fathers at a young age, and both had been abused as a result.

Matthew's hand returned to Justin's knee, and Justin looked at his brother. Matthew's eyes softened as he nodded at him.

Justin closed his eyes as Matthew's letter came to him: *You mean so much to me, Justin. I hope you know how much I love you. I'm so blessed you're my brother. You're not a bad, dirty person just because a bad man tried to ruin you.*

Justin opened his eyes and met his abuser's stare. "Do you know the difference between you and me?"

"A hundred IQ points?" King sneered.

Justin ignored that. "You didn't have a brother. A twin. You didn't have someone to love you, to sacrifice for you."

King breathed out through his nose. "You've got that mixed up. You're the one who gave yourself up for your brother. Your love made it so easy to manipulate you."

"And I would do it again," Justin said. "But you're wrong. You have no idea the sacrifices my brother made for me."

"Just…" Matthew warned.

"How'd the feds get those warrants?" King changed the subject abruptly.

"You'd like to know, wouldn't you," Matthew replied.

"So you were involved?" Wrinkles rutted the skin around King's ice-blue eyes. "It's your fault I'm here?"

Matthew scoffed. "No one's to blame but you. But yes, we know how the feds obtained the warrants. And we'll tell you if…"

King nudged closer to the table.

"If you give us a hint about the attack tomorrow."

"Fat chance."

"Your choice." Matthew shrugged. After a long silence, he asked, "What was your father like, Dr. King?"

King studied Matthew.

"He taught you about explosives, right? He was a smart man."

"Much smarter than Marco Durante," King said.

Just one punch. Justin clutched his hands together.

"Your father took good care of you after your mother died," Matthew said. "He was all you had in the world."

King said nothing.

"It shattered you when he died." Matthew paused. "And tomorrow some boy's going to lose his father in whatever attack you have planned."

A smile tugged the corner of King's mouth.

"You hate the government, but you won't hurt the government if you kill civilians," Matthew said.

"The government's supposed to keep people safe." King's nostrils flared. "However, they always fail. Their incompetence and corruption are staggering."

Matthew nodded. "They failed to keep your father safe. Even worse, they covered up their exploitation. But how will ripping another boy's father from him, sending him into foster care, help teach the government a lesson?"

King sat motionless, and Justin wanted to shake him. He wanted to shake the bombing plans out of his shriveled, rotted brain.

"We already know your plans," Justin said. "Tomorrow, you bomb a soft target in the US. You plan to attack soldiers—"

King's flinch stopped him. "What'd you say?"

"Soldiers are your target."

King's head tilted. "Where'd you hear that?"

Intrigued by King's response, Justin wanted to hear more, but he refused to bring Gideon into it. "That's what the FBI told us."

Icy eyes roamed over his face, making Justin want to run from the room.

"Safia Shaheen will tell us more," said Matthew, diverting King's gaze. "You know the FBI has her here, right?"

A slow smile spread. "You two." King shook his head. "So cute, your naiveté—it's like you're still the twelve-year-old scamps I took into my home. You think I'd tell you *anything* to endanger my intricate plans? You think you can outsmart a woman ten times cleverer than you? Safia and I will die before revealing one word."

The doorknob jangled, and Justin swiveled around to find Agent Zahran beckoning him and Matthew. Before Justin got to his feet, he met King's eyes. "Have a nice life in prison."

"You'll join me here soon," King replied, "after you molest little boys."

Justin exploded from his chair, but Matthew grabbed him and pushed him out the door before he could lunge at King.

Once Justin entered the observation room, he looked through the one-way mirror at King still seated at the table. His hands itched with the desire to backhand the bastard. "Sorry we didn't get anything. But if you let me beat the crap out of him—"

"What're you talking about?" Zahran seized Justin's shoulder with one hand and held up his cell phone with the other. "We're onto King's plans because of you two."

A female voice came through the speaker of Zahran's phone. *"Okay, we're getting Officer West's duty assignment for tomorrow—hold on."*

"What's happening?" asked Matthew, looking from Zahran to Ray Donovan, who sat typing on a laptop in the small room. Kate hovered over the prosecutor, staring at the laptop screen. "Who's Officer West?"

"King's older foster brother, Lee West." Zahran's eyes darkened. "Once King told you that tidbit from his past, we got on the horn with West Virginia Children's Services. West is now a cop in Chicago."

Justin looked at Matthew as he asked, "How do you know he's involved?"

Kate looked up from Ray's laptop. "Shaheen's credit card records came through when you were talking to King. The only place she's traveled to in the past year is Chicago. Three times."

The hairs on the back of Justin's neck stiffened.

"Sir?" said the agent from Zahran's phone. *"The commander from the Near South Side district got back to us. Officer West is assigned to patrol a music concert tomorrow. Uh...yeah, same concert tonight as well."*

Zahran frowned at the phone. "What concert?"

"U2, sir."

"Me, too?"

"The Irish band, sir."

Zahran blew out a breath. "Where?"

"Soldier Field, sir."

Justin froze. Matthew's eyes widened as they met Justin's, and both turned to the mirror, which showed King staring straight at them. But he couldn't see them, right?

"Soldier Field," Matthew mused. "You think that's what Gideon overheard?"

Justin swallowed—it was hard to think.

Kate approached Zahran, who shuffled through some papers on a table. "So King blackmails West, threatening to reveal that West sexually abused him if he doesn't set off a bomb?"

Zahran scowled. "But Shaheen said something about the bomber just graduating from the academy—West has been working the beat for years."

"However it goes down, it's happening tomorrow," Ray said.

Kate stiffened. "Maybe they changed the timeline once King got arrested. Maybe the attack happens tonight."

Justin kept staring at King. "Unless we stop it."

"Get me in touch with the SAC in Chicago," Zahran barked into his phone.

Ⅱ

Humming along to "It's a Beautiful Day," Sebastian handed Lee a cup of coffee.

"Thanks, kid." Lee opened the plastic lid, blew on the black brew, then took a sip as he watched the frenetic crowd. "You don't want one?"

The jackhammer of his heart told him the last thing he needed was caffeine. "It's their encore set—the show will be over soon."

"With this size crowd?" Lee grunted. "We won't get out of here for hours."

Or not at all. "Time to head up to our sniper station?"

"Just about, yeah." Lee yawned. "Getting too old for this shit."

Sebastian's heartbeat slowed as he watched the idiot down another gulp of coffee.

They turned to head for the stairs, but right after Lee unlocked the door leading to the stairwell, two men in shiny navy jackets rushed up to them. Sebastian's chest seized as they flashed FBI badges.

"Lee West?" asked a gray-haired agent who appeared to be in charge.

"Yeah, who wants to know?"

"You need to come with us, sir."

Lee leaned back against the door he'd unlocked, swaying a bit, like he needed the support to stay on his feet. "What's the deal?" He

255

shook his head as if to clear it. "We need to get up to our station or my boss will have my ass."

The other agent looked at Sebastian. "Let's see some ID, Officer."

A flame of fear lit up his spine. "Dude, we're just trying to do our job. We'll talk to you after the concert—we have to protect the exits."

"Yeah, don't give the kid a hard time," Lee added. "He just graduated from the academy."

The gray-haired agent recoiled, then his eyes narrowed. "ID, now."

Fuck.

The agent reached out to grab him just as Sebastian shoved Lee away from the door and pulled it shut with a clang. What the crap would he do now? The metal doorframe rattled as the agents tried to open the locked door. Sebastian spun around and leaped up the stairs, two at a time, his heart in his throat.

Fuck, fuck, fuck. Should he call the beautiful lady? No, she hadn't responded since yesterday. It was on him now. With shaking hands, he unlocked the door leading to the small room at the top of the stairs. *Shit!* He was supposed to be wearing gloves. He shook his head; it didn't matter. After he closed and locked the door, he knelt to extract two semiautomatic rifles and rounds of ammunition from their hiding place, setting them next to the department-issued rifle already lying by the small window.

He gasped as the door behind him rattled. They'd already made it up the stairs! But he knew just how to sidetrack them. With the concertgoers still in their seats, the blast wouldn't kill as many as they'd planned, but he had no choice. He'd pick them off one by one as they ran from the stadium in terror.

He grabbed his phone and was just typing in the code to detonate the bomb when a blast sounded in the room. Had his bomb exploded? Then a searing pain engulfed his back, and he realized he'd been shot. The bullet flattened him on his belly, sending his phone skidding into the wall. A weight pressed on his back, and he cried out as he felt his arms wrenched behind him. He twisted around to see which agent was on him.

"Get his phone!" Gray Hair ordered, and the other agent shoved a rifle aside to pick it up. Gold letters spelled out FBI on the back of his jacket.

The agent peered at the screen. "Looks like he's trying to set off a device remotely, sir."

"Where's the bomb?" Gray Hair pressed harder on his back as he frisked him, suffocating him.

Sebastian stayed silent, thinking of his foster father and all the evil wrought by the US government as he strained for air. He moaned when the guy pressed his knee into his wound.

"Don't think the bomb has armed, sir." The agent looked at his boss. "Should we evacuate the stadium?"

"Not yet. Get me Erickson and EMS on the phone."

Sebastian closed his eyes, overcome with failure. But he stopped breathing when the agent searched his pockets and whipped out the note.

"What the hell," Gray Hair growled after a moment of silence. "He wrote some sort of suicide note taking credit for the bomb, including the obligatory *Allahu Akbar*." He yanked Sebastian's cuffed wrists. "We stopped you this time, didn't we, scumbag?" He became quiet again. "The fuck? This note's signed by Lee West."

Sebastian felt wetness slide down his back and realized it was blood. Maybe he'd bleed out before EMTs arrived. *Sorry, Father.*

Gray Hair pushed off of him and rolled him on his side. "How's Officer West involved?"

"Sir?" The agent thrust his phone toward Gray Hair.

As Gray Hair made a report to his superior, the other agent kicked Sebastian in the kidney.

Sebastian groaned, and the agent leaned down to get in his face. "How dare you pretend to be someone who protects and serves, shit-brain? You and your co-conspirators will get the death sentence for this."

Pain obscured Sebastian's vision, but he could still see the hate in the agent's eyes.

21. Even

Matthew looked out the window at the sunlight dappling the lush greenery behind the office building. "Hot out there."

"July in Ohio," George replied. "A veritable sauna. Think how much warmer you'd be if you still had that long hair."

Matthew grinned. "You never liked my ponytail, did you?"

George's mouth twitched.

"Kate 'fessed up that she never liked it, either."

"Well, it's good to keep her happy, then." George's probing gaze met his. "And you don't have to hide behind all that hair anymore."

His psychologist was right. He didn't encounter the same recoil when people heard his last name now that Justin had been exonerated and the national media had splashed King's crimes across their outlets.

Matthew tapped his fingers on his thigh. "I've been thinking about fatherhood lately."

"Makes sense."

George's warmth enveloped him. Matthew had thought it would be difficult to be on the other side of the couch, but almost two months of therapy with George had allayed his fears. He felt free to explore any thought or feeling with the wise man across from him. Matthew hoped Justin, Cody, and Gideon had experienced the same benefit from their therapy, though he suspected it was a rougher ride for them.

"How's it going with Gideon?" asked George.

"Tough." Matthew sighed as he thought about his latest battle with the boy. "He doesn't like to take his meds."

"Sounds like a typical teenager."

Matthew frowned. "Except this one spent over a month in residential treatment."

"He knows you and Kate are trying, and that means a lot to him." George smirked. "Even when he is being a little shit."

As Gideon's foster parents, Matthew and Kate held the privilege of knowing what Gideon had shared with George in therapy. Matthew was grateful for the insider information — sometimes George's encouragement was the only thing getting him through the trials of parenting.

"We're just worried the state won't let us adopt him."

"Give it some time," George advised. "Adoptions take a while, and you all are still reeling from everything that happened."

The ticking of the clock echoed through the office. Matthew studied his hands as they curled with tension. "What if Gideon turns out like Sebastian?"

"C'mon, Matthew. You know you're nothing like King."

Matthew kept staring at his lap.

George shifted in his chair. "Sebastian was tortured by King and that woman — brainwashed and radicalized even beyond King's usual abuse. And King kept up his pattern with a foster son between Cody and Gideon, just as we suspected."

"Of course he did. I should've known." Matthew felt his eyebrows furrow. "Of course there were other boys King abused."

"How would you have known?" When Matthew didn't respond, George went on, "You didn't even know your twin had been abused. Justin buried that secret in a vault. How were you supposed to know others had been hurt?"

Matthew pressed his lips together.

"When you did discover the truth, you risked your life so your brother could live his. Don't you dare tell me you should've done more."

As his eyes closed, Matthew let out a breath. *"I should've done more*—that's a negative belief from trauma, isn't it?"

"Exactly." George sat back in his chair. "Blaming yourself for something outside of your control. King's the responsible one here. King's the one going to prison for life."

"Sebastian, too," Matthew added in a soft voice.

George's eyes creased. "Maybe. I hear they're going for not guilty by reason of insanity."

"Kate said NGRI rarely works." Matthew's throat constricted. "But you'd *have* to be insane to execute the attack they'd planned. Have you ever been to a concert at Soldier Field?"

George shook his head.

"I have, when Kate was in law school at Northwestern. It took us a good thirty minutes to get out of there. So many people—we were inching forward, shoulder to shoulder. Imagine if a sniper was up there, picking us off one by one." Matthew shuddered. "Especially if a bomb had just taken out a chunk of the stadium...we'd be even more panicked and disoriented. If we survived the blast, that is."

George exhaled. "Sickening. I can't believe you all stopped it."

"I can't believe Sebastian's locked up in a psychiatric facility just like I was."

George's office phone rang, but he didn't answer it.

"What was it like in there?" asked George.

The scratch of his white jumpsuit on his neck, the smell of sour milk, the gnarled teeth of Shaddox's smile—only flashes of those days remained with him now. He hoped King and Shaddox would share a prison cell, but King was likely headed to federal prison in Colorado.

"I had trouble keeping in touch with reality in there," he said. "Almost like I *was* crazy."

"Sounds like the Zimbardo prison study."

Matthew nodded. Just like the college students who'd pretended to be prisoners for an experiment, he'd adopted a helplessness that made it easy for the guards to control him. He was relieved that Francine Pierre had quit that place once the feds had exposed Majumdar's corruption. He knew she'd tried her best to keep Justin alive.

"Justin's not suicidal anymore, right?"

George cocked an eyebrow. "We've discussed this, Matthew."

"I know, I know. You can't tell me." He suppressed a sigh.

"There are confidentiality limitations, of course," said George. "But more importantly, I want you to start thinking about yourself. Take care of your own needs, and let Justin take care of his. He's quite adept at figuring things out."

"Have you met my twin?"

George smiled. "Justin's an adult. He's studying chemistry in college."

Matthew nodded. His brother's recent enrollment at Columbus State Community College was rather impressive.

"He needs to take his own road." George eyed him. "And you need to let him forge that path. Let him rebuild trust with you."

"Broken trust." Matthew frowned. "Another legacy of trauma."

"And of secrets. But you're not keeping secrets anymore from your family, or your clients."

"You really think I'm ready to get back to work?"

"I do." George eyed him. "What do you think?"

Matthew scratched his neck. While he and George had agreed that it would do more harm than good to notify his clients about Justin playing therapist, he'd still needed some therapy of his own before resuming his practice. He couldn't have anticipated that Justin would pull such a stupid stunt, but Matthew's actions had placed his clients' welfare at risk all the same.

"I think I'm ready, yeah."

"It'd do you some good to contribute to society again," George said.

"And Kate wants me out of her hair."

George smiled.

Matthew started on the sofa. "Crap, what time is it?" He looked at the clock and shot to his feet. "I need to pick up the rental car."

George rose. "To drive to the meet in Indianapolis? Why do you need a rental car?"

"Because mine's a little cramped for five adults. Well, four adults and a snarling teen."

A smile crinkled George's eyes. "Good luck to Cody."

"Thanks." Matthew hesitated, then shook George's hand. "Thank you." Two words were hardly sufficient to convey his feelings about all George had done for them, but he hoped the psychologist knew what he meant.

"See you next week, Dr. Durante."

Later that evening, after a trip to central Indiana, the lights of the natatorium sparkled in Kate's engagement ring. Sitting on her left in the stands, Matthew took her hand in his as he watched Cody rocket off of the block during warm-ups. He flinched as a sharp edge dug into his palm. "Ouch, your diamond hurt my hand."

Kate quirked one side of her mouth. "Proud of yourself for buying that rock, Durante?"

Relieved, actually. He'd dumped his savings into prepaying his mortgage for a year, but Kate's legal acumen had helped secure a hefty restitution payment from King's estate. With the money, Matthew had purchased a ring, Justin had paid college tuition, and Cody had trained over the summer without needing to find a job. Matthew and Kate planned to re-enroll Gideon in private school next month to pursue his artistic talent.

"Oh, he's proud," Justin said from the other side of Matthew. "Wouldn't shut up about the goddamn ring."

Kate let go of Matthew's hand to reach across him and shove Justin. "Thanks for helping him pick it out." She ogled the glittering stone. "Not that I need major bling to make up for years of stall tactics or anything."

Matthew rolled his eyes.

"So, Justin." Kate tucked her hair behind her ear. "You gonna buy Francine a ring like that?"

"Kate!" Matthew glared at her. "Don't egg him on. It'd be unethical for them to date—she was his damn therapist."

Cody's girlfriend, Hannah, peered around Kate at Matthew. "What're you guys talking about?" Her long, wavy blond hair cascaded over one shoulder, which featured a skull tattoo.

"Matty's jealous of me and a hot blonde," Justin informed her.

"Watch it, Durante," Kate hissed.

"Seriously, Just." Matthew pointed his finger at his twin. "Dr. Pierre can't be with you. It wouldn't be ethical."

After a moment, Justin licked his bottom lip. "We agreed no more secrets between us, right?"

"Oh, God." Matthew groaned. "You already slept with her."

"*Oui.*" Justin grinned. "She's teaching me French."

Kate chuckled.

"Why is this crap show amusing to you?" Matthew huffed.

Kate's smile vanished. "Get off your moral high ground, Mister Switcher."

Matthew glanced at Hannah, but she appeared enthralled by Cody toweling off his muscular shoulders on the deck below.

"This whole situation has been perverse from the start," Kate continued. "Normal ethics don't apply. If two consenting adults want to get it on, I say go for it. Life's too short."

Matthew looked at Justin, who stared back at him. George's advice swam in his mind: *"Justin's an adult—focus on yourself."*

"Welcome to US Swimming Senior Nationals," the announcer boomed, "at the IUPUI Natatorium."

As they rose for the national anthem, Matthew checked on Gideon, but the seat on the other side of Justin was empty. "Where's Gideon?"

Kate frowned. "Hmm…"

After the anthem finished, Matthew sent him a text, but there was no response.

"He's not answering me, either." Kate rubbed her lip. "Think he's run off?"

Matthew pressed down on the top of his head. "Won't look good to the adoption counselor if we lose him, in another city no less."

"Want me to look for him?" Justin offered.

When Kate got to her feet, Matthew also stood.

"No, stay with Hannah," she told Justin. She gave Matthew a fake smile as she dipped her fist down in front of her, ending with an enthusiastic punch near her chin. "C'mon, Dad, let's find our wayward son."

"You two as parents…" Justin chuckled. "That's fucked up."

Kate slugged him as they weaved toward the end of the row.

The concrete hallways behind the slanted stands were barren because the meet was starting, and whistles and shouts from the crowd pierced the air.

"We won't miss Cody's event, will we?" Kate's gaze roamed the crowd.

Matthew shook his head. "I think it's later in the meet."

They dashed from the hallway into each seating section, searched for Gideon, then moved on when they couldn't find him. They were about to cross the lobby to the other side of the stands when Matthew saw a shock of turquoise hair at the end of a row of seats. As Gideon's hair bleach had begun to fade, Kate had suggested he return to his original color. Instead, Gideon had turned to The Smurfs for inspiration.

The crowd noise swelled as Matthew hustled down the stairs to Gideon's row, with Kate on his heels. Gideon sat next to another skinny teenage boy and jumped when he saw his foster parents.

Matthew waited for the cheering to die down after the race finished. "You okay, Gid?"

"Why aren't you answering texts?" Kate demanded.

A middle-age woman leaned across the boy next to Gideon and smiled up at them. "I hate when Joey doesn't text me back."

The boy between her and Gideon scowled. "That's because you blow up my phone with texts. Unnecessary texts."

Matthew shared a look of exasperation with the boy's mother, then nodded at Gideon. "C'mon, let's go back to our seats before Cody swims."

"Can't I stay with Joey?"

The way Gideon leaned into the boy gave Matthew sudden insight into their relationship. "Oh, uh…"

"Do you have another son in the meet?" the woman asked. "Joey's sister is swimming the hundred fly."

"Ahh…" How could Matthew explain his relationship to Cody?

"Yes," Kate supplied. "Cody Keystone in the one-hundred freestyle."

The woman scanned a stapled set of papers in her hand. "Why, Gideon, you didn't tell us about your brother. He's one of the best swimmers in the meet!"

He is? Matthew tugged his ear.

Joey's mother held up the papers. "Says right here in the heat sheet—Cody Keystone's seeded second in the hundred free."

Matthew had no idea what that meant.

"And now the finalists of the men's hundred-meter freestyle!" called the announcer.

Rock music blasted as Cody and a group of seven swimmers filed onto the deck from the ready room. Cody wore massive headphones over his swim cap, along with a fierce glare.

Kate latched onto Matthew's bicep. "We better get back—Justin will worry if we're not there for Cody's event."

"I'll be okay," Gideon promised.

Joey's mother smiled. "We'll take care of him."

Matthew hesitated before he followed Kate back up the stairs.

"I guess the return of his libido is a sign of healing." Matthew rubbed the back of his neck as he trailed his fiancée. "But I don't know about this."

"Listen, you and I don't have a clue what's normal, but that little interaction back there?" Kate looked at him as they resumed their seats. "It felt kind of, well, *normal*. Maybe Gideon will be fine."

"Is he okay?" asked Justin.

Kate nodded.

The announcer said, "Lane five, Cody Keystone from Ohio State Swim Club."

Justin's shout nearly shattered Matthew's eardrums, and he added a hoot to his vigorous clapping.

"He has to finish in the top two to make the national travel team," Justin said as he elbowed Matthew.

"How'd you know that?"

Justin shrugged. "He told me."

Probably in a fake counseling session. Matthew gritted his teeth.

"Top six, actually," Hannah corrected. "They take more swimmers in the hundred free for the relay. But he has to be first or second to make the individual event."

Matthew studied her. "I thought you were a lacrosse player, Hannah."

"The best sport ever. I teach Cody about lacrosse, and he teaches me about swimming."

Matthew needed Cody to teach him more about this strange sport as well. He wanted this bad for Cody—he knew how hard he'd trained for nationals. As he watched the boy stretch and bounce behind the blocks, he felt amused. "I wonder what Joey's mom will think when she sees the size difference between the 'brothers.'"

"And she didn't even bat an eye when she thought we were Gideon's parents!" Kate grouched. "No way we look old enough to pull that off."

"Not a day over twenty-nine, my little firecracker."

"That's no compliment — that's my real age —"

His kiss right below her ear stopped her short. He let his breath warm her skin as he hovered his lips over her jaw. Her eyes closed, and a sound close to a purr rumbled from her throat. Her facial g-spot undid her every time.

"Swimmers, take your mark…"

Matthew looked up just in time to see Cody launch himself from the block. The spectators in the row in front of him stood, so Matthew jumped out of his seat and tugged Kate up with him. In one of the middle lanes, Cody's powerful strokes churned him forward, an emulsion of strength, technique, and whitewater. He flip-turned and sprinted back toward the finish.

"Holy crap, he's in the lead!" Justin hopped and hollered.

Matthew had trouble breathing as Cody barreled for the finish. The other swimmers seemed to catch up to him in the final meters. Once Cody jammed his hand against the wall, his head popped up, and he stared at a massive electronic scoreboard.

"He got second!" Hannah screeched. "His best time, too." She grabbed Kate for a hug.

"Second in the country?" Justin gaped. "Second in the freaking U S of A?"

From the water, Cody looked up at them and met Matthew's eyes. Grabbing a lane line, he thrust himself up and punched his fist in the air.

Matthew mirrored his move without thinking. "Yeah! You did it, Cody!"

The swimmer fell back into the water, submerging his huge grin.

When Matthew turned to Justin, he noticed both of them still had an arm raised in the air. They laughed at each other as they cracked a loud high-five.

"Cody rocked it out," Matthew said. He stared with love at his twin, noting the matching black hair, crooked nose, and light blue eyes. It was good to have him back.

Justin nodded, holding his gaze for a long moment. "The boy did good. And so did you." He smirked as he turned back toward the pool. "But I'm still the smarter twin, little brother."

Acknowledgments

Inspired by a dream, I started writing *Twin Sacrifice* in 2009. Two trilogies diverted my attention in subsequent years, but twins Matthew and Justin kept after me to write their story, which I'm excited to launch in 2018. Though I include psychology in every novel, this is my first stab at a psychological thriller.

Many thanks to those who sacrificed their time to guide this project:

Nicki Elson, critique partner. I don't know how I would write without you. It is *so* motivating to send a chapter at a time, and I appreciate your sharp eye for improving the manuscript. When you called this story riveting, you lit a fire to my muse!

Jessica Royer Ocken, editor. Your editing is an emulsion of speed, accuracy, and inspiration. We've become mind twins after working on eight novels together. It was a bomb to share our concert experience in Chicago!

Coreen Montagna, book designer. Your formatting is flawless and I'm grateful that Omnific Publishing brought us together.

Author buddies Nancee, Beck, Darcia, Omni Sisters, and SLOBS — thanks, chicas!

Thank you to my subject experts (any errors are mine):

Dr. Matthew W. Stoltzfus for chemistry help. Chemistry and I don't get along (talk about writing what you *don't* know) so your help was invaluable.

Author Jillian Chantal for legal assistance.

Dr. Liz R and Dr. Karen Bretz for insights into forensic psychology.

Joan val Joan Kraus for theater knowledge.

About the Author

Psychologist/author (psycho author) Jennifer Lane invites you to her world of romance, sports, and suspense! By day she's a therapist, and by night she's a writer. She can't decide which is more fun.

Jen's first psychological thriller launches in 2018: *Twin Sacrifice*. Psychologist Matthew Durante risks his own life to save his twin brother's as their foster father tries to take them down.

Jen loves to create sporty heroines and hot heroes in her college sport romances. Volleyball wonder Lucia Ramirez finds her love match in *Blocked* despite the glaring political spotlight aimed on her family. In *Aced*, the second book in the Blocked series, it's her brother Alejandro's turn to get lucky in love. *Spiked* (Blocked #3) completes the series and features Lucia's younger brother Mateo.

A swimmer and volleyball player in college, Jen writes swimming-based romances as well: *Streamline*, a military mystery, and the free New Adult novella *Swim Recruit*.

Stories of redemption interest Jen the most, especially the healing power of love. She is also the author of The *Con*duct Series, a romantic-suspense trilogy that includes *With Good Behavior*, *Bad Behavior*, and *On Best Behavior*.

Whether writing or reading, Jen loves stories that make her laugh and cry. In her spare time she enjoys exercising, attending book club, and visiting her sisters in Chicago and Hilton Head.

Visit Jen at:

JenniferLaneBooks.blogspot.com
Facebook.com/JenLaneBooks
Twitter.com/JenLaneBooks
Pinterest.com/JenLaneBooks
Instagram.com/JenLaneBooks

If you enjoyed *Twin Sacrifice*, you may also like The *Con*duct Series.
The first book in this romantic suspense trilogy is
With Good Behavior...

In the midst of organized crime and dim hopes of redemption, can love persevere? For Sophie Taylor, a psychologist who lost everything when she violated an ethical boundary, and Grant Madsen, a naval officer who sacrificed himself to protect his uncle, finding that love seems unlikely.

As they start their lives over in Chicago, both fight family influences and run as fast as they can to escape the past. When their paths cross outside their parole officer's door, attraction sparks. Too bad a hidden connection may not only shatter their fledgling love, but prove deadly to them both.

Check out *With Good Behavior* by reading the first chapter...

1. Reconviction

Jerry Stone sighed as he reviewed the list of parolees on his schedule. He tossed the printout on his desk and leaned back in his squeaky chair as he rubbed the bridge of his nose.

It was Wednesday, and the Department of Corrections always stuck it to him on Wednesdays. Two newbies in a row, right off the bat. Two inmates freshly released, about to give him the old song and dance about how they'd never return to prison—how they were *rehabilitated.* What a joke. If they weren't cons by the time they entered the Illinois corrections system, they sure were by the time they left. They should call it *reconviction.*

A knock made him straighten. "Enter!"

The door creaked open, and Jerry's eyebrows arched as his first parolee entered. She wasn't the typical bottom-dweller inmate, reeking of unwashed clothes, hostility, and despair. She was tall and thin, with reddish-blond hair, and she carried herself with an almost regal air as she floated into his office. He bet they'd eaten her up at the pen.

She swallowed. "Mr. Stone?"

"Yeah, who're you?"

"Sophie Taylor."

"Back number?"

"Seven two six three four."

"Take a seat." He gestured toward the chair facing his desk as he opened her file. What the hell had led this gorgeous chick into crime?

Sophie sat, taking in the dirty cornflower-blue walls, the steel desk piled with uneven, wobbly stacks of papers, and the moldy white blinds.

She was to report here weekly for an entire year, and the décor wasn't much different from Downer's Grove Women's Prison. She crossed her legs and hugged her handbag, studying the parole officer's salt-and-pepper hair as he read her paperwork.

After a few moments, Jerry looked up from the file. "You were a psychologist?"

She managed a tight smile. "Yes."

"Should I call you Dr. Taylor, then?"

Her chest squeezed as she looked down. It had been over a year since anyone addressed her that way. She thought back to her last therapy client to use those words, *Dr. Taylor*. His smooth, deep voice reverberated in her mind. She'd been enthralled by his rich baritone as it caressed and possessed her name with a hint of love. With what she'd *thought* was love.

Jerry noticed her blush as she lifted her head. "No, I'm not a psychologist anymore. The Illinois Board of Psychology revoked my license once I was convicted."

"I see." He continued to scan her file. "I'm not finding any reports from your sessions with a prison psychologist."

Sophie cleared her throat. "That's because I never met with one."

"Huh. Thought you'd be all over that, with your former career and all."

"I don't want therapy. Don't believe in it anymore."

Jerry sat back in his chair. "You went to prison because of a massive lapse of judgment, right?"

She nodded.

"And now after a year in prison, you're trying to get your life back." When she nodded again, he ordered, "And don't just tell me what I want to hear, young lady."

"No, sir. I really do want to start my life over. I have to."

"So if you were still a psychologist, and you knew of a woman in these circumstances — trying to figure out what led to a huge mistake to prevent it from happening again, reeling from a year in prison despite no priors, hoping to move forward — in your professional opinion, would you say this woman makes a good candidate for therapy?"

Sophie's heart thudded. "There're lots of ways to get one's life back on track. Therapy doesn't always lead to rehabilitation."

"You spent a long time training to become a psychologist. And now you don't believe in it?"

Sophie crossed her arms and pursed her lips.

"Because *I* think you're a perfect candidate. And I'm making that a condition of your parole: weekly therapy."

"Court-ordered therapy doesn't work!" Her brown eyes flared.

Jerry squinted. "What're you afraid of?"

"I'm — I'm not *afraid*." Therapy was about reliving the past, uncovering hidden motivations, diving into family dysfunction. She wasn't about to delve into those memories. "How am I supposed to afford therapy? I don't have a job yet."

"The DOC will pay for it."

He'd thwarted every objection. "What if I refuse?"

"Do you *want* to return to prison?" he thundered.

She closed her eyes. "No."

He marched around the desk. "You don't get it, do you? You're out of prison, with good behavior, but you have a whole *year* left of your sentence. I could throw your ass back inside so quick your bunkie wouldn't even know you'd left."

Her eyes widened as he towered over her, and she glanced at the handcuffs dangling from his belt. One wrong move and they'd be clasped around her wrists once again.

"I'm sorry, Mr. Stone." She studied the crease between his bushy brows. "I don't want to go back. I — I'll do whatever you say."

He stared at her. *Newbies.* He hated his first session with parolees, having to sniff out their true intentions after knowing them for mere minutes. He hated the cagey lies, the empty promises.

After thirty years in the DOC, he'd developed a keen sense about people. He could sort through all kinds of bullshit to discern the truth. But this one made him nervous: a woman with a doctorate, a *shrink* nonetheless. She could fool and manipulate. She could mind-fuck him to Mexico.

His butt cheeks found his seat again. "Doing whatever I tell you to do — that's precisely the attitude you need to stay out of prison."

"I don't want to start off on the wrong foot with you, Mr. Stone. I know you must have all kinds of cons giving you a hard time, and I don't want to be one of them."

"Glad to hear that." He reached into his filing cabinet and handed her a paper. "A list of therapists who work with the correctional system. Schedule an appointment with one of them before we meet again. Understood?"

"Yes." She exhaled when she didn't recognize any former colleagues on the list.

"Report here every Wednesday at nine. If you don't show up, you'll return to prison. There'll be random drug tests, and if you fail even one, you'll return to prison. I expect you to secure employment in the next two weeks. If you don't find a job, you'll return to prison. Are the terms of your parole clear, Taylor?"

She nodded, thinking this parole thing didn't sound all that much better than prison.

He clicked a pen. "Where're you living?"

"With a friend."

"I need an address." When she gave him a Lake Shore Drive number, he frowned. She lived downtown? "What's your friend's name?"

"Kirsten Holland."

"What does Holland do for a living?"

"She's a therapist." When he continued staring at her, she added, "We went to grad school together."

"But she's not a psychologist?"

"Oh, no, she's ABD, um, All But Dissertation? She hasn't finished her degree, so she can't call herself a psychologist yet."

"Does Holland have a criminal background?"

"No." Kirsten was nowhere near as stupid as Sophie. "She's letting me live with her as long as I kick her butt to finish her dissertation."

Jerry stifled a smile. This *had* to be the first time he'd discussed doctorates and dissertations with a parolee. "Very well. Any questions for me?"

Sophie ran her finger along the strap of her handbag. "How long have you been a parole officer?"

"Thirty years." He cocked his head. "And that's the first time I've been asked such a personal question."

"Sorry." She winced. "I don't mean to pry. I just wondered, in those thirty years…what percentage violates their parole and returns to prison?"

He looked up to his right. "I'd say, ballpark, sixty percent."

"Wow."

"It's serious business, Taylor. We're not messing around here."

"I get that. Well, I'll definitely be in the forty percent. I'm *not* going back."

"I hope that's the case." There was something about the twenty-nine-year-old woman that made him like her. Warmth and smarts shone through. But he stuffed down those fond feelings.

Jerry glanced at his watch. "It's time for my next appointment. See you Wednesday, Taylor."

"Thank you, Officer Stone." She rose and extended her arm.

He paused before shaking her hand.

Sophie let out a long breath, feeling the stress of her first parole meeting dissolve. That relief was short-lived, however, once she opened the door and found herself eye to eye with a man whose black, buzzed hair and olive skin highlighted eyes that held crystal-blue, bottomless depths. The next parolee on the docket? His nose was slightly crooked and his lips were full. His penetrating gaze bore a hole in her. She stood frozen, staring for several moments before regaining her bearings and muttering, "Excuse me."

She ducked out of the door and strode down the hallway, daring to glance behind her to see the man watching her leave. A faint smile crossed his lips, and her cheeks burned.

As she scurried off, the stranger's intriguing eyes on her mind, she decided parole wasn't all that bad.